Performative Opacity in the Work of
Isabelle Huppert

Performative Opacity in the Work of Isabelle Huppert

Edited by Iggy Cortez and Ian Fleishman

EDINBURGH
University Press

Edinburgh University Press is one of the leading university presses in the UK. We publish academic books and journals in our selected subject areas across the humanities and social sciences, combining cutting-edge scholarship with high editorial and production values to produce academic works of lasting importance. For more information visit our website: edinburghuniversitypress.com

© editorial matter and organisation Cesar Ignacio Cortez and Ian Fleishman, 2023, 2024
© the chapters their several authors, 2023, 2024

Edinburgh University Press Ltd
13 Infirmary Street, Edinburgh, EH1 1LT

First published in hardback by Edinburgh University Press 2023

Typeset in 11/13pt Ehrhardt MT by
Cheshire Typesetting Ltd, Cuddington, Cheshire

A CIP record for this book is available from the British Library

ISBN 978 1 4744 7983 7 (hardback)
ISBN 978 1 4744 7984 4 (paperback)
ISBN 978 1 4744 7985 1 (webready PDF)
ISBN 978 1 4744 7986 8 (epub)

The right of Cesar Ignacio Cortez and Ian Fleishman to be identified as editors of this work has been asserted in accordance with the Copyright, Designs and Patents Act 1988 and the Copyright and Related Rights Regulations 2003 (SI No. 2498).

Contents

List of Figures	vii
Acknowledgements	ix
Notes on Contributors	x
Introduction: Performing the Inassimilable *Iggy Cortez and Ian Fleishman*	1
1. The Unknown Huppert *Catherine Wheatley*	15
2. Huppert in the Ozon-Machine: Melodrama and Meta-Acting in *8 Femmes* *Nikolaj Lübecker*	30
3. Alter/Ego: Isabelle Huppert as Werner Schroeter's Double *Ian Fleishman*	48
4. Laughing in the Face of Death: The Comedic Force of Isabelle Huppert in *La Cérémonie* *Karen Redrobe*	70
5. White Mothers on Colonised Land, or What Isabelle Huppert Makes Visible? *Erin Schlumpf*	89
6. Isabelle Huppert's Caring, Carefree, Careless Abortionist in Claude Chabrol's *Une affaire de femmes* *Henrietta Stanford*	105

7. Horn | Huppert | Horn 123
   Lutz Koepnick

Bibliography 139
Index 149

Figures

I.1	Isabelle Huppert (playing herself) running between roles in *Dix pour cent*	2
1.1	Still photograph from the video portrait of Isabelle Huppert as Greta Garbo, 2005 by Robert Wilson	16
1.2	Pomme (Isabelle Huppert) staring intently at the camera at the end of *La Dentellière* (*The Lacemaker*, 1977)	27
2.1	Isabelle Huppert performing 'Message Personnel' in *8 Femmes* (*8 Women*, 2002)	34
2.2	The actresses as 'equal dolls' in *8 Femmes* (*8 Women*, 2002)	42
3.1–3.2	Isabelle Huppert as her own double in *Deux* (2002)	58
3.3	Isabelle Huppert in a quasi-cameo at the end of *Deux* (2002), immediately before a title dedicating the film to her	60
4.1	Sophie (Sandrine Bonnaire) attempting to decipher a note with a phonetics book in *La Cérémonie* (1995)	73
4.2	Jeanne (Isabelle Huppert) mimicking urinating with hot chocolate, aligning herself with patriarchal violence in *La Cérémonie* (1995)	81
4.3	Jeanne (Isabelle Huppert) in front of a map of Saint Malo in *La Cérémonie* (1995)	83
4.4	The Lelièvre family in their living room featuring a tapestry covering the wall in *La Cérémonie* (1995)	83
5.1	The Mother (Isabelle Huppert) regarding herself in profile in *Un barrage contre le Pacifique* (*The Sea Wall*, 2008)	91
5.2	A close-up gives us Huppert's desolate, disgusted face in *Un barrage contre le Pacifique* (*The Sea Wall*, 2008)	96
5.3	Maria (Isabelle Huppert) with her father-in-law's blood splattered on her face in *White Material* (2009)	100

6.1	Bending to pick nettles. Isabelle Huppert in *Une affaire de femmes* (*Story of Women*, 1988)	106
6.2	Enjoying jam and biscuits. Isabelle Huppert in *Une affaire de femmes* (*Story of Women*, 1988)	113
6.3	Listening to her neighbour as she recounts her reasons for wanting an abortion. Isabelle Huppert in *Une affaire de femmes* (*Story of Women*, 1988)	119
7.1	Roni Horn, Portrait of an Image (Frankfurt), 2013 (detail). 16 images from *Portrait of an Image (with Isabelle Huppert)* 2005	125
7.2	Roni Horn, *Portrait of an Image (with Isabelle Huppert)* 2005–6 (detail)	132

Acknowledgements

We would like to thank Gillian Leslie and Sam Johnson from Edinburgh University Press for their guidance on this project, which has been long in the making. Libby Saylor and Nathalie Barton offered invaluable assistance with formatting for which we are extremely thankful. The anonymous reviewers for Edinburgh University Press made vital suggestions on delineating the conceptual uniqueness of this volume and we are grateful for their careful readings and commentary.

We are indebted to Robert Wilson and Roni Horn for allowing us to republish their work, as well as to Tiffany Wang from Hauser and Wirth and Noah Koshbin and Christoph Schletz from the Robert Wilson studio.

As in so many other things, Leo Bersani was a guiding light for this volume. We dedicate it to his memory.

Notes on Contributors

Iggy Cortez is Assistant Professor of Cinema & Media Arts and English, Vanderbilt University. His writing has appeared in *The Journal of Cinema and Media Studies*, *Camera Obscura*, *ASAP/J*, *College Art Association Reviews*, and *Faces on Screen: New Approaches*. He was the co-curator with Charlotte Ickes of Itinerant Belongings at the Slought Foundation in Philadelphia. He is currently at work on a book on night-time in world cinema.

Ian Fleishman is Associate Professor of Cinema & Media Studies and Francophone, Italian & Germanic Studies at the University of Pennsylvania. He has published widely on subjects ranging from the Baroque to contemporary moving image pornography. His first monograph, *An Aesthetics of Injury: The Narrative Wound from Baudelaire to Tarantino* (2018) was the winner of the Northeast Modern Language Association's Best Book Award.

Lutz Koepnick is the Max Kade Foundation Chair in German Studies and Professor of Cinema & Media Arts at Vanderbilt University. He has published widely on film, media art, and aesthetic theory from the nineteenth to the twenty-first century. His most recent books are *Resonant Matter: Sound, Art, and the Promise of Hospitality* (2021), *Fitzcarraldo* (2019) and *Michael Bay: World Cinema in the Age of Populism* (2018). He is the co-editor of various anthologies on subjects such as ambiguity in contemporary art and theory, the culture of neoliberalism and German cinema.

Nikolaj Lübecker is Professor of French and Film Studies at Saint John's College at the University of Oxford. He is the author of *Le Sacrifice de la sirène – 'Un coup de dés' et la poétique de Stéphane Mallarmé* (2003), *Community, Myth and Recognition in 20th century French Literature and Thought* (2009) and *The Feel-Bad Film* (2015), as well as more than a dozen articles on literature and cinema. He is currently working on what has been dubbed the nonhuman turn in the humanities.

Karen Redrobe (formerly Beckman) is the Elliot and Roslyn Jaffe Professor of Cinema and Modern Media, Director of the Wolf Humanities Center, and has served as Chair of the Department of the History of Art at the University of Pennsylvania. She is the author of *Vanishing Women: Magic, Film and Feminism* (2003), *Crash: Cinema and the Politics of Speed and Stasis* (2010), and is now working on a new book, *Undead: Animation and the Contemporary Art of War*. She has co-edited two books and is the editor of *Animating Film Theory* (2014).

Erin Shevaugn Schlumpf is Assistant Professor of Film Studies at Ohio University. Her research focuses on aesthetic responses to historical trauma as well as queer and feminist counter-narratives of the past. Her recent work has been published in *A Companion to Jean-Luc Godard* (2014), *differences: A Journal of Feminist Cultural Studies* and *Comparative Literature and Culture*.

Henrietta Stanford's research foregrounds questions of subjectivity, gender, the politics of emotion, care, and violence (and its afterlives) in modern and contemporary art and film, from a psychosocial, relational and feminist perspective. Henrietta's AHRC-funded PhD was awarded in 2015 by the Courtauld Institute of Art, where she has taught a range of courses at both undergraduate and postgraduate level. Her work has most recently appeared in the *Oxford Art Journal*.

Catherine Wheatley is Reader in Film Studies at King's College London. She is the author of *Michael Haneke's Cinema: The Ethic of the Image* (2009) and a monograph on Haneke's *Caché* (2012). She has also co-authored *French Film in Britain: Sex, Art and Cinephilia* and co-edited a volume on Anglo-French cinematic relations with Lucy Mazdon. Currently, she is developing a book project on the relationship between Christianity and contemporary film and film theory.

Introduction: Performing the Inassimilable
Iggy Cortez and Ian Fleishman

In an episode of the hit comedy show *Dix pour cent* (*Call My Agent!*, 2018), Isabelle Huppert plays an exaggerated version of herself that humorously iconifies her public image as an indefatigably ambitious and prolific actress. The episode follows Huppert as she tries to shoot two films at the same time, forcing her agents to transport her covertly back and forth from one set to another in the hopes that they don't get caught (and therefore sued) for violating the terms of her contracts. The stressful scenario escalates when the overstretched Huppert throws a radio interview, a script rewrite, a Chanel fashion show, and an experimental film into her already unforgiving schedule. This wacky premise adheres to a well-trodden comedic principle that continuously escalates an increasingly stressful predicament. While it is not difficult to foresee how such zaniness will lead to hilarious hijinks, the episode's more unexpected appeal lies in the dedicated precision with which it assesses Huppert's specific career and persona. In other words, much like the devoted agents the show follows, Huppert's episode of *Dix pour cent* continuously displays a dedicated and meticulous attention towards the central subject of its regard.

As the episode's events unfold, we witness Huppert move between an American film production, a French costume drama directed by Cédric Kahn (also playing himself), and later, an experimental short by a South Korean filmmaker. This diverse gamut of projects captures not only the eclectic range but also the international scope of Huppert's career – especially in recent years – the latter of which has seen her star in an increasing number of Asian and American productions. Early in the episode, Huppert mentions having several films in Cannes in the same year, alluding to her career's close association with the festival, where she has won the Best Actress award twice and also served as jury president for the main competition in 2009. (Her affiliation with international festivals and awards far exceeds Cannes, of course, but it would be too unwieldy, either in the episode or in this introduction, to list those different venues and accolades comprehensively.) During the radio interview with journalist Laure Adler, Huppert bypasses customary anecdotal banalities to discuss instead the nature of duration and nothingness – a gentle caricature of her reputation as an actress with an 'overtly intellectual temperament', to echo critic Richard Brody's succinct summation.[1] Across these coordinates, the various producers, agents and directors searching for Huppert but never quite finding her evoke the actor's elusive public persona: a 'self', Cristina Álvarez López and Adrian Martin argue, that falls outside the grasp of fixed or facile categorization, remaining perpetually 'mysterious, fugitive, and hard to get a fix on'.[2]

But the television episode's parodic and comedic details are not solely biographical in nature. They are also tellingly attuned to the tenor and method of Huppert's performance style. In another moment, for instance, we witness Huppert intensely absorbed in a prolonged deathbed monologue, displaying an affective intensity that appears both intently focused yet also emotively detached, only for her bodily affect suddenly to recalibrate into the brisk alacrity of a sly prankster as soon as the director wraps, allowing Huppert to rush to her next engagement. Clearly, the speed with which the actress moves from character to character – keeping in mind that 'Huppert' here, too, is a fictional take on the real Huppert – appears exaggerated for farcical purposes. But there is something about Huppert's rapid yet nonchalant oscillation between the throes of death and insouciant mischief in this scene that nevertheless thematises what is distinctive about her disposition to performance across her body of work, as her method has consistently deviated

Figure I.1   Isabelle Huppert (playing herself) running between roles in *Dix pour cent*.

away from principles of psychic coherence and unity, attuning us instead to the ambiguities and discontinuities of emotional life.

We begin with *Dix pour cent*'s meta-textual vignette as an invitation to reflect upon the aims of this volume of essays, which similarly aspires at once to take stock of Huppert's long and varied career and also to explore how she has become so resonant with, one might even say iconic of, a certain image of international art cinema – a cultural sphere commonly viewed as cerebral and oftentimes even as perverse. In so doing, our contributors aim to reflect upon the points of correspondence between screen performance and cultural performance. In other words, our aim is not only to situate Huppert's star text and performance style within institutional and aesthetic discussions in cinema, but also conversely to interrogate what Huppert's relationship to acting dramatises about the aesthetics and politics of the cinematic image more broadly.

While the essays in this volume will certainly resonate with scholarly approaches to stardom and screen performance – surveying Huppert's corporeal bearing, her repertoire of gestural and emotional expressions, the affective attributes and orientations she signifies – they also take her work as an invitation for sustained reflection on the aesthetic, political and at moments even philosophical questions it raises. By rejecting conventional imperatives of psychological transparency or facile relatability, the ambiguous cadences of Huppert's acting style – at once precise and enigmatic, intensely affective yet often expressively reticent or indecipherably detached – continuously unravel deterministic limitations that conventional narrative and representational frameworks impose on the presentation of subjectivity. We will return to this point later, but first we wish to map some of the conceptual contours of this project and outline how the discursive trajectory on Huppert's career overlaps with important recent debates in cinema studies and the humanities.

'47 VARIETIES OF BLANKNESS'

This volume situates its inquiry on Huppert between star studies and the analysis of performance, approaches that might share the same object – the actor's screen presence – but that do not always methodologically overlap, as Pamela Wojcik, Kyle Stevens and Murray Pomerance have separately noted.[3] In a recent publication of essays on Huppert that explicitly assesses 'how scholarly discussions of Huppert can contribute to a broadening of the parameters of Star Studies itself', editors Nick Rees-Roberts and Darren Waldron observe how Huppert's versatility, as well as her generally successful resistance to exposing her private life to public scrutiny, have eluded the fixed imagery around which the cultural meanings imputed on star texts tend to be structured.[4]

By continuously insisting both on the opacity of her characters' psyches as well as that of her own private life, Huppert's stardom thus undermines how the conventional star paradigm, according to Michelle Cho, encodes 'the promise of self-identity and plenitude as a magical antidote to the self-estrangement that characterises the modern subject'.[5] Similarly, in an article on Huppert in *Sight & Sound*, Ginette Vincendeau, one of the leading academics on French stardom, underscores how Huppert's star image embodies a paradoxical awareness of her off-screen life's secrecy, thus making Huppert an exception within the 'frenzy of celebrity culture' of the 2010s in which 'the pressure to reveal all is constantly ratcheted up'.[6] As Vincendeau elaborates, the general public's lack of intimate knowledge about the particularities of Huppert's private life does not void her stardom but re-inflects its conventional parameters, as it helps accentuate 'her opacity on screen' – one of the most consistent descriptions of Huppert's performances across her career. Even though Huppert defaults from the way star discourses make the private life of actors part of the 'multiple but finite meanings ... a star image signifies', to invoke Richard Dyer's famous formulation, it seems undeniable that Huppert, not despite but rather because of a certain unlocatablility, serves as a locus for intersecting ideals and cultural meanings that our contributors aim to identify and bring into relief.[7]

Vincendeau, in fact, contends that Huppert signifies attributes of 'opacity, intellectualism and authenticity [that] have characterised [her] almost from the start – and apply equally to the auteur cinema she has served so well'.[8] For other critics, Huppert's career is linked to the exploration of monstrous, extreme, or unspeakable instincts that, in turn, align her with a corresponding ethos of fearlessness (on the cover of the September issue of *Sight & Sound*, for instance, the magazine boldly announced Huppert as 'Cinema's most fearless actor'). Huppert's most acclaimed roles, in fact, tend to embody turbulent and (self)-destructive drives and desires – take, for instance, *La Pianiste*'s (*The Piano Teacher*, 2001) sadomasochistic Erika Kohut; Hélène, the glibly perverse and ultimately incestuous matriarch in *Ma Mère* (2004); Jeanne, the gleeful and unrepentant murderer in *La Cérémonie* (1995); Mika, the aloof owner of a chocolate factory who poisons her husband's family in *Merci pour le chocolat* (2000); and, most recently, Michèle, the head of a video game company who treats her rape with a seemingly pragmatic coldness in *Elle* (2016). Even in roles that appear less psychically volatile in lighter comedies, such as the carefree Babou in *Copacabana* (2010) or haughty Martine in *Les sœurs fâchées* (*Me and My Sister*, 2003), Huppert's comedic timing is inflected by discordant notes of psychic distress and even fugitive moments of dissociation.

Describing Huppert's reputation for extreme or deviant roles solely from a narrative or thematic perspective, however, does not sufficiently express the specific resonance of her performative style. Her affective disposition towards abject, aberrant, or discordant characters approaches the darker recesses of the psyche as a captivating but also unpredictable and interminably fluctuating process (rather than as mere occasions for visceral but intellectively ungenerative shock and consternation). In fact, we contend that attention to Huppert's performative intonations can reframe recent discussions on the social and cultural dimensions of emotion and normativity through a compelling paradox: her roles tend to express grandiose, even overwhelming conditions but through elusive and at times resistant or diminutive forms of expression. Depravity, dispossession and trauma come to light in the microeconomy of a grimace, through subtle vocal modulations, a stillness of expression that, when held in a long-take close-up, registers transformative psychic reconfigurations through almost imperceptible surface movements and inflections.

Critics have been particularly drawn to Huppert's achievement of affective intensity via such minute physiognomic changes. In an especially ekphrastic review of Huppert's performance in Olivier Dahan's *La Vie promise* (*The Promised Life*, 2002), J. Hoberman observes, for instance, that

> this superb actress can register more fugitive shifts in expression in a single take than most actresses manage in an entire movie. (And she can always be relied upon to drop a single, slow-rolling tear.) If it was Marlon Brando's genius to render the inarticulate eloquent, it is this most introspective of performers' genius to distinguish 47 varieties of blankness.[9]

Similarly, in the remarkable video essay '"I Furrow My Own Film Inside Those I Pass Through": Isabelle Huppert', accompanying their article 'Isabelle Huppert: The Absent One', Álvarez López and Martin meticulously parse the patterns of Huppert's performative style attuned to the minor tectonics of errant corporeal and bodily affects, noting her 'concentrated facial micro expressions', 'eccentric or exaggerated hand gestures', 'vocal exclamations and intonations', 'discontinuous or suspended reactions of shock', 'inscrutable appearance' and 'restrained emotion' that can operate alongside a more pronounced physicality marked by 'restless movement, vigorous action and physical exertion'.[10] The diminutively textured distinctions Huppert is able to evoke beneath the threshold of explicitly manifested expression is not, in sum, in opposition to the spectator's affective experience of her performances. They are rather the very conduits to their powerful intensity, as well as an aleatory pathway, we argue, to the sensory recognition of obscure and fugitive registers of atmosphere and affect that tend to elude normative patterns of legibility.

In this regard, descriptive attunement to Huppert's rich gradient of diminutive gestures and expressions responds to Lesley Stern and George Kouvaros's advocacy for 'descriptive acts' about film performance that '[move] away from the invincible paradigm of the visual ... [drawing] out a notion of filmic engagement where considerations of bodily affect, tactility and memory (configured through a range of sensory responses) play a central role'.[11] In so doing, Huppert occasions a consideration of how careful attention to her performance aesthetics' famously fugitive registers might participate in the critical cultivation of enhanced descriptive practices influential in the humanities since the turn to affect. Which is to say that Huppert's work requires what Kathleen Stewart elucidates as 'kind of haptic description',[12] aiming to capture not what is intelligible and concretely manifest in advance but rather 'the resonance of nascent forms quickening or sloughing off, materialities pressing into the expressivity of something coming into existence'.[13] This, in turn, might 'suggest something of the plasticity and density of lived compositions now proliferating in ordinary scenes of living through what is happening'.[14] Indeed, what descriptive accounts of Huppert's acting seem to share is the sense of a phenomenological experience that is irreducibly aware of its own unfolding, as if perceptual alertness towards film acting's mechanics were intensified by performance's expressive recession: its movement towards diminutive registers of nuance that require a laboured descriptive specificity in light of its unyielding relation to traditional grammars of legibility and analytic scrutiny.

In other words, if Huppert's acting style is often viewed as withdrawn and non-demonstrative – committed to a certain distance between herself and the spectator's desire for assimilative identification or interpretive mastery – the kind of critical enthusiasm she generates, conversely, is often expressed in unequivocal and hyperbolic terms. 'It's Isabelle Huppert, how can you not stand for Isabelle Huppert?' the actor Gael Garciá Bernal is reported to have exclaimed regarding the standing ovation when Huppert won Best Actress at the Gotham Awards in 2016.[15] This surprise recognition for her performance in *Elle* was the first of many international accolades that year, culminating in Golden Globe and César wins. In the narrative arc of that awards season sweep (which came up just short of the Academy Award for Best Actress), this image of a transnational Mexican star expressing his admiration for Huppert as at once absolute and self-evident distils something of the global reach of her stature, as well as the passionate valence of the admiration she inspires. Especially since the release of *Elle* (2016) and *L'Avenir* (*Things to Come*, 2016), Huppert has been routinely dubbed the world's greatest living actress in various newspaper and magazine headlines, and not only in the

United States, where the extent of her critical and awards recognition has been largely seen as arriving belatedly compared to Europe.

In a review entitled 'Isabelle Huppert Is Great in "Things to Come." Discuss', *The New York Times* co-chief film critic A. O. Scott, for instance, asks 'Isabelle Huppert: great actress or world's greatest actress? Once that is settled (in favour of the second option, of course), we can turn to more advanced Huppertiana.'[16] In 2020, Scott, alongside *The Times* co-chief film critic Manohla Dargis, would in fact name Huppert the greatest actress of the 21st century.[17] In the catalogue for *Woman of Many Faces*, a traveling exhibition of portraits of Huppert taken by photographers such as Richard Avedon, Nan Goldin, and Philip-Lorca Di Corcia, among others, Susan Sontag writes in a brief accompanying essay that 'Isabelle Huppert ... is an actor of unlimited ability, with ... a body of work and a talent from which we can expect anything in the future, anything and everything.'[18] Similarly, describing her as the 'best actress working in France today',[19] philosopher Julia Kristeva, in the published transcript of a conversation at the Centre Roland Barthes, expresses that the 'concerns of Roland Barthes and the talent of Isabelle Huppert' share two similarities: 'pleasure and intelligence'.[20] If laying out this sequence of ecstatic praise seems simply to rehearse the statements' excess and exuberance, we do so precisely because the ardent attachment Huppert inspires, as well as broader questions regarding the tonal and affective disposition of reception, are at the core of what this volume seeks to explore and to interrogate through the lens of her career and performances. To put it more plainly: we ask if it is even possible to imagine contemporary art cinema without Huppert. And if so, what might this suggest about the geopolitical and historical contours of what we call cinephilia? We are thus specifically drawn to whether the fervent zeal Huppert incites – particularly among critics, actors, and humanities scholars both within and outside of cinema studies – might not in fact gesture towards something particular and unique about what her distinctive star-image lays bare about cinema's institutional trajectories.

PERFORMANCE AS A POLITICAL HEURISTIC

In order to begin exploring these issues, we offer this volume in dialogue with recent work in cinema studies that interrogates how the entwined properties of screen performance – its affective resonance and notorious elusiveness to critical analysis – can serve as a heuristic lens into the instability or fluidity of the cinematic image's ontology.[21] In this volume, contributors like Lutz Koepnick, Nikolaj Lübecker, Karen Redrobe and Catherine Wheatley lay bare how Huppert's opacity interrogates the assumption that the cinematic image's conditioning parameters are grounded in its testimonial and transparently referential qualities.

At the same time, these contributors, as well as Ian Fleishman and Henrietta Stanford, turn to assessments of performance that consider the exegetical force of performance aesthetics beyond the parameters of 'character'. Writing about American acting in the 2010s, Shonni Enelow observes that 'it's impossible to talk about acting without talking about culture. The relationship between cultural performance and professional performance is symbiotic: actors imitate what they see in the world, and non-actors in turn respond to and (consciously or unconsciously) imitate what they see on the screen.'[22] It is precisely due to this feedback loop that acting styles can serve as an index of emergent structures of feeling or paradigm shifts in national sentiment. Enelow identifies a notable shift in critically valorised aesthetics of screen performance in US independent films towards the reticent and affectively recessive, in contrast to the 'the economy of repression and release that characterises many Method performances' we associate with actors such as James Dean all the way to Daniel Day Lewis.[23] These shifts in acting style allegorise, Enelow contends, changes in how the self is conceptualised in relation to constraining cultural forces and forms:

> This is another way to read the emotional withdrawal or refusal in these performances: as a response to a violent or chaotic environment, one that doesn't offer an alternate vision of an open and embracing future. For even when representing an alienating or unfeeling world, actors of earlier eras generally appealed to the camera and their audiences to receive their feelings and implicitly trusted them to respond generously, either through vicarious sentiment or humanist compassion. Expressive acting – of which Method acting is one dominant form – is built on the conviction that audiences want an actor's emotions to be in some way available to them. There's a basic optimism in that conviction: the optimism that the world would be better if we all told each other the truth about what we feel. In contrast, many of today's most lauded American film actors give performances that evince no such optimism about emotional expression.[24]

The 'tortured mistrust of expression itself' Enelow identifies in this new paradigm for acting signals a kind of perpetual endurance in a chronically hostile environment that seems distrustful of a politics rooted in humanist principles of exposure and intelligibility.[25] While here Enelow is discussing American performance in the 2010s rather than the French and European art cinema with which Huppert is more commonly associated, the resonances between Huppert's acting style and this new aesthetic of 'emotional inaccessibility and inscrutability' should be apparent. We might thus draw a speculative link to the complexly 'undemonstrative' acting style taking hold of American film to Huppert's influence, given the revitalised visibility and acclaim in United States film institutions and criticism that she has enjoyed precisely in the period coinciding with the landscape Enelow assesses.

Needless to say, however, Huppert has been eminent internationally at different moments, and by gathering contributions assessing Huppert at varying stages of her career – from the seventies to the contemporary period – we seek to understand how her performance aesthetic and star text signifies differently in particular cultural contexts and at specific historical junctures. For example, if 'no other actress has a presence that has shaped French cinema more profoundly than Isabelle Huppert,'[26] as the blurb to Vincendeau's *Sight & Sound* article suggests, Patricia White has read her star text in Claire Denis's *White Material* (2009) as an inscription of France's hegemonic role within institutional discourses of world cinema. For White, Huppert's iconicity reflexively '[displays] and [disavows] the power and privilege of white femininity' in such a way that helps '[interrogate] white female colonial mimicry'.[27] White's reading is illuminating beyond Denis's film, as Huppert's appearance in films by Brillante Mendoza (*Captive*, 2012), Rithy Panh (*Un barrage contre le Pacifique*, 2008), Joachim Trier (*Louder Than Bombs*, 2015) and Hong Sang-Soo (*In Another Country*, 2012, and *Claire's Camera*, 2017) can be read as discursive sites in which these directors metaphorically negotiate different national cinemas' circulation within the institutional protocols of world cinema, wherein French cinema still possesses an overpowering and overdetermined influence. In these films, Huppert's corporeal presence and iconicity thematise these (neo)colonial legacies, thereby making them available for critique – a dynamic that serves as the primary theoretical concern for Redrobe's and Erin Schlumpf's essays in this collection.

Despite our contributors' discrete concerns, however, they all nonetheless share a sense of Huppert's body of work, as well as the intersection of her star text and performance aesthetic, as a dramatisation of negativity, a concept Lauren Berlant and Lee Edelman describe as 'the psychic and social incoherences and divisions, conscious and unconscious alike, that trouble any totality or fixity of identity'.[28] If Huppert's career thus embodies not only the dispossessive violence of discordant drives, but also an ambivalent identification with their disruptive force, it has consistently offered aesthetic form to complexities of the psyche that are largely inadmissible to the vocabulary of formal politics. In the context of her films' narrative grammars, the particular affective valence of Huppert's performances seems to rupture not only the fantasmatic coherence of the self but also the unity of the social and cultural regimes that constrain what that self is permitted to be.

The question of negativity returns us to an earlier, and even more fundamentally underlying question regarding the nature of screen performance as such, as the negativity attributed to Huppert's aesthetic appears to distil the enigmatic elusiveness of film acting as a property perpetually in excess of film theory's analytic taxonomies. It has become commonplace, in fact, for critics to describe Huppert as an auteur in her own right in order to designate how her performances are always reliably legible as a countervailing logic to the director's influence and intent. A. O. Scott, for instance, has observed that '[Huppert's] best performances often feel like dialogues – or outright arguments – with her directors.'[29] Similarly, in their video essay, Álvarez López and Martin observe that Huppert 'brings to a scene something apparently not scripted', as her creative contribution to her films is often viewed as equal to, and at times even more significant, than that of their directors. The aleatory, even unruly, valences these critics identify in Huppert's acting can be read as the fulfilment of the discursive excess intrinsic to screen performance – which Huppert, through her choice of roles and her particular methods, harnesses into a tool to communicate the inassimilable limits of rational subjectivity which encompass the interior life of the diegetic characters she embodies as well as the putatively totalizing authority of auteurial intent.

SECTIONS AND CHAPTERS

We conclude this introduction by parsing the overarching concerns uniting the collection's contributions despite their distinct orientations. The book's contributions can be conceptualised across three interrelated rubrics: the affect of performance aesthetics, performance as a sociocultural heuristic, and performance in relation to the expanded fields of cinematic media. Outlining the volume in this way, we hope to bring into relief how these various essays open epistemological concerns regarding the writing and description of performance into analytic lenses into social and political life, on one hand, and institutional, aesthetic, and conceptual debates into cinema and contemporary art, on the other.

The first three essays in the collection focus on performative registers consistently linked to Huppert's star persona and performance aesthetic: unknowability, exteriority, and blankness. Our collection opens with Catherine Wheatley's analysis of Huppert within existing theorizations of the female star in the writings of Stanley Cavell and Roland Barthes. Bringing a video portrait of Huppert by Robert Wilson, filmed at a time in which she was already an established actress, alongside her performance as Pomme in Claude Goretta's *La Dentellière* (*The Lacemaker*, 1977) the film that launched her career, Wheatley contends that Huppert repeatedly stages the opacities of the self not only as an irreducible condition of subjectivity but also as a deliberative insistence on the right to remain private and unknown. In so doing, Wheatley identifies how Huppert troubles the image of the star from within, unravelling the fantasmatic coherence and containment of the subject that stardom normatively enshrines. In his essay on François Ozon's *8 Femmes* (*8 Women*, 2002), Nikolaj Lübecker reads Huppert's performance through Gilles Deleuze and Felix Guattari's conceptualisation of affect as external, surficial, and relational rather than interior or psychological. In so doing, Lübecker theorises Huppert's performance in this film as a form of meta-acting that generates affect without reference to humanist principles of interior depth. Ultimately, Lübecker posits that Huppert in Ozon's film orients us towards the possibility of an aesthetic in which affect and pleasure do not reinscribe monadic (and sovereign) selfhood but point us, rather, towards an ecological recognition of our coextensiveness with the external world. In his essay on two of Werner Schroeter's collaborations with Isabelle Huppert – *Malina* (1991) and *Deux* (2002) – Ian Fleishman reads alongside and against Lauren Berlant's influential notion of flat affect in order to theorise Huppert's blank expression as a subtly but significantly distinct model of underperformativity. If the flat affect of an actor like Tilda Swinton would often appear to imply an asignifying immediacy, Huppert's blank expression instead seems to refer tautologically back to its own expressive blankness – underpinning the impression of a stable, if unknowable self and accounting, Fleishman argues, for her surprising constancy across a countless array of wildly divergent roles.

The next three essays situate Huppert's star text in relation to the social and political valences of her acting aesthetic. In her essay on one of Huppert's most acclaimed roles, the impertinent and murderous Jeanne in Claude Chabrol's *La Cérémonie* (1994), Karen Redrobe analyses Huppert's humour as an entwinement of libidinal energies and destructive death-drives. Moving beyond theorisations of humour as either intrinsically subversive or defensively reactionary, Redrobe reads Huppert's comedic mode in relation to Tiffany Lebatho King's concept of shoaling, a means of unsettling collectively binding atmospheres and perspectives to allow for unexpected relations to become visible. As a result, Redrobe contends that Huppert's humour propels the film's treatise on class politics beyond the framework of the nation-state into the larger geography of French colonial violence. Through a similar focus on colonial legacies, Erin Schlumpf's essay addresses Huppert's embodiment of motherhood and colonial France in two films, Rithy Pahn's *Un barrage contre le Pacifique* (*The Sea Wall*, 2008) and Claire Denis's *White Material* (2009). Schlumpf argues that Huppert, in these performances, deconstructs whiteness from within, embodying characters that extend the violence of 'white mythology' in such a way that ultimately destroys them to make room for those alienated in the margins of colonial whiteness. In her essay on Claude Chabrol's *Une affaire de femmes* (*Story of Women*, 1988), Henrietta Stanford is similarly invested in how Huppert's performances of motherhood undermine its cultural figuration as an impregnable and totalizing ideal that is often conscripted into patriarchal agendas. In dialogue with the work of Adriana Cavarero and Bonnie Honig, Stanford explores how Huppert's performance of an abortionist and mother in the Vichy era oscillates between affective registers of recklessness and care, selfishness and compassion, in order to reconceptualise care outside its associations with self-abnegation or selflessness.

Throughout the book, then, but perhaps especially in its final chapter, we consider Huppert in the expanded field of other discourses and media, concluding with an exploration of her collaborations with artists and photographers, as well as her relevance to debates outside of film studies. Lutz Koepnick's concluding essay on Roni Horn's *Portrait of an Image* (2005) analyses Huppert's collaboration with the American photographer – for which the artist took different photographs of the actress, each summoning a different role from her body of work. Contextualising Horn's portraits of the actress in relation to the artist's photographs of shifting, unfixed environments, such as the weather or an adolescent's face, Koepnick reads Horn's encounter with Huppert as a ruminative treatise on photography and performance in which their ontologies are not defined by the determinism of fixed or calcified resemblances but rather by principles of permeability, becoming and mutability.

As these chapter summaries will have made evident, our volume is not uniquely concerned with Huppert's stardom nor with her approach to acting and authorship but seeks instead to explore the aesthetic, cinematic, political and philosophical stakes of her idiosyncratic performative style and the conceptual complications it engenders through its rejection of received models of psychic interiority and cinematic transparency. Indeed, several of these contributions use questions of Huppert's characterisation and performance style as catalysts for ideological analysis. The notoriously slippery, elusive subtleties of Huppert's performances and public persona require sustained attention not only to her acting itself but also to the different directions in which her work so enigmatically and suggestively gestures, including questions of film narrative, auteurship, mise-en-scène and the politics of national and transnational cinema's circulation. The various contributions to this volume thus all seek to situate their readings of Huppert's performances within the larger context of these discourses, within the oeuvres of the auteurs and artists with whom she has collaborated and with regard to the broader implications of such dialogues and discussions. In so doing, these chapters map how Isabelle Huppert at once expands and blurs the contours of the position occupied by an international art cinema within the contemporary media landscape. We can think of no figure who better embodies this position and its evolution than Huppert.

NOTES

1. Richard Brody quoted in David Ehrlich, 'Who Is the Greatest Actress in the World? – IndieWire Critics Survey,' *Indiewire*. December 5, 2016. https://www.indiewire.com/2016/12/best-actress-in-the-world-isabelle-huppert-tilda-swinton-greta-gerwig-1201752582/.
2. Cristina Álvarez López and Adrian Martin, 'Isabelle Huppert: The Absent One,' *The Third Rail* 10. http://thirdrailquarterly.org/isabelle-huppert-the-absent-one/.
3. See Pamela Robertson Wojcik, ed., *Movie Acting: The Film Reader* (New York: Routledge, 2004); Murray Pomerance and Kyle Stevens, eds, *Close-Up: Great Cinematic Performances Volume 1: America* (Edinburgh: Edinburgh University Press, 2018).
4. Nick Rees-Roberts and Darren Waldron, 'Introduction—Against Type: Isabelle Huppert's Unorthodox Stardom,' in *Isabelle Huppert: Stardom, Performance, Authorship*, eds Nick Rees-Roberts and Darren Waldron (London: Bloomsbury, 2021), 11.
5. Michelle Cho, 'Face Value: The Star as Genre in Bong Joon-Ho's *Mother*,' in *The Korean Popular Culture Reader*, eds Kyung Hyun Kim and Youngmin Choe (Durham, NC: Duke University Press, 2020), 172.
6. Ginette Vincendeau, 'Isabelle Huppert: The Big Chill,' *Sight & Sound* 16, no. 12 (2006): 38.
7. Richard Dyer, *Stars* (London: British Film Institute, 1979). See also *Heavenly Bodies: Film Stars and Society* (New York: Macmillan, 1986).
8. Vincendeau, 'The Big Chill,' 38.
9. J. Hoberman, 'Pill-Popping Prostitute Driven Mad by Crashing Piano Chords.' *Village Voice*. February 24, 2004. https://www.villagevoice.com/2004/02/24/pill-popping-prostitute-driven-mad-by-crashing-piano-chords.
10. Álvarez López and Martin, 'The Absent One.'
11. Lesley Stern and George Kouvaros, 'Introduction: Descriptive Acts,' in *Falling for You: Essays on Cinema and Performance*, eds Lesley Stern and George Kouvarous (Sydney: Power Publications, 1999), 20.
12. Kathleen Stewart, 'Atmospheric Attunements,' *Environment and Planning D: Society and Space* 29, no. 3 (2011): 445.
13. Ibid., 446.
14. Ibid., 446.
15. Jada Yuan, 'Isabelle Huppert is Having a Great Fall,' *Vulture*, December 1, 2016. https://www.vulture.com/2016/12/isabelle-huppert-is-already-having-a-great-fall.html.

16. A. O. Scott, 'Review: Isabelle Huppert Is Great in "Things to Come." Discuss,' *New York Times*, December 1, 2016, https://www.nytimes.com/2016/12/01/movies/things-to-come-review-isabelle-huppert.html.
17. Manohla Dargis and A. O. Scott, 'The 25 Greatest Actors of the 21st century (Thus Far),' *New York Times*, November 25, 2020, https://www.nytimes.com/interactive/2020/movies/greatest-actors-actresses.html.
18. Susan Sontag in *Isabelle Huppert: Woman of Many Faces*, eds Ronald Chammah and Serge Toubiana (New York: Harry N. Abrams, 2005).
19. Julia Kristeva, 'Isabelle Huppert – le Plaisir du jeu' in *Le Plaisir des formes* (Paris: Seuil, 2003), 169. All translations from the French are our own.
20. Ibid., 171.
21. Writing on sexploitation movies, for instance, Elena Gorfinkel theorises how 'bad acting' renders labour visible owing to its failure to adhere to classical standards of naturalism and invisibility, delaminating the distinction between the diegetic and profilmic in the process. Focusing on 'the physically excessive performance style of [Giulietta] Masina' in *Nights of Cabiria*, Karl Schoonover, in turn, observes how her gestural performance brings into relief 'the semantic indeterminacy that haunts all filmic bodies' since 'we cannot tell whether Masina's physical expressions represent an affectation or a spontaneous natural response.' See Elena Gorfinkel, 'The Body's Failed Labor: Performance Work in Sexploitation Cinema,' *Framework* 53, no. 1 (2012): 79–98; Karl Schoonover, 'Histrionic Gestures and Historical Representation: Masina's Cabiria, Bazin's Chaplin, and Fellini's Neorealism,' *JCMS: Journal of Cinema and Media Studies* 53, no. 2 (2014): 99.
22. Shonni Enelow, 'The Great Recession,' *Film Comment* 52, no. 5 (2016): 56.
23. Ibid., 60.
24. Ibid., 60.
25. Ibid., 59.
26. Vincendeau, 'The Big Chill.'
27. Patricia White, 'Pink Material: White Womanhood and the Colonial Imaginary of World Cinema Authorship,' in *The Routledge Companion to Cinema and Gender*, eds Kristin Lené Hole, Dijana Jelača, E. Ann Kaplan, and Patrice Petro (London: Routledge, 2016), 223.
28. Lauren Berlant and Lee Edelman, *Sex, or the Unbearable* (Durham, NC: Duke University Press, 2013), 9.
29. Scott, 'Things to Come.'

CHAPTER 1

The Unknown Huppert
Catherine Wheatley

Robert Wilson's nine-minute-four-second video portrait of Isabelle Huppert frames the actress in medium close-up. She appears at first as if motionless, cradling her head in her hands. Her nails and her downturned lips are painted a matching shade of scarlet. Her hands emerge from the sleeves of an oversized knit made of soft fabric that cloaks her tiny frame; the left is ever so slightly higher than the right. Her hair is parted on the left and smoothed down to the right, creating a frame for her alabaster face: her familiar freckles veiled with powder. Her lips are downturned, her eyes thickly made-up under perfectly arched brows and heavy lidded. She seems bored, drowsy. Eighteen seconds in she closes then opens her eyes languidly, almost in slow motion.

For nearly ten minutes, Huppert's eyes are the only thing that move. Each time they open and refocus we are reminded that Huppert knows she is being watched. More than that, she watches us back.

This chapter began life as an intuition, while reading Stanley Cavell's *Contesting Tears: The Melodrama of the Unknown Woman*, that Isabelle Huppert has something in common with the women who inhabit the titular genre. Ingrid Bergman, Barbara Stanwyck, Bette Davis, Marlene Dietrich. But most of all Greta Garbo, the actress Cavell calls 'the greatest, or most fascinating cinematic image on film of the unknown woman'.[1]

You can imagine my delight, then, when I came across Robert Wilson's video portrait of Huppert, in which she poses as Garbo. This portrait of Huppert is part of a series, inaugurated in 2004, that involves about 50 celebrity subjects, including Salma Hayek as Marlene Dietrich, Winona Ryder as the character Winnie in Samuel Beckett's play *Happy Days*, and Robert Downey Jr in a modern-day version of Rembrandt's 1632 'The Anatomy Lesson of Dr Nicolaes Tulp'. Each of these portraits is shot in high definition; in Wilson's touring exhibition they are displayed on separate

Figure 1.1 Still photograph from the video portrait of Isabelle Huppert as Greta Garbo, 2005 by Robert Wilson (Courtesy Robert Wilson)

plasma screens, playing on a loop. Some of the subjects perform gestures, but many remain still. Seen from a distance they look like a photographic image, but on closer inspection we see the subject is breathing, blinking, perhaps swaying gently. Sometimes the subject is posed in a re-creation of a painting, sometimes they are presented as cultural icons. Wilson states that for each image, he and his team 'take into account the subject's biography, the subject's personality ... so that can inform the creative direction'.[2]

Why pose Huppert as Garbo? What is it in her biography, her personality, that inspires this creative decision? What, exactly, do the two actresses have in common? Wilson is not alone in seeing the similarity between Huppert and this particular constellation of stars. The graphic artist ShinRedDear recasts the famous optical illusion Young Woman, Old Woman (or My Wife and My Mother in Law) as a shifting portrait of the two stars.[3] Photographer Andreas Larsson shot Huppert as Garbo once again for Acne Paper in 2013, while Carole Bellaïche dressed her in tuxedo and top hat to resemble Marlene Dietrich for her photoshoot. In films, she is often styled to resemble stars such as Dietrich (*Violette Noziére*), Stanwyck (*La Pianiste*), and Davis (*8 Femmes*), in which Huppert's self-proclaimed 'dowdy spinster aunt' is a deliberate homage to Davis's performance in *Now, Voyager*. Nor is Huppert herself insensible to the connection. The actor and director Patrice Chéreau recounts commenting to Huppert, once, on her resemblance to Garbo. 'To my astonishment', he recounts, 'she agreed completely'.[4]

A FATHOMLESS FACE

Perhaps the best-known piece of writing on Garbo is Roland Barthes's essay, 'Garbo's Face', in which he argues that whereas Audrey Hepburn's face is an Event, Garbo's face is an Idea.[5] Huppert's impersonation here is an uncanny reflection of Barthes's description of Garbo, in which he writes that 'the star's makeup has the snowy density of a mask; it is not a painted face but a face in plaster, protected by the surface of its shadow and not by its lineaments; in all this fragile and compact snow, only the eyes, black as some strange pulp ... are two rather tremulous wounds' (the crimson gash of Huppert's mouth is a stark difference between the two faces: Garbo was of course shot in black and white).[6]

For Barthes, Garbo's face is one we may become lost in. It participates in a realm of 'amour courtois, where the flesh develops certain mystical sentiments of perdition'. This is a 'Platonic idea of the human face ... virtually sexless'.[7] At the same time, Garbo 'is always herself, frankly revealing under her crown or her wide-brimmed felt hats the same countenance of snow and solitude'.[8]

Cavell agrees with Barthes that Garbo is always herself. In *The World Viewed*, he cites Erwin Panofsky's claim that while theatrical characters have an existence beyond any particular incarnation, screen characters live and die with the actor who plays them. Watching *Grand Hotel*, for example, we do not see Grusinskaya played by the actress Greta Garbo, but rather 'Greta Garbo' incarnate in a figure called Grusinskaya.[9]

Film gives full expression to the individuality of its performers: their demeanours and dispositions, their gestures, intonations, gaits and mannerisms. In so doing, it assures the possibility of individuality. These things remain remarkably consistent across their performances: hence the proof of the great stars' distinction, according to Cavell, lies in their ability to be impersonated. The source of their glamour, their appeal, lies not in any objective or Platonic ideal of physical perfection, but in their uniqueness. In the face of the world's pressure to conform, film stars assert their distinctiveness.

The drama embodied in stardom – the struggle between conformity and self-reliance – plays out at a narrative level in the melodramas of the unknown woman. These films are concerned with a woman's search for a story, or the right to tell her story. They share certain features: most significant of which for Cavell is their rejection of the idea that their heroines might find satisfaction or self-fulfilment through marriage. This is in contrast to the heroines of the adjacent genre that Cavell discusses in his earlier book on film, *Pursuits of Happiness*.[10] In the films that Cavell refers to as 'comedies of remarriage', the women played by Katharine Hepburn, Irene Dunne and Rosalind Russell enter into relationships with men who are their equals, with whom they are able to establish a 'meet and happy conversation' that results in a mutual journey of moral and intellectual education.[11]

In the melodramas of the unknown woman, however, no such reciprocity is possible. Charlotte Vale in *Now, Voyager*, Paula Alquist Anton in *Gaslight*, and the eponymous heroines of *Stella Dallas* and *Letter From an Unknown Woman* do not reject marriage per se – a good marriage is a thing to be much desired – but they turn their backs on a marriage that is not between equals, a marriage of 'irritation, silent condescension, and questionlessness'.[12] They are the descendants of Nora, in Ibsen's *A Doll's House*, in which Nora leaves her husband in search of what she calls an education, but which, according to Stephen Mulhall, 'might equally be called a transformation or metamorphosis – an entry into a new mode of existence'.[13] Both the remarriage comedies and the melodramas are concerned with the creation of the woman, then. The women who inhabit these films throw down a challenge to their male counterparts to seek a mutual education. In the remarriage comedies, the men rise to the challenge. In the melodramas, they do not. And so lacking a man who is up to the task, these women, like Nora, must 'think things over for [themselves] and get to understand them.'

These women are deliberately, willingly unknown. And their rejection of the couple is, moreover, a rejection of the social. They test the world as they test their male counterparts and find it wanting. Their unknownness is therefore a rebuke to society, because while they are unknown, they are not unseen. Far from it. It is contingent on them to affirm their existence by theatricalising the self, performing their unknownness. Such performances remind others that they are beyond their knowledge. But importantly, this enacted unknownness also functions as a proof to themselves of their own existence: a kind of internal cogito ergo sum. As Cavell explains, '[m]elodrama may be seen as an interpretation of Descartes' cogito, and contrariwise, the cogito can be seen as an interpretation of the advent of melodrama – of the moment (private and public) at which the theatricalization of the self becomes the sole proof of its existence.'[14] With no one else to rely on for affirmation of their values or even their being, the melodramatic heroines become self-reliant.

LA DENTELLIÈRE (THE LACEMAKER)

Huppert has made over 140 films over the course of her career, so it is impossible to pigeonhole her work into any one genre. Nonetheless, we can say that many of her films accord central roles to mothers and motherhood (fathers are notable for their absence); feature an ambiguous relationship to the past, which is frozen, mysterious, isolated; and a relative geographical stasis – the action and characters begin and end in the same place. Most importantly, it is highly unusual for Huppert to finish a film as half of a happy couple. From her very earliest starring role in Claude Goretta's *La Dentellière* (*The Lacemaker*, 1977) through mid-career films such as Werner Schroeter's *Malina* (1991) and Michael Haneke's *La Pianiste* (*The Piano Teacher*, 2001) to more recent works such as Mia Hansen-Løve's *L'Avenir* (*Things to Come*) and Paul Verhoeven's *Elle* (both made in 2016), Huppert frequently ends her films in solitude, having turned her back on romance and often on society at large.[15] More often than not, too, she reaches this position through a series of ordeals, which range from heartbreak and rejection to rape and (self-)mutilation. Indeed such is the persistence of her characters' suffering that the French film magazine *24 images* was prompted to ask: 'More than any contemporary actress, we have seen you die in the cinema ... Don't you want to have a little fun?'[16]

This template is set with *La Dentellière* (adapted from Pascal Lainé's novel of the same name, itself inspired by Johannes Vermeer's portrait of an unknown girl). Here she plays Béatrice, otherwise known as Pomme, a sweet, unworldly young woman who works as an assistant in a hairdressing salon and who embarks upon a love affair with the older, sophisticated François. Pomme begins the film, like most of Cavell's unknown women, as an adolescent (the rule-proving exception is Charlotte Vale who exists in a state of suspended adolescence). She lives alone with her mother, who coddles her, letting her drink chocolate milk from the bowl and tucking her into bed at night. Her father has been absent since childhood. The closest thing she has to a friend is Marylène, an older woman prone to falling in and out of love dramatically and frequently and who treats Pomme like a younger sister, sidekick or pet. It is while accompanying Marylène on a trip to the coast that Pomme is approached by François, who pursues her, relieves her of her virginity, convinces her to move in with him, and ultimately casts her aside. After returning to her mother, Pomme has a breakdown and ends the film in an institution, silent and alone. The film's epigraph, taken from Lainé's original text, reads:

> He would have passed by without seeing her, because she was one of those souls that do not show any sign, but those it is necessary to question patiently, and you must know how to look at them. At another

time, a painter would have made her the subject of a genre painting. Seamstress. Water girl. Lacemaker.

While there are clear overlaps with Cavell's description of the melodramas of the unknown woman, the narrative of *La Dentellière* is in many ways more that of classical melodrama: a poor, uneducated and naïve young woman is seduced by a man from the upper classes who impregnates and abandons her, leaving her shattered.[17] And yet Pomme's retreat from the world at the film's end seems to involve a deliberate turning away from a relationship and a world that is not able to recognise what she has to say, and this aligns the film with Cavellian conceptions of the genre.

Cavell's melodramatic heroines often wrestle with the question of voice. While the comedic heroines of the remarriage films are able to verbally spar with their partners, their melodramatic equivalents find themselves voiceless, either because their voices have been suppressed, or because they deliberately censor themselves, believing that what they have to say will fall on deaf ears. Importantly, when their voices are denied, the consequence is madness – they lose 'the capacity to count, to make a difference'.[18] Through choice, so it seems, Pomme speaks rarely, at least at the outset of the film. What dialogue she has comes largely in response to questions that others have posed of her, and gives little away. Her quietness is not a refusal to engage but a simple question of choosing one's words wisely. Pomme, who is self-contained, straightforward and easily satisfied (though not simple) says what she needs to and little more. Witness, for example, the following exchange between Pomme and François, in which he pries into her background and romantic history:

> François: You've come to Cabourg to meet men?
> Pomme: We came to see the sea.
> François: You've never seen the sea before?
> Pomme: No.
> François: You know nothing then … and what about your life in the city?
> Pomme: Work, and then home.
> François: Boyfriends?
> Pomme: No.
> François: You've never had one?
> Pomme: No, never.
> François: You're a virgin then?
> Pomme: Yes.

The critic Murielle Joudet understands François's responses during this exchange as an admixture of fascination and exasperation: Pomme's lack of curiosity and her manner of being satisfied with so little both irritate him and incite a desire to show her the world she has yet to encounter.[19] Pomme's muteness lends her an air of mystery which is both appealing (her silence allows her friend and lover to pontificate uninterrupted) and alluring (suggesting a still water that runs deep), but also, ultimately, frustrating. If Pomme is a blank slate onto which François projects his own desires, he also projects onto her his insecurities. His parting monologue expresses the discomfort and anxiety that her muteness and inscrutability engender:

> **François:** I don't know what you're thinking. I don't know if you're happy or displeased. You're here, you're there. You never request anything. What do you expect of me?
> We'll never be happy. We're too different. You're bored, that's obvious. It's my fault, I should have realised sooner. You have the right to hold it against me, I should never have dragged you into it. But I really thought you wanted to change.
> In any case, I haven't made a fool of you, although I can understand you might think that. I've been sincere throughout. I haven't made a fool of you. I understand that you'll be upset with me, but it's the only solution. Don't you agree?

François delivers this speech in a single medium close-up shot, pacing the small apartment that he shares with Pomme. When he comes to a pause in his speech, the film cuts to Pomme; but she is not with him in the apartment, rather out walking the streets of Paris, shopping at a market, disembarking from the metro. Behind François are sketches of young women, eyes downcast, anonymous. It is as if he has already substituted the living, breathing woman for these mute objects. Finally, he reaches a mirror, looks over his own shoulder and then turns to stare directly at what the next shot tells us is Pomme herself, now standing at the kitchen sink, briskly washing lettuce, her hands making quick sharp, movements. Now they are in the same room, but they do not inhabit the same frame, just as they do not share a common understanding. The camera lingers on Pomme as she shakes the leaves, wraps them, and presses them to her face. Finally posed a question, 'Don't you agree?', she assents with a single syllable: the French word 'si', which is hardly even a gesture of assent, since it signals a 'yes' only after a negative question or affirmation. François removes a sketch of Pomme from the wall, and hands it to her. She stands, doubled, before yet another drawing of an anonymous woman and slides it into her suitcase, kissing him briefly on each cheek before leaving. If François's half-hearted, shifty dismissal is a cruel provocation designed to evoke weeping and clinging, he is left once more disappointed.

WITHDRAWAL FROM THE WORLD

Throughout the film, those surrounding Pomme attempt to change her to suit their vision of the world and her place in it, to educate her in their ways. For Marylène, this education consists of make-overs, seduction tips and swimming lessons; from François it prompts class consciousness and upward mobility. Time and again he exhorts Pomme to change her job, to get an education, to demand more from life. By the film's end she has learned to tell him what he wants to hear: she has been travelling to Greece, she says, where she saw white windmills (we suspect, as François perversely seems not to, that this is a lie; a closing shot of the breakroom where Pomme sits knitting, adorned with posters of Mykonos, seems to confirm as much). Her answers – more expansive than ever before – are platitudes: she has ceased trying to communicate, understanding that François cannot hear the significance of what she has to say. That François takes her reassurances at face value confirms his inability to speak her language. (The sequence is dripping with irony, a state that Cavell describes as the negation of the state of conversation in the remarriage comedies.) But what about us, the spectators? As the film draws to a close the camera circles around Pomme and she simultaneously turns, lifting her eyes to stare directly into the camera. Her gaze, unblinking, unreadable, offers a challenge to the viewer. She seems to ask: I am indeed one of those souls who give little sign of what rests beneath the surface – do *you* know how to look at me? It is a gaze that, according to Joudet, 'seems to usher in all the madnesses and the cruelties to come' for Huppert.[20]

Pomme's suffering is not in vain. Admittedly, her ultimate isolation is not presented without ambivalence, and, as with many of the films Cavell writes about, it is hard to know whether to read this ending as tragical or triumphant. If we are to follow Cavell, however, the answer would be both. The female characters who inhabit the melodramas are unknown to those around them: 'their existence as independent beings is systematically denied or missed, particularly by the men with whom they are paired.'[21] That may be tragic, but it is not a tragedy, since these women suffer through no fault of their own, but are the victims of a failure of a world unwilling or unable to recognise them for who they are. More than this, these women are deliberately, willingly unknown – and that is something to be celebrated. As Cavell puts it, 'there is surely a sense of sacrifice in this group of films; they solicit our tears. But is it that the women in them are sacrificing themselves to the sad necessities of a world they are forced to accept? Isn't it rather that the women are claiming the right to judge a world as second-rate that enforces this sacrifice; to refuse, transcend, its proposal of second-rate sadness?'[22] The sacrifice that Pomme would have to make to live with François would be the very annihilation of her identity. Better alone, perhaps, with her knitting and her postcards of Greece, than yoked to a man who cannot acknowledge her and who would turn her into something she is not. Her withdrawal from the world is also a declaration of her independence from it.

Something more is happening here, too. In his extended analysis of the ending of *Stella Dallas*, Cavell makes the argument that as Stella, played by Barbara Stanwyck, strides towards the camera, smiling, what we see is not only the Stella striding towards independence, but Stanwyck emerging as a star. That is, she is presented here as a star ('the camera showing her that particular insatiable interest in her every action and reaction'), which entails the promise of return.[23] One way of thinking about this is that Stella is walking into Barbara Stanwyck's future. Just so, watching Pomme/Huppert languidly turn her head to face the camera we know we are looking at a star, and that she might be gazing past us towards her future.

We know now that Barbara Stanwyck will go on to star in *The Lady Eve*, *Double Indemnity* and *Ball of Fire*, just as we know that Huppert will go on to star in *Violette Nozière*, *La Cérémonie*, *La Pianiste*, *Valley of Love* (in which she will play an actress named Isabelle) and *Greta* (in which she will play a mysterious woman called Greta). But even those audiences watching *La Dentellière* at the time of its release knew that Huppert was a star because that film – like so many of her subsequent works – presented her as a star, the camera showing her precisely that attention that Cavell sees with Stella Dallas/Stanwyck, whether she is bathing or ironing or eating ice-cream.[24] Little wonder the film won her the award for best newcomer at the BAFTAs. Even when stripped of ornament, hair short, face bare, Huppert's screened presence is centripetal, forcing the camera and the eye always towards her. When she is on screen, we notice little else.

A SINGULAR STYLE

La Dentellière traces a narrative arc that recurs throughout Huppert's later work. But it also announces her as an actress with a unique performance style, one that will be deployed with remarkable consistency throughout her ensuing career. After only one or two films, we come to recognise Huppert's idiosyncrasies, immaculately catalogued by Cristina Álvarez López and Adrian Martin in their video essay 'I Furrow My Own Film Through Those I Pass Through'.[25] Here they describe, drawing on examples from across her career, Huppert's repeated reliance on 'concentrated facial microexpressions, eccentric or exaggerated hand gestures, vocal exclamations or intonations [and] discontinuous or suspended reactions of shock'.[26] All of these stylistic gestures are in evidence in *La Dentellière*. Pomme paces the streets hastily, licking greedily at ice creams; runs her tongue back and forth over her teeth in a strange, vulgar gesture that suggests the sensual pleasure of emerging from a cold swim; scrutinises herself in mirrors, scurries over shingles and swoops to pick up seashells that have caught her eye, all the while embodying a strange combination of energy and stillness. In one early scene, Huppert demonstrates all three of the characteristics that Álvarez López and Martin detail within the space of a minute. Watching Marylène plead with her lover on the phone Pomme wrings her hands, touches her fingers to her lips, raises and lowers her gaze from the dramatic scene playing out on the other side room, exclaims and flutters her arms as Marylène runs towards the window in an apparent attempt at suicide, and then stands stricken, gazing down after Marylène launches her large toy bear out instead of herself.

All of these movements are relatively restrained compared to the grand, histrionic tantrum that Marylène engages in. And yet despite suggestions to the contrary, Huppert is not an especially subtle or understated actor. Here, as well as in her body of work, her performance is deliberately, provocatively stylised; the repeated mannerisms and abrupt, jerky gestures call attention to themselves in fact in a manner that demands our attention more urgently than Florence Giorgetti's flamboyant theatrics, in part because of the interplay between absolute stillness and sudden movement. This stylisation becomes exaggerated no doubt as her career progresses, occasionally even – as in *La Cérémonie* (Claude Chabrol, 1995), *Greta* (Neil Jordan, 2018), and *8 Femmes* – bordering on camp. But all her performances call attention to themselves as performances: as theatricalisations of her individuality. They are proof of her existence, to herself and to us. But no gesture makes this declaration more plainly than Huppert's trademark gaze to camera, introduced in *La Dentellière* and reprised throughout her career.

Jacques Aumont, in his book *Du visage au cinéma*, argues that it is through the actor's face that their distinctiveness most visibly asserts itself. 'The face has only one appearance with which to represent both actor and character', he claims.[27] Across films and performances, an actor's clothes, hairstyles, movements and accent, amongst other things, may vary. But the face remains the same. And so it is the close-up – the shot that lingers, lovingly, on the face – that in any given film best reveals the actress (and not just the character), at least according to Aumont. Just so, it is Garbo's face that is the subject of so much critical attention, from Barthes to Cavell and beyond.

As Álvarez López and Martin make clear, and as I have argued elsewhere, Huppert is a remarkably mobile actress, much more so than she is usually given credit for.[28] She performs with her whole body. But since we began this essay, as Huppert began her career, with her face in close-up, let's return to it (for all unknown women end where they started, after all), to see what final insights it might yield.

For theorists such as Béla Balázs, Jean Epstein and André Bazin, the facial close-up closes the distance between screen and spectator.[29] This artificial, illusory proximity that it offers intensifies relations between the star and the spectator emotionally as well as sensually, erotically and psychologically, allowing the viewer a sense of bodily intimacy with the star. It calls for empathy. It prompts us to wonder what is fomenting beneath the surface, of both the actor and the character. Certainly aspects of Huppert's performance style – the concentrated micro-gestures that Álvarez López and Martin describe, her invitation to the camera to come close and scrutinise her face for signs of an inner life – make her particularly well suited to Balázs's interest in 'microphysiognomics': the tiny details that reveal 'the invisible face behind the visible'.[30]

What both Barthes and Cavell realise with regard to Garbo, however, is that her exposed face screens (from us) as much as it is screened (for us): it invites intimacy only to declare its impossibility. Her 'absolute expressiveness' engenders ultimately a 'sense of failure to know her, of being beyond us'. The fact she is 'visibly absent ... is itself the proof of her existence'.[31]

Garbo's face thus reveals something opposite to us about the condition of the medium. It signals to us that what seems to be present is in fact absent, and it is not recoverable: there can be sympathy on the audience's part, but not intimacy. In *The World Viewed*, Cavell describes how the film audience's absence from the world presented in film is something that we desire: our absence mechanically assured and not a function of our subjectivity. Garbo's absence, on the other hand, *is* a function of her subjectivity. Cavell finds her 'within a private theatre, not dissociating herself from the present moment, but knowing it forever, in its transience, as finite, from her finitude, or separateness, as from the perspective of her death'.[32] We bear witness to her own knowledge of her separation, her acceptance – indeed her embrace – of her distinction. She embodies 'the lucidity of self-consciousness, the capacity to exist for others, to acknowledge and [at the same time] accept the limitedness of others' views of herself'.[33] Like Stanwyck, Davis and Bergman, Huppert's quality of stardom or magnetism is not to do with her personal beauty but with her declaration of distinctness.[34] Huppert is sometimes unbeautiful, perhaps even ugly; she is never unremarkable. She is unique, and she is endlessly, often hyperbolically, expressive. At the same time she remains out of reach, beyond our knowledge. Like these women, too, she is rarely pitiful, even at her (or her character's) most abject. In her demeanour is a refusal to accept a world that is second-rate. She stands above the fray.

ALONE, AGAIN

If, for Cavell, the greatest stars are those who – because of their distinctness – lend themselves most readily to impersonation, then what does Huppert's impersonation of Garbo in Wilson's video-portrait tell us? Here, this most distinctive of contemporary actresses assumes the role of the most distinctive actress in history and rather than subsuming her identity to that of Garbo, emerges forcefully as *always herself*. Huppert, like Garbo, epitomises what it is to be self-reliant.

But there is a crucial difference between Garbo and Huppert.

To understand this difference and its import, we must first note that Cavell believes Garbo's most emphatic proclamations of her unknowability take place when she is posed alongside a man. In such photographs, Garbo looks away or beyond or through him, 'as if in an absence ... hence as if to declare that this man, while the occasion of her passion, is surely not its cause'.[35] Cavell gives the specific example of a widely reprinted photograph in which she is posed with John Gilbert, her eyes slightly raised, seeing elsewhere. Even when Garbo is alone, she seems to look elsewhere. In the indelible closing image of *Queen Christina* (Rouben Mamoulian, 1933), for example, Garbo's face fills the entire screen. Her eyes look to the left of the screen, out of shot, as the wind pushes her hair off her face. In her lucid analysis of the sequence Louise Hornby recounts Rouben Mamoulian's direction to Garbo in preparing the shot: 'I want your face to be a blank sheet of paper. I want the writing to be done by every member of the audience. I'd like it if you could avoid blinking your eyes, so that you're nothing but a beautiful mask.'[36] For Hornby, Garbo's beautiful mask implies secrecy. For Barthes, as we have seen, it is an archetype. For both, it is bound up with stillness, stasis, and spectacle: the mask, that is, is all surface, a physical barrier (the surface of which is a blank slate that can be written on, no less) between the person beneath and the audience looking on. It dangles before us the possibility – however slim – of its removal.

Huppert is rarely shot as part of a couple. In a majority of her films, especially those centring on a romantic male-female pairing, both camerawork and editing tend to separate her from her male companions, intercutting between the two or placing them on opposite sides of the screen: even, as in *La Dentellière*, placing Huppert at a temporal and spatial remove from the actor with whom she is sharing a scene. Just so, her look is not towards an unseen elsewhere. Her trademark gaze to camera, captured head-on by Wilson, reconfigures the relationship between subject and object, making permeable the skin of film. It acknowledges our look and accepts its limits. At once wry, contemptuous, knowing, and blank. It is a gaze that both sees us and sees beyond us and sees through us.

Figure 1.2   Pomme (Isabelle Huppert) staring intently at the camera at the end of *La Dentellière* (*The Lacemaker*, 1977).

And yet even this familiar look shifts through the course of her career. Staring into the camera at the end of *La Dentellière*, Huppert, like Garbo, does not blink (since the shot runs for nearly thirty seconds, we can assume her stillness is deliberate: it is hard work, not to blink for thirty seconds). In response perhaps to this lack of motion her image in this shot has been read by feminist scholars as, by turns, both 'opaque ... private'[37] and 'passive ... controlled'.[38] Meanwhile Huppert herself has commented on the dangerous potential the image had to overwhelm her as a performer:

> For a long time, you are followed around by the first image, by the first role that brought you success and it hangs like a weight around your neck for years. For me it was in effect *La Dentellière*. After that I had to do three or four films in a certain mode of interior expression and about silence, hardly anything more [...]. Before, I emitted an enormous amount of passivity which the director took advantage of completely. I have gone towards something more rebellious, and I now wish to express this revolt completely.[39]

What better example of an unknown woman could there be than this actress, who having thrown down a challenge to her directors and found them wanting, determines to take control of her own image, to furrow her own film through those she passes through? Huppert's career inscribes a trajectory from conformity to self-reliance (a trajectory that may in fact be mirrored within her roles). So when, in *Malina*, in *The Piano Teacher*, in *Greta*, in *Elle* and in Robert Wilson's video portrait, Huppert stares into the camera and *blinks*, fracturing the smooth, still, mask, bringing it to life – is it too much to call that blink a claim for personal freedom?

Of course Huppert, like Garbo, is still absent. Visibly so. The blink serves as a reminder of this absence, functioning as a minute turning away, an interval of blindness in an otherwise apparently uninterrupted exposure. But her look to camera anticipates ours, and smirkingly declares that even when the mask is removed, there can be no ingress, no access to the woman beneath. Her mobile gaze – focusing, blurring, shutting down, opening up, while all the time the camera remains fixed in place – openly declares the actress's performance of privacy, her knowing unknownness.

Now we see her, and now we don't.[40]

NOTES

1. Ibid., 106.
2. Wilson is speaking in *LIVING PICTURES / A Brief history of Robert Wilson's Video Portraits*, directed Jakub Jahn, available at: https://www.youtube.com/watch?v=lllDq0TIPHwo.
3. ShinRedDear, "Garbo or Huppert." https://www.deviantart.com/shinreddear/art/Garbo-or-Huppert-791887448.
4. Patrice Chéreau, 'The Abyss as Blank Page,' in *Isabelle Huppert: Woman of Many Faces*, eds Ronald Chammah and Serge Toubiana (New York: Harry N. Abrams, 2005), 37.
5. Roland Barthes, 'The Face of Garbo,' in *Mythologies*, trans. Annette Laver (London: Vintage, 2009), 61–3.
6. Barthes, 61.
7. Barthes, 63.
8. Ibid.
9. Cavell, *The World Viewed: Reflections on the Ontology of Film* (Cambridge: Harvard University Press, 1979), 27.
10. Stanley Cavell, *Pursuits of Happiness: The Hollywood Comedy of Remarriage* (Cambridge: Harvard University Press, 1981).
11. Cavell, *Pursuits of Happiness*, 146.
12. Cavell, *Contesting Tears*, 11.
13. Stephen Mulhall. *Stanley Cavell: Philosophy's Recounting of the Ordinary* (Oxford: Oxford University Press, 1998), 237.
14. Stanley Cavell. *In Quest of the Ordinary: Lines of Skepticism and Romanticism* (Chicago: University of Chicago Press, 1988), 130.
15. In *Elle*, in fact, the heroine ends in what Cavell calls the world of women, having chosen to move in with her female friend Anna after both sever their romantic ties with Anna's husband Robert.

16. Ginette Vincendeau, 'Isabelle Huppert: The Big Chill.' *Sight & Sound* 16.12 (2006): 34.
17. See for example, Peter Brooks, *The Melodramatic Imagination*. (New Haven and London: Yale University Press, 1976).
18. Cavell, *Contesting Tears*, 58.
19. Murielle Joudet, *Isabelle Huppert: Vivre ne nous regarde pas* (Paris: Capricci, 2018).
20. Joudet, *Vivre ne nous regarde pas*, 28.
21. Mulhall, *Philosophy's Recounting of the Ordinary*, 241.
22. Cavell, *Contesting Tears*, 127.
23. Cavell, *Contesting Tears*, 219.
24. Ibid., 219.
25. Cristina Álvarez López and Adrian Martin, 'Isabelle Huppert: The Absent One,' *The Third Rail*, 10 http://thirdrailquarterly.org/isabelle-huppert-the-absent-one/.
26. Álvarez López and Martin, 'The Absent One.'
27. Jacques Aumont. *Du visage au cinéma* (Paris: Éditions de l'étoile, 1992), 80.
28. See Álvarez López & Adrian Martin, 'The Absent One,' and Catherine Wheatley, 'Isabelle's Espadrilles. Or, *les chaussures d'Huppert*,' in *Shoe Reels: Footwear on Film*, eds Elizabeth Ezra and Catherine Wheatley (Edinburgh: Edinburgh University Press, 2020), 279–91.
29. Epstein is less enamoured with static close-ups, which seem to undermine the very essence of cinema: motion. But of course as Wilson's video-portraits make clear, a moving image is never motionless.
30. Béla Balázs, *Theory of Film: Character and Growth of a New Art*, trans. Edith Boone (New York: Dover Books, 1970), 40.
31. Stanley Cavell, 'Psychoanalysis and Cinema: The Melodrama of the Unknown Woman', in Joseph Smith and William Kerrigan, *Images in Our Souls: Cavell, Psychoanalysis, Cinema* (Baltimore: Johns Hopkins University Press, 1987), 36.
32. Cavell, 'Psychoanalysis and Cinema,' 36.
33. Cavell, *The World Viewed*, 205.
34. Here I am paraphrasing Cavell. See *Contesting Tears*, 128.
35. Cavell, *Contesting Tears*, 106.
36. Louise Hornby, *Still Modernism: Photography, Literature, Film* (Oxford: Oxford University Press, 2017). See chapter 'Stilling the Subject: From Composite to Close-Up', esp. pp. 106–7.
37. G. Parker, 'The Lacemaker,' *Film Quarterly* 32, no. 1 (Fall 1978): 51–5.
38. Bridget Birchall. 'From Nude to Metteuse-en-scène: Isabelle Huppert, Image and Desire in *La Dentellière* (Goretta, 1977) and *La Pianiste* (Haneke, 2001),' *Studies in French Cinema* 5, no. 1 (2005): 5–15.
39. Huppert is speaking here with Danièle Parra, in an interview quoted in Birchall, Ibid., 11.
40. Available to view at https://vimeo.com/356686543.

CHAPTER 2

Huppert in the Ozon-Machine: Melodrama and Meta-Acting in *8 Femmes*

Nikolaj Lübecker

François Ozon's *8 Femmes* (*8 Women*, 2002) brings together eight of France's best-known actresses for an Agatha Christie-like murder mystery set in a luxurious country mansion: Fanny Ardant, Emmanuelle Béart, Danielle Darrieux, Catherine Deneuve, Virginie Ledoyen, Firmine Richard, Ludivine Sagnier and Isabelle Huppert. At its release the film was widely seen as a tribute to these actresses, and their participation secured the film a strong commercial success in France and abroad. However, when asked about the casting and the homage that it paid to the women involved, Catherine Deneuve answered: 'I am not sure Ozon likes women, but he likes actresses.'[1] This slightly cryptic answer seems to express a certain ambivalence about participating in *8 Femmes*, an impression further strengthened when Deneuve goes on to characterise Ozon as 'a charming boy, but first of all a hard worker. A boy scout who controls everything'.[2]

If I begin by quoting these statements (which did not prevent Deneuve and Ozon from collaborating again on Ozon's similarly successful *Potiche* [2010]), it is not to speculate about the relation between actress and director. Rather, it is because the pages that follow give one possible reading of why an actress – any actress – might feel conflicted about *8 Femmes*. However, they also aim to show that such reticence in no way marks the performance of Isabelle Huppert. The argument will advance through three main stages: the first part will focus on the film's relation to the genre of the melodrama. With this comes a temptation to concentrate on psychological or intersubjective relations. However, looking at Huppert's performance in one of the film's key scenes, it will be argued that such an approach is partly undercut by an almost mechanical aesthetic that brings the women closer to puppets. A final part then considers the relation between the melodramatic and the machinic, before concluding that Huppert's performance is at once non-psychological, nonhumanist, and communicative of an exhilarating confidence in the world's ability to make sense.

8 FEMMES AND THE MELODRAMA

One way into *8 Femmes* and the performance of Huppert goes through Douglas Sirk, Rainer Werner Fassbinder, and the genre of the melodrama. This story is well-known: Sirk took a low-status genre (the 'women's weepie'), further enhanced the stylisation and anti-naturalism, and loaded the genre with politically poignant material. Rather than being *à l'eau de rose* or tacky, his films delivered sharp political critiques of an American way of life that was really just, as Sirk demonstrated, an *Imitation of Life* (1959). Sirk explored racism, sexual prejudice, ageism, and multiple other forms of bigotry without alienating the public that loved the melodramas, thereby squaring the circle of making Hollywood movies at once popular and political. The French New Wave directors and *Cahiers du cinéma* critics loved Sirk and considered his films through a Brechtian lens, viewing the non-naturalistic lighting, colours and mise-en-scène as *Verfremdungseffekte* that allowed the spectator sufficient distance to engage with the politics as well as enjoying the visuals. Fassbinder largely saw Sirk's films through the same lens, sharing the enthusiasm of Jean-Luc Godard and others. He collaborated with Sirk when Sirk returned to Europe, and of course he transposed one of Sirk's masterpieces about class, gender and ageism in small-town America (*All That Heaven Allows*, 1955) into another masterpiece about gender, ageism and xenophobia in 1970s Munich (*Ali: Fear Eats the Soul*, 1974).

It is easy to take this route into *8 Femmes*. It has often been done, and to some extent it should be done. Ozon's admiration for both Sirk and Fassbinder is well-attested. Just a couple of years before *8 Femmes*, he adapted *Gouttes d'eau sur pierres brûlantes* (*Water Falling on Burning Rocks*, 2000) from a manuscript Fassbinder wrote shortly before his death, and *8 Femmes* begins with a reference to the final scene in *All That Heaven Allows*: a deer sniffing around a snow-covered fairy-tale house. Not only does *8 Femmes* make reference to Sirk, but Ozon more generally seems to adopt the Sirkian method. He builds a highly colourful 1950s-inspired universe, dominated almost exclusively by women.[3] He then fills this female universe with themes that betray the postcard setting: infidelity, murder and incest. Most persistently, he explores female homosexuality and gender politics in a manner that is resolutely post-millennial. It is therefore logical to consider Ozon's film as a Sirk-variation, more frivolous than Fassbinder's, but nevertheless a popular film with a gender-political edge. As Andrew Asibong eloquently put it, *8 Femmes* is 'a bright pink candy box of pulsating kitsch, perversion and sweet-smelling cruelty'; it played a key role in establishing Ozon, in the words of Kate Ince, as 'France's first mainstream queer *auteur*'.[4]

However, there are also reasons to be cautious about this parallel with melodrama. This becomes clear if we consider a short text by Christian Viviani on the continuing attraction of the melodrama.[5] Drawing on recent releases by Lars von Trier, Pedro Almodóvar, Todd Haynes and Curtis Hanson, and comparing these with classic films by Douglas Sirk, Vincente Minelli and many others, Viviani reminds us that melodrama is an affective genre that invites spectators to empathise with its characters. Melodramas are usually played out in everyday settings, taking up problems found in everyday life. They are stylised, and will frequently trigger the reaction 'c'est trop', but that does not mean the genre is insincere. On the contrary, good melodrama is – writes Viviani – always literal, non-ironic. Furthermore, it is political and ethical, frequently challenging conventional moral frameworks: in the 1950s Sirk made viewers wish for the female characters to act on their socially unacceptable desires (for example in *All That Heaven Allows* and *Written on the Wind*, 1956), while in the 1990s Almodóvar encouraged spectators to empathise with an HIV-positive nun and a transgender sex worker (*All About My Mother*, 1999).

Given these remarks, it is hardly surprising that Viviani considers *8 Femmes* to be melodrama only 'at the level of style, not of content'.[6] Although Ozon makes references to specific examples of melodrama and to melodramatic conventions more generally, and although he had recently released the great modern melodrama *Sous le sable* (*Under the Sand*, 2001), Viviani finds *8 Femmes* too ironic and not sufficiently literal to fit the category. It may be set in a home, but there is little engagement with the everyday, and more importantly Ozon seems uninterested in generating empathy for his characters. Viviani describes the 33-year-old director as 'cunning and talented' – the first of these adjectives pointing to a duplicity that the second adjective does not redeem.[7]

Nevertheless, Viviani tempers his critique of Ozon (instead directing it towards Lars von Trier's *Dancer in the Dark* [2000]). This is not least because *8 Femmes* contains a number of scenes where the director drops the irony, and produces raw, unmediated emotion. Prime among these scenes are the musical interludes. Each actress was given a solo performance in the form of a well-known French song.[8] These were recorded in a studio session by the actresses themselves and then performed to the camera, in a play-back version, with more or less stylised (though not too elaborate) choreography. Viviani highlights Huppert's performance of Françoise Hardy's 'Message personnel' (1973) and Danielle Darrieux's performance of Georges Brassens's 'Il n'y a pas d'amour heureux' (1953) from a poem by Louis Aragon (and he could also have mentioned Firmine Richard's performance of Dalida's 'Pour ne pas vivre seul' [1972]).⁹ For Viviani, these performances somewhat save the film, adding emotional depth and sincerity to the pastiche. Huppert's song-performance is indeed the most arresting and fascinating scene in the film, but is it literal? Is it non-ironic?

'MESSAGE PERSONNEL' AND THE ART OF META-ACTING

Huppert first appears in the third scene of the film and is immediately introduced as the spinster of the house, Aunt Augustine. Her hair is tied up, she wears glasses, and she speaks in a high-pitched voice at breakneck pace – in some scenes rattling off an impressive twenty words in less than five seconds. Her expressions and movements are abrupt and expansive. Thibaut Schilt makes a surprising but evocative comparison when he writes of Huppert's 'Louis de Funès-like performance'.¹⁰ The comparison with the much-loved de Funès (1914–1983) brings to mind a high-energy performance style where the pitch of the voice, the gestures, and elements such as the clothing, lighting and décor are so stylised that we hardly need to listen to the meaning of the words to understand what is being communicated.

Most of this changes when she sings. The scene, which lasts three minutes and 20 seconds, begins as Huppert sits down at the grand piano to perform 'Message personnel'. This ballad opens with a long spoken-word section over a simple piano figure. Huppert delivers the monologue while four of the other actresses gently hum in the background. In comparison with previous scenes, her voice has dropped an octave. The lyrics refer to the speaker's inability to inhabit a voice and express her desire. Many of the sentences are incomplete, and the verbs oscillate between the conditional and the indicative, gesturing towards an intense desire that lies just beyond the possibility of articulation.¹¹ Initially, the camera focuses on Augustine's hands on the piano, then it moves back to show her in a mid-range shot. In the background, a birdcage with two white cockatoos can be seen. These are not live birds, but wooden models, ironically signposting Augustine's trapped emotions. Ozon then slowly zooms in on Huppert's face, at times cutting to the four background singers who sit on the stairs across the room, gently singing, gently swaying, looking at Augustine as she expresses her torment. When the zoom has brought us close up to Huppert, the piano riff, the background singers and Huppert all fall silent – the film holds its breath. Backlit and in close-up, Huppert takes off her glasses, the depth of field is shallow, her face fills the screen.

At this point she gets up and leaves the piano. Ozon focuses on the four women sitting on the stairs; as Huppert goes across the floor their heads move synchronously, almost as though they were watching a tennis match in slow motion. Alone in the middle of the floor, she now breaks into song, initially *a cappella*, then with cello accompaniment. Huppert performs directly to the camera, her hands framing and at times covering her face (like in Madonna's video for 'Vogue' [1990]). The focus is so shallow that we have no choice (and no other desire) but to lose ourselves in Huppert's face. The four women externalise the spectators' position, gazing with awe and empathy. The camera zooms to extreme close-up, the cello is replaced by a violin, Huppert's voice begins to crack, her eyes well up, and the song jumps an octave. Tears run down her cheeks, she clutches her hands, closes her eyes, continues to move her head, but no longer sings: Huppert retreats to the unfathomable depths she has been singing about. Ozon gives no reaction shot, but leaves it to the spectator to respond. Then the music stops and the four women approach Huppert. Ten seconds later, the glasses are back on her nose, and she is speaking at six words per second.

It is difficult to disagree with Viviani that this performance stands out. It produces emotion in a manner that sets it apart from the rest of Huppert's performance – and from most other scenes in the film. This change invites a psychological reading of Huppert's (melodramatic) character, and most critics have been keen to deliver such a reading. It can then be said that on the surface Aunt Augustine is a cold, anti-romantic, speed-talking spinster, but beneath the surface – as the song reveals – she is a romantic, tormented, sensitive woman. She warns her youngest niece (Sagnier) against the reading of trashy romantic magazines, but reads them in secret herself; she scolds her other niece (Ledoyen) for being promiscuous, but she secretly yearns for her brother-in-law, the patriarch of the house. This behaviour not only invites

Figure 2.1 Isabelle Huppert performing 'Message Personnel' in *8 Femmes* (*8 Women*, 2002).

us to think in terms of a very clear-cut dichotomy between appearance and truth, it also brings to mind another keen reader of trashy romances, Gustave Flaubert's Emma, and another sexually frustrated, pianist living with her mother, Elfriede Jelinek's Erika Kohut – two roles Huppert famously played in Claude Chabrol's *Madame Bovary* (1991) and Michael Haneke's *La Pianiste* (2001).

Indeed, it is worth noting how *8 Femmes* echoes *La Pianiste*. This becomes clear if we compare Alison Taylor's insightful analysis of Huppert's performance in Haneke's film to her performance in Ozon's film. It is tempting to apply what Taylor writes about Erika Kohut to Aunt Augustine:

> [She] seems to occupy a precarious identity between child and adult, prudish spinster and melodramatic heroine [...] Characteristic of Huppert, Erika's eyes bespeak a soul that is ruthlessly intelligent and hardened by experience at one moment, and innocently childlike at the next. One gets the sense that inside, however, is a tensely knotted psyche.[12]

It is precisely this kind of psychological complexity that Aunt Augustine seeks to claim at the end of 'Message personnel.' As the other women approach, she laments that 'Nobody understands my love, they think it's hate.' Following the plot of *8 Femmes*, we could then say that Ozon's film gives a happy ending to Jelinek's Erika, taking her in the direction of liberation: in the remainder of the film we witness how, with the help of the vampish maid Louise (Béart), Augustine connects with her own sexuality, borrows the dresses of her older sister (Deneuve), and finally emerges as a character closer to Rita Hayworth than to Louis de Funès.

But *8 Femmes* is obviously not *La Pianiste* with a happy ending. The film tempts us to speak about desublimation and the lifting of repression, but it is difficult to follow through on a psychological reading. We cannot really take seriously the idea of a 'tensely knotted psyche', since we do not suffer with Aunt Augustine (or any of these characters) like we do with Erika Kohut – or with Lana Turner when she struggles as an ambitious single mother (*Imitation of Life*) – or with Brigitte Mira when she fights social and racial prejudice (*Ali: Fear Eats the Soul*). In fact, we may care very little about Aunt Augustine's emotional life, but Huppert's interpretation of 'Message personnel' still produces emotion.

The scene delivers what I shall call a form of meta-acting. At no point do we forget that we are watching a performance; rather it is as if we are attending a masterclass in how to produce emotion through acting and mise-en-scène. And this masterclass is delivered with such virtuosity that it easily achieves its goal of producing pathos. Throughout the scene we repeatedly get more than we dared to hope for ('c'est trop ... bon'): wondering whether she will she go from spoken word to song, if she will she move away from the piano, if her voice will break, if the song will modulate,[13] if she will cry – and each time the answer is *yes*! The birdcage, the pause, the removal of the glasses, the reaction shots (and the absence of reaction shots), the shallow focus and backlighting, the clutching of hands ... these are all highly visible tricks and games, but they still work on us. Like good pop music – and Huppert's song performance is impressive – this is affecting and entirely without depth.

DIDEROT, KLEIST AND THE ABSENCE OF PSYCHOLOGY

The idea of meta-acting implies that a certain style of acting is put on display. In the present case, this style can be placed between two great classics of performance theory. The first is Denis Diderot's polysemic dialogue *Paradoxe sur le comédien*, written between 1773 and 1777, posthumously published in 1830. Here the main character famously argues that the talent of an actor, 'depends not, as you think, upon feeling, but upon rendering so exactly the outward signs of feeling, that you fall into the trap'.[14] Good acting is about technique, craft, deception; an actor's own emotions, on the other hand, will only get in the way of a performance, for instance by making performances uneven (because no actor feels the same every evening). Diderot's character is not afraid to sum up his argument emphatically. He stresses that from the actor's point of view there is no immersion, only the moulding of what he (in an earlier version of the text) called 'the external symptoms of the soul one adopts'.[15] He therefore argues that only the 'complete absence of sensibility' makes sublime acting possible, and that '[the] player's tears come from his brain'.[16]

Obviously, the point is not that only insensitive people can be actors, but rather that only those who are able to bracket off their own sensibility, and to study analytically, can be good actors. This is why another key passage instrumentalises the actor – but in such a way that it allows the instrument to be ever-changing, entirely depending on the text:

> A great actor is neither a pianoforte, nor a harp, nor a spinet, nor a violin, nor a violoncello; he has no key peculiar to him; he takes the key and the tone fit for his part of the score, and he can take up any. I put a high value on the talent of a great actor; he is a rare being – as rare as, and perhaps greater than, a poet. ... A great actor is also a most ingenious puppet, and his strings are held by the poet, who at each line indicates the true form he must take.[17]

The reference to the puppet ('pantin') and later references to the 'mannequin' point us to another famous dialogue, written approximately 40 years later, but published 20 years before Diderot's: Heinrich von Kleist's 'Puppet Theatre' (1810).[18] In this text the principal voice distances himself even further from ideas of empathy, immersion and psychological depth by arguing for the superior elegance of the puppet in comparison with live performers (the dancer, first of all). Kleist's speaker offers a very abstract, formal gaze on the puppet (drawing both on contemporary mathematics and the aesthetics of William Hogarth). He speaks about the lines that can be drawn with the puppet, and the grace that can be achieved with the strings. Asked about the advantage of puppets, he replies:

> First of all, my friend, a negative one, namely, that they would always be without affectation. For affectation sets in, as you know, when the soul, the vis motrix, is elsewhere than at the centre of gravity, during its movement.[19]

Again, the ideal performer must strive to nullify herself, so that she does not get in the way of the performance. With this idea of nullification, it follows that in terms of grace 'a human [is] simply incapable of rivalling the marionette'.[20]

For reasons that will become apparent shortly, it is worth adding that this emphasis on the external dimension of a performance also features in Kleist's short, thought-provoking essay 'On the Gradual Production of Thoughts Whilst Speaking'.[21] As this title indicates, the topic is now thinking and speaking, not theatre and performance, but the text is worth mentioning for the view of subjectivity that Kleist presents. He offers what we today might call an 'ecological' theory of what it means to think and speak. Whereas common sense suggest that we must think *before* we speak, Kleist's text argues that we only produce our ideas as we speak. We therefore have to throw ourselves into the electric forcefield of a conversation (the reference to electricity is in Kleist's original), and as we swim about, beginning sentences without knowing where we are going, we can harvest the intersubjective intensities in such a manner that ideas crystallise as fully formed thoughts.

Going back to Huppert's performance of 'Message personnel' we can now offer a non-psychological reading of the scene. When Huppert sings, the meta-acting is in the tradition of Diderot and Kleist's two dialogues. Like Diderot's first speaker, and with the help of Ozon's mise-en-scène, Huppert is presenting acting as the job of moulding a performance, with simple stylised gestures, a nuanced vocal performance and the tears to top it off. And we can push this reading harder by rethinking Huppert's talents, and suggesting that they have something to do with abandoning the subject position and becoming a gracious puppet.[22] When tears run down her cheeks, they affect us not as the sign of any psychological truth, nor even because of her craft, but because of the interplay between everything that is visible and audible in the film. The colours, the song, the blurring of the background, the close-up, the gestures ... all these elements create an environment that Huppert draws in, allowing pressures and tensions to push on the spectators too. Rarely has a performance been more obviously technical – and affecting. The pleasure that comes from watching Huppert sing has to do with her being given a platform, and then delivering with a virtuosity that carries us away – even if her 'message personnel' expresses no depth at all.[23]

One way to conceptualise this shift away from psychology and immersion is to work with the distinction between affect and emotion as it has been presented by thinkers such as Gilbert Simondon, Gilles Deleuze, Brian Massumi and many others.[24] A good presentation of what is at stake can be found in Eugenie Brinkema's *The Forms of the Affects*, particularly when Brinkema goes via Deleuze and etymology to outline the broader framework of her volume:

> This turn to the exterior [...] accompanies another turn, from the word 'emotion' to the word that will be used henceforth in this book: 'affect.' As in Deleuze's reading of the priority of force on force, the word 'affect' – far more so than the often taken synonyms 'emotion' or 'feeling' or 'sensation' – is redolent of a topology that de-privileges interiority, depth, containment, and recovery. While the etymological trajectory of emotion gestures at moving out, emission, and migration (*e-movere*) – and therefore evokes a communicative, transferential relationship – 'affect' etymologically allows for a proliferation of concepts related to forces that act on themselves. Derived from the Latin *affectus* (a completed action) and the *afficere* (to act upon), 'affect,' according to the first definition in the *Oxford English Dictionary*, is 'the way in which one is affected or disposed; mental state, mood, feeling, desire, intention.'[25]

If Huppert's performance is affective (rather than emotional), it is because the Huppert-puppet seems capable of drifting anywhere. Like with Diderot's instrument comparison, she goes through registers and coagulates in different and contradictory manners. Her vocal performance signals this most clearly.[26] From the high-pitched machine-gun voice reeling off full sentences at a staggering pace, to the slow tempo of the lower pitched song performance delivering fragmented, hesitant sentences laden with conditionals, to the more measured, self-assured voice found at the end of the film: Aunt Augustine comes across as corrosive, almost anarchic, and arguably no truer at the end than anywhere else in the film.

Considering Ozon's film more generally, there are many other ways in which he moves us out of the psychological register, presenting his actresses as marionettes rather than live women. Let me briefly mention three of these: symbolism, intertextuality and genre (again). Already from the opening credits it is clear that this film offers characterisation without psychology. The name of each actress is associated with a flower that symbolises her character. Fanny Ardant gets the red rose because she plays the character who has lived out her sexuality most fully; Huppert, the most prickly and shape-shifting character, is associated with an orange-red thistle on a green stem.[27] These colours match her hair and eyes, and (as with the other actresses) the colour scheme carries over into her costumes, thereby flattening the relation between character and objects such as shirts, flowers, blouses and housecoats.

In the credit sequence, Ozon is borrowing from George Cukor's *The Women* (1939), the film he originally wanted to remake (but the rights had been purchased by Meg Ryan and Julia Roberts). In Cukor's credits each actress is associated with a feline animal (panther, cat, tiger ...). This points to another – already mentioned – aspect of Ozon's film: intertextuality. The film contains multiple references to both Anglophone and French classics, including snippets of dialogue lifted from François Truffaut's *La Sirène du Mississippi* (1969) and *Le Dernier métro* (1980). Ozon is asking actresses to redo scenes from films that they first shot many years ago, and to offer variations of performances by other famous actresses (such as Ardant reworking – and queering – Rita Hayworth's performance in *Gilda* [1946]). Numerous critics have played the cinephile 'spot the reference' game, and there is pleasure to be found at this level too. These references function in multiple, complex ways. On the whole, however, they not only break the frame of this particular film but weave a web so complex that the overall effect is one of de-individuating the characters presented in *8 Femmes*.

Furthermore, there are the generic intertexts, such as the Agatha Christie-inspired whodunit.[28] What is the attraction of Hercule Poirot and Miss Marple stories? The task of the reader (and spectator) is to determine how things connect, reconstruct the story, find the murderer. For this to work, a number of characters are introduced. These are generally stereotypes (the posh mother, the promiscuous daughter, the mysterious butler), and one of their character traits is exaggerated (greed, desire, insecurity ...). As the plot unfolds, this allows the characters to take turns at occupying the position of potentially guilty. We are interested in these character traits only to the extent that they provide the characters with a motive. In other words, we are interested in the plot at a very formal or abstract level – as a beautiful piece of machinery. Ozon's whodunit pushes in the exact same direction. We do not need to invest ourselves in the psychology of the characters, we do not have to care (too much) about the conflicts, but we can still enjoy watching the plot machine do its job. In the whodunit it is therefore not really the case that plot determines character (as Aristotle advocated); rather, character and psychology are hollowed out to allow for the smooth running of the plot-machine.

At this point it may be helpful to summarise and to distinguish between two different approaches to Ozon's film. The first considers *8 Femmes* as a Sirk-inspired variation on the melodrama. Ozon has taken a popular genre – or several genres: musical, whodunit, melodrama – and packed them with potentially provocative themes. This reading pays attention to the relations between the various characters, the theatre of desire and in particular to the multiple manners in which *8 Femmes* subverts heterosexual and paternalistic norms. As mentioned, this reading is widespread in the critical literature about the film. For it to be possible, we must – to some extent – take seriously the identities of the various characters. We must consider their development throughout the film, pay attention to their queering. The second approach is less plot- and character-oriented, and it is less psychological. It emphasises the puppetry and dollhouse setting of *8 Femmes*, its mechanical dimension. Elements of this reading can also be found in the scholarship about the film. Andrew Asibong, for instance, recounts how Ozon has spoken about his childhood love of dolls and dollhouses, and how this love impacted on *8 Femmes*.[29] Other critics similarly make reference to dolls and to the mechanical dimension of the film.[30] What is less common, however, is an explicit discussion of how these two readings – or rather, how these two dimensions of the film – relate: the melodramatic and the machinic.[31] To engage such a discussion, we will now briefly turn to Deleuze and Félix Guattari's writings about Kleist.[32] We will see how these writings can help to conceptualise the relation between the melodramatic and the machinic in Ozon, and we shall argue that Huppert's performance plays a key role for its articulation. Ultimately, this performance therefore becomes instrumental for the experience of a form of pleasure that shall be called 'nonhumanist'.

THE OZON-MACHINE

Deleuze and Guattari describe Kleist's literature as a 'war machine'.[33] Some of its principal characteristics should now sound familiar: Kleist's machine goes up against the conventional emphasis on interiority and identity, and offers instead an image of thought as exterior (knowledge is outside ourselves), resulting from intensities generated in encounters, constantly metamorphosing. In *Mille plateaux*, Deleuze and Guattari famously explain the war machine via a distinction between two board games: chess and Go. Chess operates with pieces that have different properties and move according to these properties. Go operates with identical 'stones', which take on different functions according to the situation in which they are placed. Chess is about identities and psychology; Go is relational and external. Deleuze and Guattari associate chess with the structure of the state ('l'appareil d'état') which concentrates power in the king; and they associate Go with the 'war machine', with nomadic subjects that deterritorialise and create smooth spaces without monolithic power concentrations.[34] Kleist's is a literature of smooth spaces: it is whirlwind-like, disruptive, fast. In Kleist's text, the 'subject' is nothing but the temporary coagulation of affect, a result of the clash of forces. Whereas sentiment is internal (as Deleuze and Guattari put it), affects are external, relational.

It is important to mention two further dimensions of Deleuze and Guattari's systematisations. First, *Mille plateaux* explains that we must not think of the relationship between the state apparatus and the war machine as that of two forces exterior to each other. Rather, these forces are always already entangled. The state apparatus will necessarily seek to appropriate the war machine, to turn the nomads into an army. The war machine will resist this appropriation, and try to undermine the state as it engages in its attempt of annexation. Therefore the 'relation' is one of internal tensions, not a dichotomy or a dialectic. Secondly, Deleuze and Guattari specify that the aim of the war machine is not (necessarily) war. The aim, rather, is the creation of smooth spaces where desires can express themselves more freely; spaces that are produced by the movements and relations, rather than limiting movements and relations. The name 'war machine' must not therefore be reserved for situations of armed conflict. Writing can be a war machine (as in Kleist's and Kafka's work); love can be a war machine. One may then object that the name seems slightly misleading, but of course the name is deliberate and gives to the concept an edge and a tonality that has been carefully conceived.

A first reason for introducing Deleuze and Guattari's remarks on Kleist is that an affective, geometrical, machinic reading of *8 Femmes* is appropriate too. As already suggested, the eight women make for a kind of antipsychological machinery that opposes the idea of centralisation. The film begins with the murder of the father. This gets the machinery going ('who did it?') and produces clashes and infighting that bring out secrets, sometimes creating new and surprising alliances. At the end of the film – coup de théâtre! – we then learn that the father only *staged* his own death. He teamed up with the youngest daughter and has been following the action from behind his bedroom door. Having seen how mischievous the women are, having witnessed the exposure of secrets he shared with each of them, he commits suicide – arguably attempting to make all eight women responsible for his death. This leads to the final scene in which Danielle Darrieux sings 'Il n'y a pas d'amour heureux.' For this performance the choreographer

(Sébastien Charles) has chosen a slow, almost mechanical dance with symmetries and patterns that break and recompose, flattening relations among the eight women. Whereas Sirk is famous for what he called his 'unhappy happy end[ings]', *8 Femmes* ends with what can best be termed a 'happy unhappy ending'.[35] As the women spin like figurines on a music box, before holding hands and theatrically facing the spectators, there is the clear sense that a job has been done. The film has delivered on the promise of its first song ('Papa t'es plus dans le coup') and even if there is no happy love ('il n'y a pas d'amour heureux'), there is clearly a form of solidarity.

And such is the film: a machinic game of combinations. The colours and patterns pull away at identities, which are further undone by extra-texts and inter-texts, by previous roles and genre-variations. In that process the nomadic women encircle (and thereby eliminate) paternal authority. It can therefore also be argued that the puppet-machinery brings about a smooth space. In this space, only stars feature. Two of these were nominated for best female lead at the Césars – Isabelle Huppert and Fanny Ardant – and with Ozon's many interfilmic references, it is tempting to say that these nominations also involved the performances the same actresses delivered in films by Truffaut, Chabrol, and Haneke – not to mention the performances of Lana Turner, Gene Tierney, Marilyn Monroe, Bette Midler and others, in films by Sirk, Preminger, Hitchcock, Vidor and many others. Consequently, and despite the fact that Ozon keeps his dolls on tight strings, we may argue that *8 Femmes* delivers a remarkable illustration of filmmaking being a team effort. The actresses are *equal* dolls, equal also to the film's flowers and wooden cockatoos. Furthermore, the rarely recognised artisans that keep the machinery of

Figure 2.2 The actresses as 'equal dolls' in *8 Femmes* (*8 Women*, 2002).

cinema going are all playing starring roles: the costumes (Pascaline Chavanne), hair (Jean-Charles Bachelier), choreography (Sébastien Charles), set design (Marie-Claire Quin), and music (Krishna Levy) all contribute to the hollowing out of psychology, making sure that this is a film where shapes, colours and symmetries take centre stage.

But before this description of a geometrical machinery begins to seem exaggerated, it is important to mention that the second reason for drawing on Deleuze and Guattari has to do with the dynamic, conflictual relation they establish between state apparatus and war machine. *8 Femmes* presents a similar relation between centralising, psychologising, and interiorising tendencies (that can be associated with the melodrama) on the one hand, and the depsychologising, exteriorising tendencies of the puppet machinery on the other. The Ozon-assemblage is machinic and puppet-like, but it also pays homage to Sirk and Fassbinder. It is possible to argue that some characters and performances are more psychological and centralising than others. For instance, it can be said that Deneuve is closer to the psychological and Huppert to the machinic. Deneuve endows her role with a certain layered mystery: she is the one around whom things are organised, the big sister, the owner of the house. Huppert, by contrast, speaks too fast and changes too fast. She plays without psychology, without depth. She is all nerves and tachycardia (a condition her character claims to suffer from). But, on the whole, it is precisely the combination of the melodramatic and the machinic that must be emphasised.

Therefore, *8 Femmes* walks a tightrope, doing two numbers at the same time. On the one hand, it is doing a number *like* the one Sirk did, reworking a cathartic, bourgeois form of entertainment. Ozon brings non-normative gender politics to what seems like pure entertainment, whilst holding on to a much larger spectatorship than with any of his other films at the time. On the other hand, and more provocatively, *8 Femmes* is also doing a number *on* Sirk – and on most other directors – by challenging the humanist worldview that their films express. Rather than making us suffer with characters who are struggling to hold on to agency and authenticity in the ideological maze of Western capitalist societies (as Lana Turner does in *Imitation of Life*), Ozon finds pleasure in hollowing out their psychologies and flattening relations between characters and settings, text and intertexts, thereby setting up a centrifugal machinery that challenges the spectator to seek enjoyment beyond the values that cinema (and other arts) so frequently promote: depth, authenticity, humanism, empathy, and a liberal understanding of the individual.[36]

In the light of this, we may understand why Deneuve suggested that Ozon, or at least *8 Femmes*, likes actresses more than it likes women. If the film is a homage to its actresses, it is a homage that works partly by turning them into puppets, into 'Go stones' in a machinic assemblage. No one seems willing to do this more (play)fully, more happily and more effectively than Isabelle Huppert. How can we understand this happiness?

EXHILARATION BEYOND HUMANISM

One last time, we may return to Huppert's performance of 'Message personnel'. We saw that Viviani read the scene as a rare moment of authentic emotion in a film dominated by post-modern irony, but this chapter has offered a different reading. The scene can be read as an exercise in meta-acting, with Huppert and Ozon creating a performance somewhere between Diderot's version of acting as a form of exterior sculpting and Kleist's even less psychological (and more ecological) ideas about the superiority of puppets and the capacity of interlocutors to draw from environmental intensities such as those created in conversations. Huppert is here drawing intensity from the environment; she is coagulating (and is seemingly aware of this).

It is tempting to speak of cynicism in relation to the performance of 'Message personnel' – to argue that it demonstrates how an actress can manipulate emotions whilst not being involved herself. And many critics do view *8 Femmes* as a cynical film. However, an alternative reading is possible. If this scene produces emotion in the spectator (for some of us, even exhilaration), it is because it allows us to glimpse a form of nonhumanist pleasure. It signals something that lies closer to Kleist, Deleuze and Guattari: the liberating potential of a form of being-with that requires no depth. We see a human being bringing together an environment, affecting us. If this performance feels so satisfying it is because it points to the pleasures of giving oneself over to an environment, of participating in this environment as it seeks expression through elements such as music, colour, rhythm and light. This is not a question of finding a sense that precedes us, nor is it a question of denying oneself a role in the sense-making process, rather, it is a question of participation. Just like one must have confidence in the impersonal power of conversation in order to begin a sentence without knowing how to end it, Huppert's performance communicates a contagious confidence in the ability of the world to make sense.

NOTES

1. Catherine Deneuve, "'8 femmes'': "L'arbre de Noël d'Ozon,'" interview by Gérard Lefort, *Libération*, August 12, 2020, https://www.liberation.fr/cinema/2002/02/06/catherine-deneuve-8-femmes-l-arbre-de-noel-d-ozon_392926/. Unless otherwise indicated, translations from French are my own.

2. Ibid.
3. To some extent, the plot revolves around the father of the house. However, he is only shown from the back in a few very short sequences. He has no proper role.
4. Andrew Asibong, *François Ozon* (Manchester: Manchester University Press, 2008), 72; Kate Ince, ed., *Five Directors: Auteurism from Assayas to Ozon* (Manchester: Manchester University Press, 2008), 113.
5. Christian Viviani, 'Permanence Du Mélo: Variations Folles et Élaborées,' *Positif: Revue mensuelle de cinéma* 507 (May 2003): 70-74; For a more detailed analysis of Ozon's use of melodrama see for instance Fiona Handyside, 'Melodrama and Ethics in François Ozon's *Gouttes d'eau sur pierres brûlantes/Water Drops on Burning Rocks* (2000),' *Studies in French Cinema* 7. 3 (2007): 207-18. Handyside focuses on *Gouttes d'eau sur pierres brûlantes*, but many of her observations can stimulate a reading of *8 Femmes* also; she places her argument in relation to some of the canonical texts on melodrama (Peter Brooks, Thomas Elsaesser and Laura Mulvey).
6. Viviani, 'Permanence Du Mélo,' 72.
7. Ibid., 72.
8. The song-interludes are reflective of Ozon's record collection, dominated by the sixties, seventies and eighties, not of a desire to build the 1950s universe.
9. There is also a famous version of this song by Françoise Hardy from 1968. Hardy and Dalida are both homosexual icons.
10. Thibaut Schilt, *François Ozon* (Urbana, IL: University of Illinois Press, 2011), 73.
11. For instance: 'Je voudrais arriver / je reste, je me déteste / je n'arriverai pas / je veux, je ne peux pas / je devrais vous parler / je devrais arriver.'
12. Alison Taylor, 'Isabelle Huppert in *The Piano Teacher*,' in *Close-Up: Great Cinematic Performances*, eds Murray Pomerance and Kyle Stevens (Edinburgh: Edinburgh University Press, 2018), 218.
13. As mentioned: better than a modulation, the song jumps an octave.
14. Denis Diderot, *The Paradox of Acting*, trans. Walter Herries Pollock (London: Chatto & Windus, 1883), 17.
15. Denis Diderot, 'Observations sur une brochure intitulée Garrick ou Les Acteurs anglais (1770),' in *Paradoxe sur le comédien* (Cork: Éditions Ligaran, 2018), non-paginated, ProQuest Ebook Central.
16. Diderot, *The Paradox of Acting*, 17.
17. Diderot, *The Paradox of Acting*, 61-2.
18. Both Diderot's and Kleist's texts are constructed as dialogues. Diderot associates his own name with the main voice (who presents the theory), whereas Kleist attributes the theory to a famous ballet dancer he has met in a puppet theatre. In both cases these fictional framings complicate the reading of the texts, and in the case of Diderot's dialogue in particular, readings have varied wildly. (Kleist's text is of course also known by its alternative title: 'On the Marionette Theatre'.)
19. Heinrich von Kleist, 'Puppet Theatre (1810),' *Salmagundi*, no. 33/34 (1976): 83.
20. Ibid., 86. A third (and, in discussions of melodrama, more common) reference point for anti-psychological acting could be Bertolt Brecht. (In 1936, tellingly,

Brecht planned to establish a Diderot society. See Mordecai Gorelik, 'Bertolt Brecht's "Prospectus of the Diderot Society."' *Quarterly Journal of Speech* 47.2 [April 1961]: 113.)

21. Heinrich von Kleist, 'On the Gradual Productions of Thoughts Whilst Speaking,' in *Selected Writings: Heinrich von Kleist*, ed. David Constantine (London: J. M. Dent, 1997), 405–9.
22. There is of course a tension between Diderot and Kleist in so far as the first emphasises the methodological, analytic approach to acting, whereas Kleist's text about thinking seems to recommend a more improvisational approach. This is not the place for a discussion of the relation between Diderot and Kleist. Let me just make the obvious point that improvisation is a skill that must be practised too.
23. Scholars of melodrama have often noted that the mise-en-scène is affectively charged. Classic melodramas present characters in emotional turmoil; they harbour conflicted desires, run themselves up against social norms, and are unable to articulate their violent emotions. Instead, their turmoil seems to find expression in cluttered settings, non-naturalistic lightning, stark colour schemes and dramatic framings (including the widespread use of mirrors). In this manner, research on melodrama has tended to psychologise props and settings. In these years of the nonhuman turn, it may be time to read this relation less anthropocentrically. What Huppert's performance suggests is that props and settings, lightning and colour, symmetries, music and costume can coagulate in characters that are as psychologically affecting as a wooden cockatoo. Richard A. Grusin, ed., *The Nonhuman Turn* (Minneapolis: University of Minnesota Press, 2015).
24. When Kleist uses the term 'affectation' in the passage previously cited, he is not referring to anything that comes close to the modern (or Spinozist) notion of 'affect'. In the original German, Kleist writes that the puppet 'niemals zierte'. See Heinrich von Kleist, 'Über Das Marionettentheater,' (Heilbronn: Kleist-Archiv Semdner, 2007), http://kleist.org/phocadownload/ueber_das_marionettentheater.pdf. 'Zieren' could also be translated as 'adorn', 'decorate', or 'embellish' and it refers to an attempt at passing oneself off as more elegant or sophisticated than one actually is. It therefore has to do with a play-acting that results from an excess of consciousness – precisely the danger Kleist's text is warning against.
25. Eugenie Brinkema, *The Forms of the Affects* (Durham, NC: Duke University Press, 2014), 24.
26. In these paragraphs, my analysis also resonates with Brinkema's article about *Gilmore Girls* in so far as both Brinkema and I emphasise how intertexuality and speed of dialogue allow *8 Femmes* and *Gilmore Girls* to disturb our cultural preference for depth over surface (I thank the editors of the present volume for pointing me to Brinkema's article). Eugenie Brinkema, 'A Mother Is a Form of Time: *Gilmore Girls* and the Elasticity of In-Finitude,' *Discourse* 34, no. 1 (Winter 2012): 3–31.
27. Schilt writes about 'a carnivorous flower', Waldron about the 'austerity of a dark red thistle'. Schilt, *François Ozon*, 66; Darren Waldron, '"Une Mine d'or

Inépuisable": The Queer Pleasures of François Ozon's *8 Femmes/8 Women* (2002),' *Studies in French Cinema* 10, no. 1 (2010): 72.
28. Unable to secure the rights to *The Women*, Ozon and his co-writer Marina de Van instead based their manuscript on the 1958 boulevard play *8 Femmes* by Robert Thomas. Thomas's play provided them with the whodunit format, but Ozon and de Van largely rewrote the characters.
29. Asibong, *François Ozon*.
30. For example, Frédéric Bonnaud, 'French Filmmaker François Ozon Directs an All-Femme All-Star Cast,' *Film Comment* 38.2 (March 1, 2002): 23; Waldron, '"Une Mine d'or Inépuisable."'
31. One of the most Sirkian directors working today, Todd Haynes, spans the same two kinds of film. On the one hand, we have melodramas such as *Carol* (2015) and the remakes of *All That Heaven Allows* (*Far from Heaven*) and *Mildred Pierce* (2011), on the other, his student film *Superstar: The Karen Carpenter Story* (1987), made exclusively with Barbie dolls. As I have noted elsewhere (with regard to Haynes's *Safe* [1995] and *Superstar*), the difference between Julianne Moore and a Barbie doll is not always as big as one would think. Nikolaj Lübecker, *The Feel-Bad Film* (Edinburgh: Edinburgh University Press, 2015), 5.
32. There are of course limits to this comparison between *8 Femmes* and Deleuze and Guattari, not least because it risks putting too much political weight on Ozon's film, which does not come with the anti-capitalist ambitions of Deleuze and Guattari's nomadology. However, I hope to demonstrate that a dialogue with Deleuze and Guattari's readings of Kleist can help to systematise the relation between the melodramatic and the machinic in Ozon.
33. Gilles Deleuze and Félix Guattari, *Mille plateaux* (Paris: Les Éditions de Minuit, 1980), 439, 468, 498.
34. Ibid., 436.
35. Bert Cardullo, Jonathan Rosenbaud, and Michael Stern, '"An Unhappy Happy End": Douglas Sirk,' in *Action!: Interviews with Directors from Classical Hollywood to Contemporary Iran*, ed. Gary Morris (London: Anthem Press, 2009), 34.
36. With 'liberal understanding of the individual', I have in mind the kind of individualism sharply outlined by John Dewey in *The Public and Its Problems:* 'The liberalist school made much of desires, but to them desire was a conscious matter deliberately directed upon a known goal of pleasures. The mind was seen as if always in the bright sunlight [...]. Its operations were like the moves in a fair game of chess.' John Dewey, *The Public and Its Problems: An Essay in Political Inquiry*, ed. Melvin L. Rogers (University Park, PA.: Pennsylvania State University Press, 2012), 96.

CHAPTER 3

Alter/Ego: Isabelle Huppert as Werner Schroeter's Double
Ian Fleishman

'Isabelle Huppert once described herself as a canvas [*Leinwand*], which is then filled', recalled Werner Schroeter in one of his final interviews, using a word that could mean either a surface for painting or a projection screen, '[t]his is how I see myself too'.[1] Speaking, on another occasion, specifically of his film *Deux* (2002), he describes Huppert's roles, or possibly Huppert herself, as 'a kind of alter-ego and ... a transposition of everything I had in myself when I was creating the scenario and when I was filming this film with Isabelle'.[2] But if the actress, in a seemingly dated and gendered cliché, is a blank slate to be inscribed with the auteur's fantasies and self-projections, here it is only because he recognises himself as equally empty of inscription, or at least as awaiting the *trans*cription she makes available to him. This chapter proposes an interpretation of Huppert's work with Schroeter as a self-conscious staging and performance of such cinematic (mis)recognition.

Following the death of his muse, Magdalena Montezuma, and a five-year break from filmmaking, Schroeter 'reemerged with a new star, Isabelle Huppert, with whom he made two films preoccupied with doubles', James Quandt reminds us in *Artforum*.[3] In the first, *Malina* (1991), Schroeter is tasked with bringing the divided self of Ingeborg Bachmann's enigmatic fiction to the screen, with Huppert incarnating the novel's unnamed narrator and Mathieu Carrière playing her most likely only imaginary other half. ('You don't realise I'm double! Double!' she cries at one point.) A decade later, in *Deux*, Huppert plays both parts, embodying the estranged twins Maria and Magdalena. ('It's as if I were divided in two!' explains the latter early on.) *Deux* thus offers Huppert the opportunity to play both halves of the same kind of split identity she could only hint at in *Malina*. But her approach here, as generally, is not to distinguish between these figures through any obvious visual cues, gestural or verbal tics, and indeed Schroeter's narratively challenging montage often leaves room for doubt about which double is which, upsetting any stable sense of self and other.

Taken together, then, these two films provide an apt occasion to consider Huppert's famously understated embodiment of different characters and what one might call her method, which is emphatically not one of identification. In an interview with Daniel Kothenschulte for the *Frankfurter Rundschau*, she insists: 'It has nothing to do with identification. On the contrary: you keep your distance. ... It's much more interesting that way, because the character isn't eclipsed.'[4] Huppert in fact frequently describes acting as an exhibitionist experience at once narcissistic and dissociative. To André Müller, in an interview for *DIE ZEIT*, she explains: 'I don't reflect when I'm acting. It's strange. There is nothing going on in my head, even in extreme situations. And I do cry in almost every film. In "Malina" I cry continuously. But I'm not thinking about anything while I do. I look at the lights. Tears come out of my eyes. I'm completely taken up by this process. The only thing I feel is the joy of acting. It's fun for me to show myself. Even the crying is a pleasure. This is surely a very narcissistic procedure.'[5] The cloven self of *Malina* and double role of *Deux*, I will argue, can be understood as dramatisations of precisely this narcissistic-dissociative operation. An examination of the concluding death scenes of each film – in which the protagonists are murdered, in a sense, by their respective double – will provide insight into how Huppert at once projects and exorcises herself as an onscreen other.

In interviews and at press events, Huppert and Schroeter make explicit their mutual admiration for one another – after their work together on *Malina*, Schroeter both wrote *Deux* for Huppert and dedicated the film to her; Huppert, for her part, dedicated the lifetime achievement award she received at the 2014 Munich Film Festival to Schroeter – as well as the collaborative, quasi-improvisatory quality of their work together.[6] But whereas Schroeter's cinema is rightly characterised by his penchant for the operatic and the excessive, for baroque ornamentality and passionately disjointed allegory,[7] Huppert's performances, as this current volume posits, even at their most dramatic, have something smoothly muted and unforthcoming about them. This tension between Schroeter's spectacularity and Huppert's quiet restraint is perhaps nowhere more pronounced than at the climax of the films in question, where the director's (literal) pyrotechnics are married to the actor's expressive blankness. This chapter will first build on Lauren Berlant's notion of flat affect in order to theorise what I'm dubbing Huppert's particular variety of *blank expression*, before observing both the continuities and the evolution of this affective mode across *Malina* and *Deux* in order to explore its implications for her role as Schroeter's desired double. Finally, with an eye to Jackie Stacey's further elaboration of the concept of flat affect and/as gender performativity, I'll examine the queer(ing) connotations of this collaboration with the goal of sketching the larger repercussions of the interpretative challenges posed – but also the methodological promise made possible – by our engagement with Huppert's unique approach to acting.

BLANK EXPRESSION

Huppert's self-description as a blank canvas, quoted by Schroeter above, is paradigmatic of this approach. In an interview with Robert Chalmers, she confesses (or mythologises) that 'I had this strange idea of myself, as a child – almost as though my face was a blank page. Because I had red hair, and a pale complexion, it felt like having no face at all.'[8] I'll return to another version of this anecdote later on, as this blankness provides a leitmotif to her career and its reception both popular and scholarly. In a *New York Times* interview from 2016, for instance, at the height of the Oscar buzz surrounding Paul Verhoeven's *Elle*, Huppert elevates this blankness to an artistic merit, highlighting such stillness, passivity and apparent vacuity as what distinguishes her acting from American colleagues: 'just to dare to be nothing. ... A sense of what it means to listen, what it means to have a blank face.'[9] But already in her earliest film appearances, writes Ginette Vincendeau, Huppert expressed a 'bruised passivity ... through the *blankness* of her performance: she could make her dull, vacant stare speak volumes'.[10] This is what J. Hoberman, in a passage quoted in the introduction to this volume, calls Huppert's 'genius to distinguish 47 varieties of blankness'.[11] To think of this in terms of either chameleonlike character acting or of rigid typecasting would miss the point: rather, what unifies Huppert's diverse roles are the protean nuances of subtle fluctuations against a serene and steady baseline.

While stillness is not the actor's only mode, it somehow seems to permeate even her most dynamic and daring performances. Most recently, introducing Huppert to American audiences of Neil Jordan's thriller *Greta* (2018), in which she plays the titular psycho killer, David Ehrlich reminds us that the 'actress is notorious for her illegibility – her almost Bressonian lack of expression, and the profound unrest she's able to convey from behind the stillness of her freckled resting face. Pauline Kael once complained that "when [Huppert] has an orgasm, it barely ruffles her blank surface."'[12] Huppert's subtler but similarly depraved performance as Erika Kohut in Michael Haneke's *La Pianiste* (2001) is perhaps emblematic of her staid frostiness and has, for this very reason, I would argue, become one of the most iconic of the actor's long career. Repeatedly referring to Huppert's 'performative blankness' in this role, Alison Taylor takes it to be an armature concealing inner turmoil:

Huppert's mastery of the contradictions within Erika is evident in the nuances of discomfort, as latent desire surfaces against Erika's will. While ... Erika toys with disclosure, albeit contrived, for much of the ... film she is at pains to conceal her interiority, performing a blankness that is increasingly undermined by the obstinacy of her body.[13]

Rather than her dramatic extremes, what seems both to attract and to repel viewers and critics alike is Huppert's seductive inscrutability.

What can be gleaned, though, from the above attempts to reveal the turbulence behind a placid surface, the depth beneath still waters, is that Huppert both invites and rebuffs – invites *by* rebuffing – the very 'faith in exposure' Eve Kosofsky Sedgwick identifies as the purview of what she dubs paranoid reading practices: hermeneutic strategies invested in revealing deeper truths behind deceptive surfaces.[14] This corresponds to how Huppert herself talks about her acting, as Cristina Álvarez López and Adrian Martin summarise: 'The crux of her performing craft is a condition she calls *interiority*, the dead opposite of actorly exhibitionism. She often appears to be in a state of internal retreat or withdrawal.'[15] This manifest withdrawal is, in fact, the very signal of a latent interiority, an index and expression of an ostensibly inexpressible introspection. Far from signifying nothing or remaining neutral, Huppert's blank expression expresses just that: blankness.

I mean for the notion of *blank expression* elaborated here to build on Lauren Berlant's influential understanding of what they variously describe as 'styles of underperformed emotion, flat affect or diffused yet animated gesture'.[16] Befitting the reticent demeanour I've been identifying in Huppert's performances, Berlant understands '[u]nderperformativity [as] a mode of flat or flattened affect that shows up to perform its recession from melodramatic norms, foregrounds the obstacles to immediate reading, without negating the affective encounter with immediacy'.[17] In this view, by highlighting illegibility the physiognomy of Huppert's flat affect would offer up unreadability itself to be read – and at face value. There is, though, a potential slippage in this apparently tautological self-reference, in that by presenting itself as absent, flat affect *presents* absence: like the presentation of a symptom, underperformativity is a making-present of what is not immediately available to further interpretation but is nonetheless immediately *felt* in, through and as this withdrawal from presentation.[18] (I'll return to the question of symptomaticity in conclusion.) Rather than 'rely on the transparency of performance', Berlant argues, the 'recessive aesthetic does not promise sentimental participation' but instead, precisely through its occlusion, provides a hint of what always '*remains to be sensed*'.[19] In a sense, then, though I'm not sure Berlant would put it quite this way, such structures of *un*feeling, to borrow a phrase from their title, might provide an immediate sensation of feelings that purport to be beyond mediation.

And this might also be where I draw a distinction between Berlant's understanding of flat affect and the variety of blank expression I'm highlighting in Huppert: whereas the former constitutes an attempt, on the methodological level (or as withdrawal from method), to engage with surfaces without presuming that they will offer up their hidden depths, or even that they have depths to offer, the blankness of Huppert's affect, it seems to me, appears to promise just that: its expressive emptiness operates as a guarantor of inexpressible profundity. It points to the ostensibly empty and invisible space around which the performance orbits, it discloses by refusing to disclose, expresses by dint of failing to express, gives access to the seemingly inaccessible. In so doing, it also bolsters a fantasy of an underlying self, providing the apparent ontological assurance of a core identity – however mutable, however hollow – across a diversity of performed personalities. As Álvarez López and Martin have it:

> It is almost impossible to distinguish Huppert's 'characterisation' from one performance to the next. The same placid reactions, movements, and gestures – such as that flatliner smile – recur in unexpected permutations and combinations, no matter the fictional situation or historical period. And yet we never have the sense that Huppert "plays herself" in the way that many actors do. Huppert's 'self' is more mysterious, fugitive, and hard to get a fix on.[20]

It is, however, and this point is crucial, precisely the sense of mystery and fugitivity of the self-as-cypher in Huppert's performances and public persona that *guarantees* its fixity as a riddle that cannot be solved, an infinite regress of the secret self: it's enigmas all the way down.

In interviews over the course of her career Huppert has teased an obstinate privacy, responding to questions about her personal life coyly at best, often with more than a hint of irritation. Across decades, this strategy has allowed her to foster a personal mythology of secrecy and blankness, an anonymity that is itself distinctive. Her most prominent journalistic interlocutors repeatedly comment on the performative aspect of her interviews, the scripted feel of her responses.[21] They also obsess over her time in psychoanalysis, a detail she let slip in the early 1980s and regarding which she gives competing, vague accounts when asked, as she repeatedly is, if she thinks of acting as a form of therapy. Chalmers, for instance, excavates an older exposé by the novelist François Weyergans, who reports that Huppert confessed to having suffered from 'Depersonalization Syndrome', defined, he tells us, as 'prolonged or recurrent experience of a feeling of detachment and of having become an external observer of one's own physical or mental functioning'.[22] In the Müller interview, she describes the therapeutic quality of acting as a kind of self-purification: 'You might compare it to a form of exorcism. I'm driving the demons out.'[23] And if Huppert ceaselessly insists that her artistic procedure is not one of identification but rather a form of dissociation, this also necessarily involves a degree of self-dissonance. Asked further if she ever saw herself in danger of becoming schizophrenic (symptoms of which include both emotional blunting and the disorganised speech and behaviour that characterise her roles in *Malina* and *Deux*), she responds,

> I had to avoid falling into the trap of believing I was identical to the characters I play. You get very lazy if you believe that. You slip into a role like putting on a slipper. You're not doing any work. So, I say to myself, I'm not the person I'm playing, although I know that I'm making use of all of my personal experiences and feelings.[24]

Expertly disseminated insinuations of narcissism, exhibitionism and dissociation converge in Huppert's carefully curated public face, which at once outwardly performs and at the same moment appears psychologically to internalise what we might, with Berlant, call the 'intimate distance' of her professional countenance, transforming this idiosyncratically syndromic cluster of alleged symptoms into an artwork.[25]

MALINA (1991)

The collaborations with Werner Schroeter can be read as illustrative of this art of self-difference not only because they are shot through with *Doppelgänger* and dissolving selves but also, in a more cinematically self-reflective sense, because of the seemingly inherent dissonances between Huppert's trademark underperformativity and Schroeter's own brand of operatic excess. These would appear, on Berlant's understanding of flat affect, to be ineluctably opposing registers:

> The recessive aesthetic ... cannot rely on the transparency of performance. At the same time, it is not merely ironic, paranoid or untrusting in relation to surfaces. ... Thus it cannot rely on the self-evidence of 'excess.' A concept oft-invoked but rarely conceptualised, 'excess' points to an intensity that, encountered in relation to an action or an atmosphere, is irrational, outside of ratio. But the recessive style always ports with it the potential for denial, disavowal, and foreclosed experience. It might genuinely represent a big emotion under the discipline of

comportment and crisis. Or, it might actually be expressive of a non-, or a light-touch, or a diffused experience. But it might also not be hiding anything. In the underperformative scene, one can always say nothing happened, because little happens when it does, it can point at once in many directions. The nothing might mask an event, or not.[26]

At issue in this argument is both a chiastic correlation of scale and the very procedure of figuration itself (for our purposes, in the rather literal sense of making visible on the face): if affective excess, as Berlant defines it, is relatively transparent (and transparently out of proportion) as an exaggeration of emotional intensity, flat affect's opacity is not only an underperformance but also an undercutting of causal relations – its manifestations do not necessarily symptomatise anything at all. The marriage of these two ostensibly incompatible modes in Huppert's performances for Schroeter thus offers an occasion for the reconsideration of how affective surface makes apparent or withholds access to interiority and subjectivity through the disclosure of or refusal to disclose an inner self, be it 'genuine' or performed.

'Isabelle is very intuitive and has a calm centre,' wrote Schroeter in his autobiography, 'a harmonious strength, that she has worked to find for herself, making it her own by dint of experience'.[27] And, tellingly, it is nothing other than this very serenity and harmony (the opposite of a schizophrenic tendency to the copresence of incompatible or contradictory features) that appeals to a director otherwise known precisely for his oeuvre's histrionic excesses, since it makes her body, unmarked by its own desires or emotions, available as a surface for projection: 'She was like a blank canvas on which I could paint. I asked her to shed tears more often than any other actress. Tears are a natural expression of her nature, a product of her body, emotional but not sentimental.'[28] The distinction Schroeter draws here between (natural, bodily) emotion and (artificial, performed) sentiment recalls Berlant's description not only of how the recessive aesthetic subverts melodramatic norms and expectations by rebuffing sentimental participation but also, if less obviously, of how flat affect teases the withheld presence of what remains unfelt and therefore remains *to be* felt – not dissimilar from what Schroeter designates emotion. It also demonstrates how the excessive, like Huppert's lachrymose performance in *Malina*, can itself come to constitute an impenetrable and uninterpretable surface, mirroring the withdrawal or opacity of the recessive.

Recalling that, in his published interview with Michel Foucault, Schroeter 'makes clear his dislike of psychology and Freudian depth psychology in particular', Fatima Naqvi, in a recent essay on the two films in question, reminds us that what the French philosopher lauded in the German director was precisely that his films 'are not interested in interiority, in confessing an inner being'.[29] Of *Malina*, specifically, she contends that

> the psychology behind the figures remains opaque, if not to say peripheral. The film's 'immediate' or 'impassioned evidence' is aesthetic rather than psychological – the gorgeous hues, the beautiful costumes, the tasteful interiors, the camera's ballet, the arias sung by Jenny Drivala. Enshrining beauty in the agitated (*agitato*) movements of *montage* and camera becomes Schroeter's way of 'exiting altogether from the psychological film,' as Foucault argues. *Malina* evades categories of the self and self-knowledge as the precondition for truth.[30]

This withdrawal from psychologisation by way of aesthetic surfeit is nowhere more in evidence than in the play of flames and reflections at the conclusion of the film. While Huppert has spent much of the movie in wild hysterics, as she notes in her interview with Müller, here she is quiet and deliberate, keeping a steely gaze directed at first almost straight into the camera lens, returning the spectator's glance, face pressed against a wall-length mirror, as she delivers her final lines to her eponymic other half before stepping slowly away to reveal one double after another as a crack in the wall of mirrors pivots open, creating an indecipherable prism of reflected selves. It is the most solemnly introspective moment in the entire film and yet it provides no answers to the mysteries of the inscrutable plot, let alone any insight into character motivation. Instead a fragmentary montage is drawn into the image itself, into the continuity of a rather long take, the blocking of which begins to resemble a film strip: an overabundance of reflecting surfaces among which the apparently original image becomes impossible to identify.[31]

In his memoir, Schroeter recalls his aversion to 'technically manipulated special effects', emphasizing that the pyrotechnics one sees in *Malina* were entirely genuine: 'of course everything in *Malina* was for real, directly in front of the camera, no tricks, no dissolves, no double exposures, nothing computer generated. The flames shown on film were real.'[32] And while inventorying the various technical difficulties, dangers and near-disasters this insistence on actual fire occasioned, Schroeter notes that '[o]nly Isabelle Huppert made her way through the flames without showing a drop of sweat'.[33] The deification pertains more to Huppert's persona as an actor than it does to the character she plays. (In these final shots, she is, in fact, glistening with sweat, whereas Mathieu Carrière, whom Schroeter praises as 'cold-blooded' in the same passage, has somehow kept his face dry for the camera although a flame flickers just in front of him.) The vision of a coolly composed Huppert surrounded by Schroeter's inferno also emblematises in a single image the balance struck between control and chaos throughout the film.

Richard Brody, who praises Huppert's performance in *Malina* as 'one of her best' notes that it is

> both contained and hectic. Though Huppert is often seated or recumbent or totally slouched, even then she seems to be in reckless motion – and, when she's in motion, the sense of frenzy is nonetheless infused with a sense of intellectual possession. Her wild gestures and heedless behaviour are tightly strung with her thoughtful concentration, and her poised contemplations and languid passions vibrate with the tension of her barely restrained emotions and the propulsion of her creative drive.[34]

Revealingly, Huppert herself describes Schroeter's cinema in similar terms: 'What's, I think, very special about Werner Schroeter is that there is what we call a sort of craziness and there is this baroque style, you know, but at the same time it's very controlled ... nothing is just at random.'[35] Finding method in the madness, bringing Huppert's 'harmonious strength' to bear on Schroeter's inchoate allegorical fragments, these collaborations achieve an unexpected compromise between flat affect and the aesthetic (of) excess which Berlant had thought beyond its purview.

In the Bachmann source text, the moment of the protagonist's disappearance into the wall is intended as a passing of the torch, as the unnamed female figure gives her stories over to be told by her masculine double, who might then be seen as the narrator of the remainder of the unfinished *Todesarten* (Ways of Dying) series – of which this novel is the first instalment. It is worth recalling here that, at the time of the film's release, Schroeter's treatment irked or outright enraged some critics both for its alleged exploitation of the author's untimely death in a fire and for the purportedly patriarchal manner in which it appropriates her narrative. But one ought not ignore how the dynamic between Schroeter and Huppert (as well as between the director and his cinematographer Elfi Mikesch, perhaps) subtly reverses gender clichés associating hysteria with femininity and mastery with masculinity: here the hyperbolic frenzy occurs primarily in the montage and the mise-en-scène, while the acting (like the cinematography) exerts a studied care and self-control.

As Schroeter himself puts it: 'Isabelle mastered her role in her own way, reflecting the woman's inner conflict in her motionless face, creating a profile of her own, a transcendent Bachmann character.'[36] If the ending of the film indeed in some way represents Schroeter's relationship with 'my alter ego, played by Isabelle Huppert', as the director says of *Deux*, it is by providing the calm core to his cinematic chaos.[37] What might instead raise eyebrows here is the slippage in Schroeter's account from inner conflict to transcendence: Huppert's flat affect – which, as Berlant theorises it, should not to be assumed to signal anything at all – becomes at once a marker of an underlying interiority, a suspected psychological turmoil or even trauma *and*, in some strange sense, its overcoming.

DEUX (2002)

If *Malina* infuses Schroeter's frenzy with composure; *Deux*, avowedly his most personal and most defining feature ('I considered the film my masterpiece'[38]), chiastically inscribes his work into the context of Huppert's oeuvre: it is perhaps as much a film about her as it is about him. This chiasmus is also operative in the relation of interiority to expression: if the conclusion of *Malina* draws inward the excesses of Schroeter's aesthetic into the flat affect of Huppert's blank expression, *Deux* ends, I will argue, with an exorcism of interiority in favour of a transparently surface-level expressivity.

As the oneiric storyline of *Deux* – based, as Schroeter insists, on 'intense autobiographical experiences and dreams'[39] – proves recalcitrant to any kind of summary, it is perhaps easiest simply to borrow the director's:

> At the center of *Two* we meet a pair of identical twins, Maria and Magdalena, both lesbians, one living in Paris, the other in Sintra on the Atlantic coast of Portugal. Separated at birth, they know neither each other nor their fantastical mother, Anna. Each lives her own life, depicted in a kind of surreal overview of her friendships and love stories, her search for beauty, sex, poetry, and music. The remarkable lesbian double nature of the twins stood not for the simple opposition between good and evil but for something split into multiple parts that finds itself in itself, painfully misses its mark, and finally kills itself.[40]

The final lines of this description, while hardly unambiguous, would seem equally to characterise the death (teased by the book's back cover as a question of murder or suicide, 'Mord oder Selbstmord?') with which *Malina* concludes: the same sort of purging of the self of inner alterity that Schroeter envisions in *Deux*.[41]

For Huppert, this means not only playing out this fantasy of the alter ego and giving corporeal form to Schroeter's obsessive 'idea that I really have an opposite number', but also doing the difficult work of playing two characters at once and, as the director puts it, 'incorporating the fine nuances in the various parts of the twins' lives'.[42] In this sense, *Deux*, perhaps more than any other of Huppert's myriad films, allows for insight into the actress's approach to characterisation – rightly noted by Álvarez López and Martin, in a passage cited above, to be vanishingly subtle – as she embodies both Maria and Magdalena. As Michelle Langford summarises the personalities of these two figures:

> The primary distinction between them is that 'Maria' has a deep love of music, which she pursues variously via opera, cabaret and dance, while 'Magdalena' is depicted as a somewhat more melancholy, or distant figure who does not appear to be invested with the same degree of passion for music. At times she is highly practical, for example, telling her female lover that she does not love her or that she is tired of all the clichéd metaphors used to describe love[.][43]

In this sense, reading for an autobiographical allegorisation of the collaborative process, one might posit Maria as the representative of the opera-besotted Schroeter and Magdalena as a stand-in for Huppert herself, with her cold and distant affect. But, as Langford's scare quotes around these two names imply, and as she herself remarks, over the course of the film 'it becomes more and more difficult to differentiate between the sisters, although, by the end of the film it is very clear who is who'.[44] This potential for conflation is engendered not only by Huppert's muted approach to distinguishing between the two sisters, which provides no obvious cues to the audience in determining which is which, but also by Schroeter's feverishly muddled montage, which not only cuts perplexingly and often seemingly indiscriminately between Maria and Magdalena but jumbles his screenplay's apparently specific temporal markings to an extent that would frustrate even the most careful repeat viewer's attempts at re-establishing any chronological ordering.

Figures 3.1 and (opposite) 3.2   Isabelle Huppert as her own double in *Deux* (2002).

I might, then, put a finer point on Langford's assertion that the conclusion of the film brings a greater semblance of clarity to the characterisation of the two sisters and suggest that it is *only* at the moment of the culminating sororicide that the audience comes to be able to distinguish meaningfully and definitively between the two. The death of the alter ego is indeed the *sine qua non* for the individuation of the self, as Maria embraces Magdalena and fatally stabs her in the back in what would appear to constitute the start of a death ritual drawing on a confused pastiche of appropriated cultural traditions.[45] As Maria, Huppert trembles and frets in an uncharacteristically non-naturalistic way, going through the motions of these rites – pacing circles around her wounded double, the knife held awkwardly in front of her, repeatedly stabbing Magdalena before consuming her vomit – with the unthinking jitteriness of a Skinner pigeon. She is, as Langford astutely formulates it, 'afflicted by a similar crisis of the gestural sphere as that which affects Huppert's character in *Malina*, moving in the same disjointed manner',[46] one which severs each gesture from the last, thereby rupturing any discernible psychological continuity: Huppert appears frenetic, disgusted and ecstatic in quick succession. This inventory of transparently overplayed affects stands, of course, in stark contrast to Huppert's usual subtlety. If in *Malina* it is the more hysterical half who is survived by her icily placid other, here the fractural nature of Schroeter's montage has been incorporated into the actor's disarticulated performance. But like in *Malina*, the affective surface this produces in *Deux* is surprisingly consistent with Huppert's recessive aesthetic. Her gestures here are so directly legible as to become two-dimensional. Recalling Schroeter's distinction between emotion and sentimentality, this flattening of signifier and signified gets to the whole problem of involuntary affect as an organic, unperformed – as opposed to merely underperformed – expression

of the body.[47] Langford notes how 'the viewer's increasingly limited ability to distinguish between "Maria" and "Magdalena" ... tends to make ... dichotomies collapse'.[48] And here that would appear to include the distinction between interiority and outward expression: instead of depth psychology, we get automatism.

As if in illustration of this principle, Maria proceeds, with the help of a Djinn (played by Arielle Dombasle) and other figures, to parade Magdalena on stilts, in something vaguely resembling bunraku, to a beach where she is to be buried. 'The idea of the actress as a puppet letting herself be led to the grave', insists Schroeter, 'was not an image of horror to Isabelle but a key scene relating to her career, as she said at many presentations of the film'.[49] Indeed, the conception of an Isabelle Huppert emptied of agency connects this moment to the mythology of blankness surrounding her person; fully assuming the non-identity of a marionette to be manipulated somehow makes it all about *her*. Fittingly, the film ends with neither of the sisters but rather with Huppert herself, I would argue, in a quasi-cameo, looking defiantly into the camera and then dancing, dressed almost as a ballerina doll, behind the closing credits, which pointedly begin by dedicating the film to her: 'pour ISABELLE HUPPERT'. The repeated insinuation of the self-as-cypher on which this puppet imagery draws allows Huppert to achieve in *Deux* the kind of transcendence Schroeter describes in *Malina*: it is not Schroeter but Huppert who survives the fleeting incarnations of Maria and Magdalena, the film and the filmography in which they are embedded.[50]

Figure 3.3 Isabelle Huppert in a quasi-cameo at the end of *Deux* (2002), immediately before a title dedicating the film to her.

SYNDROMIC READING

That there is again subtle inversion of outmoded gender clichés – the male auteur and his female muse – at work here gets to the heart of the political implications of Huppert's blank expression. Building on Berlant, and taking the example of Tilda Swinton, Jackie Stacey has argued that the recessive aesthetic foregrounds a 'sense of the performativity of gender' inasmuch as 'a flatness of affect ... contradicts the centrality of emotional legibility to the place of the woman in the history of cinema'.[51] Swinton, the mistress of flat affect, as Stacey's title has it, mobilises the aesthetic to (gender)queer ends irreducible to simple androgyny, instead revealing both the performativity and the mutability of gender norms: 'It is not merely that we find here atmospheres of muted affect, but that these registers reshape scenarios conventionally defined by melodramatic aesthetics.'[52] Refusing feminizing melodrama, flat affect, when employed by an actress like Swinton or Huppert, upsets gender expectations.

One might see this as the inversion, albeit arguably to similar ends, of a camp deconstruction of gender through hyperbole. Ulrike Sieglohr has defended Schroeter's work against charges that he 'depicts images of femininity in terms of artifice and emotional excess' by pointing out that his 'hypermelodramatic and operatic films' only '*appear* to be primarily concerned with female suffering and yearning'.[53] Instead, Sieglohr insightfully argues that

> In all of his films the actors/performers never strive for psychological realism; instead, the role is played as a role and through over-the-top acting and maneristic gestures, the actors embody a part rather than a psychologically fleshed-out character. Yet ... his representations of excessive femininity are in fact not representations of women. If anything, his performers would appear to be drag queens, irrespective of the fact that actually they may be transvestites or female actors. These representations invoke the drag queen through their flamboyant performance of 'femininity.' Not only do the transvestites wear 'femininity' as a mask, but the female performers also flaunt their 'femininity' with their accentuated makeup. The latter can be read as female drag queens by viewing Schroeter's cinema through a camp perspective. Paradoxically through exaggerating their 'femininity' the female performers denaturalise their biological gender. It is through this double take and turning ground of 'femininity' and by rendering appearance as artificial, that they invoke the drag queen.[54]

While Huppert never, even at the campiest moments of *Deux*, adopts quite the same drag queen aesthetic so unforgettably embodied by Magdalena

Montezuma, Schroeter's earlier leading lady, or the incomparable diva's flair of Maria Callas, whom he revered (these being the two figures for whom the sisters of the film are named), her performances for Schroeter nevertheless cause gender trouble through both understatement and exaggeration.[55] Or perhaps, put more precisely, if somewhat paradoxically, her deconstruction of gender expectations operates in a register of understated exaggeration made possible within and highlighted by the context of Schroeter's own excessive aesthetic.

Schroeter's cinema thus becomes a privileged site for scrutinising how Huppert's 'resting bitch face' as the *New York Times* once characterised it[56] makes of her an 'affect alien' in the sense elaborated by Sara Ahmed to characterise how feminist killjoys and unhappy queers (to take just two of Ahmed's examples) subvert sentimental norms and ideological expectations.[57] According to Berlant, after all, 'passive aggression' of the sort Huppert might be observed occasionally to exhibit when her interviews become too personal 'sneaks around the codes of sincerity and intelligibility that make possible normative social trust and trust in the social. Abjuring the inevitability of or self-evident value in the dramatic, its gestural style destabilises the conventional relation between high intensity and importance.'[58] This is not only a matter of scale but an issue of what and *who* is entitled to an unmarkedly neutral affect – and from whom such affect is understood to be aggressive or even duplicitous.

Alisa Solomon, summarising work by Aaron Devor, has asserted that 'as the presumed universal, maleness is more invisible in its artificiality. Sociological studies have demonstrated that maleness is assumed unless proven otherwise. ... Femininity, on the other hand, is always already associated with spectacle, masquerade and illusion.'[59] For similar reasons, Stacey raises the concern that the underperformativity of flat affect – a staple of male actors such as Marlon Brando – might be reductively 'read as merely a "masculine masquerade"' while neglecting the continued presence of femininity in such performances.[60] Instead, she argues, Swinton achieves an 'off-gender flux' that is 'less the in-between-ness of androgyny' than a strategy through which the historical conditioning and 'mutability of gender becomes visible'.[61] Although Schroeter had dreamed of making a film in which Huppert would star as Frederick the Great, she is not, to my mind, quite so off-gender as Swinton is in Stacey's reading and this has much to do with how the two actors go about blankness.[62] Noting that Robbie Duschinsky describes blankness as 'unmarked training in heteronormativity, alongside class and race norms,' Stacey cautions that 'to read Swinton the tomboy as an "empty slate", inviting adult projections, is to ignore how her embodiments of flatness are encoded as a stylish and desirable knowingness about how to do and undo masculinity and femininity, whose ingenuity is itself to be admired.'[63] Yet such an emphasis on agency and intent stands in stark contrast to Huppert's description of an actress as an empty canvas and her repeated assertion that acting is an ideal form of expression for a woman.

This is not to reproach Huppert for what might seem an embarrassing gender conservatism but rather to investigate how she owns her purported emptiness, repurposing it to surprising ends. To return, then, briefly, by way of concluding example, to the guiding anecdote Huppert relates about her childhood feeling of facelessness, to Weyergans she relates what she proclaims 'an extremely precise memory' from adolescence:

> I didn't have a face. For me, my face was blank white [*blanc*]. There was an outline and in the middle something blurry. A completely blank white [*blanc*] face, completely pale. It wasn't a source of an anxiety or something missing. I was a blank page [*une page blanche*]. My face is a tool for transmission more than a precise projection. And that lets me have anything I want pass across it. When I see actresses with faces much more defined than my own, I see that this can be cumbersome. I'm not burdened by myself.[64]

Huppert at once asserts an innate right to an expressionlessness (billed here as an inherent facial feature) otherwise withheld from female bodies by the gender policing of melodramatic folkways and, within the context of her other statements on the actress's metier, appropriates this blank expression as something specifically feminine. If the ambiguity of the French *blanc*, which means both *white* and *blank*, betrays, perhaps, a tacit normative assumption about the presumed or perceived neutrality of racial whiteness, here Huppert would seem to extend such a claim to unmarked anonymity into the sphere of gender, refuting the demand that femininity manifest itself melodramatically and taking recourse, instead, to what Stacey calls 'the absent presence of "the affect which is not one"'.[65] By the same token, however, Huppert crafts this professed facial featurelessness itself into her defining feature. *Markedly* anonymous, she is, to borrow a phrase attributed to Ingeborg Bachmann, there by not being there.[66]

Berlant concludes their essay on flat affect with methodological reflections on the question of symptomaticity, noting that

> a symptom is itself a genre of underperformativity, as it conveys and diffuses processes that cannot be tracked back causally through the formalism of a close reading, surface reading, distant reading or any preferred norm of encountering a surface as though it actually expresses all of the intensities it mediates in its aspiration to make something

available for an encounter[.] ... A symptom is a blockage to method. An impersonal gesture, as it reaches out it recedes.[67]

Further recognising that 'all symptoms are symptom clusters', Berlant ultimately calls for a 'syndromic protocol [requiring] competence in allowing the discernment of the senses to work, follow things out, and to develop forensics, logistics, and heuristics. The challenge of capturing its constitutive movement is a discipline in allowing, while attending to, recessive action.'[68] But attention to Huppert's peculiar variety of absent presence, her blank expression, as part of such a symptom cluster (attributable, for example to the Depersonalization Syndrome from which she is said to have suffered) might point up the difficulties of this interpretative challenge and issue a particular obstacle for Berlant's syndromic protocol – summarised by Stacey, with reference to Sedgwick's 'famous diagnosis of critical reading tendencies' as '[s]imultaneousy "paranoid" and "reparative"' – by highlighting how even gentle, non-dogmatic attention to the surfaces of what Berlant alternately dubs flat affect and the recessive aesthetic still nevertheless cannot seem to keep from assuming that something, whatever it might be, has in fact receded.[69] For if Berlant's explicitly stated aim is to 'resist the methodological impulse to overread the body that is unforthcoming, while maintaining attention to the multiple forces expressed through that body',[70] Huppert's odd admixture of narcissism and dissociation, which at once invites and rebuffs, invites *by* resisting paranoid reading, tends to screen – in the contranymic senses of projection and concealment, covering and uncovering – the as-yet-to-be-interpreted as the site of a mysterious subjectivity kept intact by its inaccessibility. Flat affect, Stacey admits, 'leaves a vacuum that we try and fill with context'.[71] But whereas, in Stacey's reading of Swinton, this encounter exposes a productively protean queerness, with Huppert it rather tends to bring us face to face with the immutable countenance of an actress who is somehow always nothing other than herself.

NOTES

1. Werner Schroeter, '"Gegen das Rohe und Brutale steht die Verfeinerung": Werner Schroeter auf der Viennale 2008,' interview by *artechock* Filmmagazin, https://www.artechock.de/film/text/interview/s/schroeter_2010. Unless otherwise indicated, all translations are my own. Huppert has made similar statements as recently as 2017. See, for example, Jocelyn Noveck, 'Isabelle Huppert: I'm Not an Artist, I'm the Canvas.' *AP News*, February 15, 2017, https://apnews.com/article/971f97e64e8a44988ef17dd93dca3122.

2. These comments are drawn from a press conference, in English, given by Schroeter and Huppert on the occasion of the second annual French Film Week and the coinciding Huppert retrospective at the German Film Museum in Frankfurt on 8 July 2009. Katja Simon and Nicolai Jürgens, 'Isabelle Huppert und Werner Schroeter zu Besuch in Frankfurt.' Cowboy Angels Filmproduktion, 2009. Mediathek Hessen. https://www.mediathek-hessen.de/medienview_5744_Nicolai-Bockelmann-OK-Offenbach-Frankfurt-Isabelle-Huppert-und-Werner-Schr%C3%B6ter-zu-Besuch-in-Frankfu.
3. James Quandt, 'Magnificent Obsession: The Films of Werner Schroeter,' *Artforum* 50, no. 9 (May 2012), 261.
4. Isabelle Huppert, '"Ich nenne das eine Art von Unschuld: Isabelle Huppert im Interview,' interview by Daniel Kothenschulte, *Frankfurter Rundschau*, July 26, 2009, https://www.fr.de/panorama/ich-nenne-eine-unschuld-11485025.
5. Isabelle Huppert, '"Ich treibe die Teufel aus": André Müller spricht mit der Schauspielerin Isabelle Huppert,' interview by André Müller, *DIE ZEIT*, July 4, 1991, https://www.zeit.de/1991/02/ich-treibe-die-teufel-aus.
6. For instance, at the Frankfurt press conference, where Schroeter contends, with reference to Jelinek's screenplay for *Malina* that 'the freer you are with the scenario when shooting, the better the film becomes, because it starts to ... breathe'. Schroeter distinguishes here between the source novel by Bachmann, Jelinek's script and 'our creation: Isabelle and my person, created something new.' Simon and Jürgens, 'Besuch in Frankfurt.' When asked about the aleatory aspects of acting, Huppert tends to cite Robert Wilson's dictum that acting is always improvisation.
7. Take, for instance, just the titles of Quandt's piece for *Artforum*, 'Magnificent Obsession,' or of Ulrike Sieglohr's in *Film Comment*, 'Divine Rapture,' *Film Comment* 48, no. 3 (May/June 2012): 50-55. Such descriptions can be traced back to the earliest scholarship on Schroeter: for example, Timothy Corrigan's essays 'Werner Schroeter's Operatic Cinema,' *Discourse* 3 (Spring 1981): 46–59; and 'On the Edge of History: The Radiant Spectacle of Werner Schroeter,' *Film Quarterly* 37, no. 4 (Summer 1984): 6–18.
8. Isabelle Huppert, 'I don't have a reputation for being difficult. Because I've been shrewd enough not to let it show,' interview by Robert Chalmers, *Independent on Sunday* (July 4, 2010), 12.
9. In Rachel Donadio, 'The Enduring Allure of Isabelle Huppert,' *New York Times Style Magazine*, November 30, 2016, https://www.nytimes.com/2016/11/30/t-magazine/isabelle-huppert-elle-movie-interview.html.
10. Ginette Vincendeau, 'Isabelle Huppert: The Big Chill,' *Sight & Sound* 16, no. 12 (2006), 37. Original emphasis.
11. J. Hoberman, 'Pill-Popping Prostitute Driven Mad by Crashing Piano Chords,' *Village Voice*, February 24, 2004. https://www.villagevoice.com/2004/02/24/pill-popping-prostitute-driven-mad-by-crashing-piano-chords.
12. David Ehrlich, 'Killer Instinct: Why Isabelle Huppert Is Still the Most Dangerous Actress in the World,' *IndieWire*, February 28, 2019, https://www.indiewire.com/2019/02/isabelle-huppert-interview-greta-1202047935/.

The quotation from Pauline Kael is frequently cited, but I have been unable to find its source in any of the published collections of her reviews and writings on film.
13. Alison Taylor, 'Isabelle Huppert in *The Piano Teacher*,' in *Close-Up: Great Cinematic Performances*, eds Murray Pomerance and Kyle Stevens (Edinburgh: Edinburgh University Press, 2018), 224, 225.
14. See Eve Kosofsky Sedgwick, 'Paranoid Reading and Reparative Reading, or, You're so Paranoid, You Probably Think This Essay Is About You,' in *Touching Feeling: Affect, Pedagogy, Performativity* (Durham: Duke University Press, 2002), 123–51; here: 139.
15. Cristina Álvarez López and Adrian Martin, 'Isabelle Huppert: The Absent One,' *The Third Rail* 10 http://thirdrailquarterly.org/isabelle-huppert-the-absent-one/. Original emphasis.
16. Lauren Berlant, 'Structures of Unfeeling: Mysterious Skin,' *International Journal of Politics, Culture, and Society* 28, no. 3 (September 2015): 193.
17. Ibid., 193.
18. I have in mind here Werner Hamacher's helpful notion of the *afformative* as that which exceeds (linguistic) presentation but also threatens to undo it: 'The afformative is the ellipsis which silently accompanies any act and which may silently interrupt any speech act.' See, in particular, Werner Hamacher, "Afformative, Strike: Benjamin's "Critique of Violence",' trans. Dana Hollander, in *Walter Benjamin's Philosophy: Destruction and Experience*, eds Andrew Benjamin and Peter Osborne (Manchester: Clinamen Press, 2000), 110–38; here: 128n12. I am thankful especially to Dominik Zechner, but also to Zachary Sng and others, for encouraging me to a more careful consideration of Hamacher's work, which continues to be informative for various projects.
19. Berlant, 'Structures of Unfeeling,' 195. Original emphasis.
20. Álvarez López and Martin, 'The Absent One.'
21. Chalmers senses a shift in her demeanour, for instance, from small talk to formal interview:

> Once I turn on the digital recorder, the mood changes. … And now that she's speaking for the record, Huppert is, so to speak, "on" in much the same way she would be in any other dramatic performance. The flow of conversation stops. She waits for questions. She uses silence rather as management trainees are taught to do, saying nothing in the expectation that the person on the other side of the desk (asking for a pay rise, say) will feel awkward and blurt out a retraction. The less she likes what she's asked, the longer the pause. (Huppert, 'I don't have a reputation,' 11)

François Weyergans notes that

> [a]fter just an hour of conversation, Isabelle has dropped phrases like "mystery," "hiding oneself," "a mystery if not revealed, at least explored," "getting close to something mysterious," "controlling oneself and losing oneself". She finishes all of her sentences. One has the sense that they

are not improvised. I am watching her play her role as actress giving an interview. It's solid work. (François Weyergans, 'Isabelle Huppert: Drapée dans son mystère.' *Paris-Match* 2885 [September 2, 2004]: 57)

22. Huppert, 'I don't have a reputation,' 12; Weyergans, 'Drapée dans son mystère,' 58.
23. Huppert quoted in Müller, 'Ich treibe die Teufel aus.'
24. Ibid.
25. Berlant, 'Structures of Unfeeling,' 196, 207.
26. Ibid., 195.
27. Werner Schroeter with Claudia Lenssen, *Days of Twilight, Nights of Frenzy: A Memoir*, trans. Anthea Bell (Chicago: University of Chicago Press, 2017), 202.
28. Schroeter with Lenssen, *Days of Twilight*, 203.
29. Fatima Naqvi, '"Psycho" Biography: *Malina* (1991),' in *Werner Schroeter*, ed. Roy Grundmann (Vienna: Österreichisches Filmmuseum, 2018), 140–57; here: 151–2.
30. Ibid., 152.
31. For a more detailed reading of this sequence, see my chapter on the film and the novel upon which it was based. Ian Fleishman, 'The Woman on the Wall: Ingeborg Bachmann's *Malina* (1971) – Elfriede Jelinek's and Werner Schroeter's *Malina* (1991),' in *An Aesthetics of Injury: The Narrative Wound from Baudelaire to Tarantino* (Evanston: Northwestern University Press, 2018), 139–65, esp. 161–4.
32. Schroeter with Lenssen, *Days of Twilight*, 179.
33. Ibid., 179.
34. Richard Brody, 'The Literary Frenzy of Werner Schroeter's *Malina*,' *The Front Row* (Blog), *The New Yorker*. November 15, 2020, https://www.newyorker.com/culture/the-front-row/the-literary-frenzy-of-werner-schroeters-malina.
35. In Simon and Jürgens, 'Besuch in Frankfurt.'
36. Schroeter with Lenssen, *Days of Twilight*, 179.
37. Ibid., 11.
38. Ibid., 207.
39. Ibid., 203.
40. Ibid., 204.
41. Ingeborg Bachmann, *'Todesarten' – Projekt*, eds Robert Pichl, Monika Albrecht and Dirk Göttsche (Munich: Piper, 1995), 3, 1: 141.
42. Schroeter with Lenssen, *Days of Twilight*, 204, 205.
43. Michelle Langford, *Allegorical Images: Tableau, Time and Gesture in the Cinema of Werner Schroeter* (Bristol, United Kingdom: Intellect Books, 2006), 58.
44. Langford, *Allegorical Images*, 58. Langford also notes the film's 'very complex temporal structure, cutting randomly between the years 2000, 1955, 1977, 1963, 1993, 1981,1984, 1971, 1978, 1985, 1962 and 1999, which are, however, almost never concretely stated in the film'. Ibid., 58. Langford, who had access to the film's unpublished dialogue list, admits that '[i]t is almost impossible, however, for the viewer to know the years in which the events take place, except via the

costumes and gestures of the characters'. Ibid., 84n20. Compounding this is the spatial disorientation produced by 'cutting between diverse locations in Marsailles [sic], Sintra, Arles, Lisbon and Paris, our only clues being our own scraps of cultural memory of these places'. Ibid., 58.
45. Schroeter admits that while he 'drew inspiration from Indian myths; I made them a part of my personal universe, as a ritual between life and death'. Schroeter with Lenssen, *Days of Twilight*, 205.
46. Langford, *Allegorical Images*, 62.
47. Ibid., 60.
48. Ibid., 60.
49. Schroeter with Lenssen, *Days of Twilight*, 206.
50. This is because, as Rei Terada summarises it, affect is not traditionally assumed to imply subjectivity in the same way emotion does: 'Auto-affection, the mode of transparent self-reflexivity, ensures passage from affect – mere corporeal sensation – to meaningfully interpretative emotions that can be ascribed to subjects.' Rei Terada, *Feeling in Theory: Emotion After the Death of the Subject* (Cambridge: Harvard University Press, 2003), 17. Huppert's automatism, her feeling that she just acts on autopilot, reduces emotion, or perhaps rather distils it, into two-dimensional affect.
51. Jackie Stacey, 'Crossing Over with Tilda Swinton—the Mistress of "Flat Affect",' *International Journal of Politics, Culture, and Society* 28, no. 3 (September 2015): 243–71; here: 237, 249.
52. Ibid., 253.
53. Ulrike Sieglohr, 'Why Drag the Diva into It? Werner Schroeter's Gay Representation of Femininity,' in *Triangulated Visions: Women in Recent German Cinema*, eds Ingeborg Majer O'Sickey and Ingeborg von Zadow (Albany: State University of New York Press, 1998), 164, my emphasis.
54. Ibid., 165.
55. Langford also points out the inescapable Biblical association with 'the thematic dichotomy of the "virgin" and "whore" that is [...] conjured by these names'. Langford, *Allegorical Images*, 60.
56. Ruth La Feria, 'Isabelle Huppert: The Best Way to Please Is Not to Please,' *The New York Times*, February 23, 2017, https://www.nytimes.com/2017/02/23/fashion/isabelle-huppert-oscar-nominee-elle.html.
57. Sara Ahmed, *The Promise of Happiness* (Durham: Duke University Press, 2010).
58. Berlant, 'Structures of Unfeeling,' 195.
59. Alisa Solomon, 'It's Never Too Late to Switch,' in *Crossing the Stage: Controversies on Cross-Dressing*, ed. Leslie Ferris (London: Routledge, 1993), 145. See also Aaron Devor, *Gender Blending: Confronting the Limits of Duality* (Bloomington: Indiana University Press, 1989).
60. Stacey, 'Crossing Over,' 259.
61. Ibid., 267–8.
62. Schroeter with Lenssen, *Days of Twilight*, 203.
63. Stacey, 'Crossing Over,' 262.
64. Weyergans, 'Drapée dans son mystère,' 59.

65. Stacey, 'Crossing Over,' 268. Stacey perhaps has in mind the double sense, more pronounced in French than English, of the word *mannequin* – either a human model or a dummy – when she describes Swinton 'as if [in] a fashion show, and as if a model', noting that 'she appears at one remove from us and yet is intensely physically present'. Ibid., 258.
66. 'Ich werde da sein indem ich nicht da bin [I will be there by not being there].' Quoted on the back cover of Elfriede Jelinek's printed version of her screenplay for *Malina*. Elfriede Jelinek, *Isabelle Huppert in Malina: Ein Filmbuch. Nach dem Roman von Ingeborg Bachmann* (Frankfurt am Main: Suhrkamp, 1991).
67. Berlant, 'Structures of Unfeeling,' 209.
68. Ibid., 210.
69. Stacey, 'Crossing Over,' 244.
70. Berlant, 'Structures of Unfeeling,' 199.
71. Stacey, 'Crossing Over,' 268.

CHAPTER 4

Laughing in the Face of Death: The Comedic Force of Isabelle Huppert in *La Cérémonie*
Karen Redrobe

In the course of an interview with Isabelle Huppert, Nick James observes that her humour has been somewhat overlooked: 'One of the things that attaches itself to you is the idea that you play a lot of cool characters who are quite intellectual, but I also see you in many comedy roles.'[1] Critics tend to associate Huppert, Ginette Vincendeau points out, with 'the cerebral cachet of auteur cinema'.[2] But it is precisely this conflation of auteur cinema's intellectual aura with art cinema's characters that Huppert rejects:

> I don't think I have played intellectual roles. I never know what that means. ... It is more because I was in certain types of films that have a certain depth and a certain amount of reflection and a certain vision of the world, so you tend to identify the actress as the director in a way ... No role is intellectual or not, all roles are both, and carnal too. So it is hard for me to make the difference between intellectual and the lighter roles. But you do have dramas, you do have comedies, you do have more or less light films and that makes a difference. (James, np)

This insistence comes up more than once: 'Even in the 'The Piano Teacher,'' she states, 'there are a few moments where it's very, very funny ... if you don't put this sense of humour in films, you don't have cinema ... it's up to the actor to extract the potential of a line to be funny. I think that's really my contribution.'[3] In the spirit of Huppert's refusal to align the comedic with the lighter genres and her remarkable suggestion that the essence of both cinema and her own acting might ultimately be comedy, I ask how employing the lens of comedy to analyse one of Huppert's most violent roles, Jeanne, the postmistress in Claude Chabrol's *La Cérémonie* (1995), impacts our understanding of the film.[4]

Sometimes described as Chabrol's greatest film, *La Cérémonie* is an adaptation of Ruth Rendell's 1977 novel, *A Judgement in Stone*, already adapted for the screen in 1986 as *The Housekeeper* by the Iraqi filmmaker Ousama Rawi (who also advised on *La Cérémonie*).[5] Chabrol shifts Rendell's setting from the United Kingdom to the French region around Saint-Malo in Brittany. In Chabrol's version, the story depicts the relationship between Jeanne (Huppert), a playful and defiant postal worker, and Sophie (or 'la bonne') (Sandrine Bonnaire), who is hired by Catherine Lelièvre (Jacqueline Bisset) to work as a maid for her family, which includes her second husband, Georges Lelièvre (Jean-Pierre Cassel), Georges' daughter Melinda (Virginie Ledoyen), and Catherine's son, Gilles (Valentin Merlet). Sophie hides that she is illiterate, and Sophie and Jeanne become close in part because they have each been suspected of – and perhaps got away with – murdering a relative (Sophie, her father, and Jeanne, her four-year-old daughter). Georges dislikes Jeanne and so forbids her to enter their home to visit Sophie. After he fires Sophie for various acts of disobedience, the two friends ultimately execute the family with shotguns during a performance of Mozart's *Don Giovanni* televised live from the Salzburg Festival in an unplanned eruption of brutal violence that is disturbingly funny.

Huppert's performance as Jeanne is defined by brilliantly-controlled physical and verbal comedy, yet this aspect of her role has been largely diminished, or pathologised.[6] While there are aspects of madness to Jeanne's character, it is not enough to collapse madness and comedy, in part because these moments of madcap extremity are often nuanced by quiet intimacy between Sophie and Jeanne, as when, shortly before the two wreak havoc at the Catholic centre, Jeanne describes being utterly abandoned in pregnancy, with no one to talk to, dry her tears or help her get an abortion. Similarly, after their shooting rampage, the script states that Jeanne 'looks at [Sophie] with infinite gentleness', and she affirms their action with a rational 'on a bien fait' ('we did a good job').[7] The confusion Huppert's humour causes may be one reason that critics avoid it. But in thinking about what to do with this inassimilable humour, I am inspired by the Black feminist scholar Tiffany Lethabo King, who introduces the oceanic metaphor of 'Black shoals' as a slowing space to 'disrupt the movement of modern thought, time, and space to enable something else to form, coalesce, and emerge'. Furthermore, King argues, the shoal functions as an explicit critique of the way that a Marxist-inspired humanism's focus on labour can erase the anti-Black and genocidal violence that sustains white domination not only in past conquests, but 'in the present motion of the now'.[8] King's project puts Black feminism and Native and Indigenous feminism in dialogue with each other in order to make visible the violences that 'make White and human world-making possible'.[9] *La Cérémonie* depicts late 20th-century France as an entirely white world, at least at first glance; and I am interested in thinking across Huppert's comedy and the critical avoidance of it; bell hooks's claim that film theory perpetuates white racial domination; and King's shoal methodology as a tool with which to disrupt white world-making scholarship. Studies of comedy often explore humour as an aspect of performance to which a fixed value can be ascribed, seeing it, for example, as intrinsically subversive or reactionary. Yet *La Cérémonie* refuses such an approach, and to grapple with this refusal, I focus on the politics inherent in what Huppert's comedic performative style makes visible. Like King's 'shoaling', Huppert's comedy in this film resists any allegorical or too-systematic interpretative mode and requires distinctions to be made between the exegetical power and political affordances of Huppert's performance of Jeanne and Jeanne as a character who embodies colonial and authoritarian complicity, even as she is subjected to misogyny and class hierarchies.

SAME/DIFFERENT

Chabrol describes *La Cérémonie*, wryly, as 'the last Marxist film'; but how does class conflict manifest itself in relation to Huppert's comedy?[10] Chabrol elaborates: '[I]n truth, the happier the industrialists are, the more worried I am. People's frustrations have to go somewhere, and if they don't go into dreams, they explode.'[11] He roots the explosive, murderous, and, I would add, comedic energy that erupts at the end of the film in the combination of Jeanne's character with Sophie's illiteracy, and he describes their relationship through an intricate linguistic analogy with the 'P' sound, which belongs, because it requires a burst of air, to the phonetic category known as 'explosives'. Chabrol explains: 'In Sophie's case, she could recognise the letter "p" and the letter "e" but she could not join them to say "pe" … On their own, each is a victim of no importance … But when you bring them together, they become a dangerous weapon. Jeanne is the vowel and Sophie the consonant.'[12]

At times, it is as if Jeanne embodies, expresses and magnifies the frustrated energy that is packed, for Sophie, into the letter 'p'. After Sophie receives her employer's written command to retrieve a white pant suit from the cleaners, opening with the ultra-polite 'Pourriez-vous', Sophie sits down with a phonetics book to decipher the note's meaning, scouring the pages until she finds the letter 'p'. This page features two photographs of a little boy who translates the letter's utterance into a manual gesture. While the first depicts his tight little fist held up to the camera like a threat, by the second image, his fingers have detonated, open like a blossoming flower. Repeatedly, Huppert's comedy embodies the intense shift of energy to which

Figure 4.1 Sophie (Sandrine Bonnaire) attempting to decipher a note with a phonetics book in *La Cérémonie* (1995).

Sophie aspires in this failed literacy effort, from fist to flower, leading Janet Maslin to say of Huppert's performance that she is 'simply astonishing as the loose cannon capable of blowing up the film's small, tidy world' and Huppert to say of Jeanne, 'She is a human bomb.'[13] This alignment of her comedy with exploding bombs makes it easy to see her as a figure of derisive feminist rebellion, but I want to shoal or slow that interpretive trajectory in case it forecloses other ways of understanding these comedic moments that throw the film's geographic, temporal and political coordinates into some productive confusion.

Huppert's performance shifts often from tightly wound tension into frenetic verbal and physical activity, but occasionally, the energy moves in the other direction, with a scene of activity giving way to a sudden stillness or retreat, as when Melinda stops on a country road to help Jeanne, whose 2CV has broken down. Confounding class expectations, Melinda tells Jeanne that she's 'good with cars' while Jeanne turns away from the ocean that we see only here, in the opening credits, and in the home's artwork, as in the painting above Sophie's TV, informing Melinda, 'Poetry's my thing.' Melinda tinkers with the engine and asks Jeanne to try it; but rather than doing so graciously, Jeanne turns away from Melinda and gazes silently out at the ocean. Has Jeanne here entered a moment of poetic reverie? And/or is she enacting some resistance akin to a work slowdown? The bewildered expression on Melinda's face suggests her displeasure. It is comedy that shifts the tempo of this strange, slowed moment. Jeanne meanders back to the car, which now works. Speeding up like a hand-cranked film, Jeanne's dynamism returns suddenly when Melinda dispenses unthinkingly with the now-oily handkerchief that Jeanne had offered her through Jeanne's car window. Quick as a flash, Jeanne tosses it over her shoulder, refusing, gratitude, her assigned role of trash collector and Melinda's filth all in one gesture. But this does not mean that Jeanne's explosions are those of the proletariat.

These tempo shifts mark some of the funniest, but often also the most shocking or violent moments of the film (the fact that violence and humour are not systematically aligned gives all the film's humour its unsettling edge, especially when viewed retroactively through the lens of the bloody conclusion). These fluctuations in Huppert's performance affect and tempo are usually relational rather than isolated, and individual examples of such humour seem to stack or build upon each other in a way that amplifies their overall effect. Recall the moment in Jeanne's apartment, when, after Jeanne has reflected on her lonely pregnancy and the (possibly accidental) death of her 4-year old child, she reads aloud a newspaper article about the fire that killed Sophie's father then asks, mischievously, 'Did you kill your father?' Jeanne reclines on her single bed as a smirking Sophie responds, 'They couldn't prove it.' Jeanne turns her face and shoulders into the mattress with a sustained cackle that seems magnetic in its force, drawing Sophie towards her for a full-blown tickle-fest. This bathetic shift of tone and tempo, from the tragic to the raucous, is swiftly followed by a rallying cry that is funny in a different way as it ironically lays bare the feel-good-factor that lies behind most charitable acts: 'Enough of that. Let's go help the poor! We need a change!'

Huppert's comedy escalates from here as the two volunteers head to the Catholic centre to sort through smelly bags of donated clothes. Jeanne energetically flings away trashy donations, and her discarding actions, echoed in her treatment of the oily cloth, are accompanied by bursts of laughter at the hole-ridden clothes, the rehearsing choir and the fact that the priest, like Sophie's dead father, smells of pee. 'Pfff' – the sound of laughter's outburst – recasts the limitations of Sophie's illiteracy – p-p-p – as a rude and playful force that ecstatically unites the two. We see a similar pattern when the friends arrive back at the Lelièvres' home and sneak up to Sophie's bedroom to watch TV. Jeanne approaches the set to switch channels, but, as if triggered by the appearance of a baby in a laundry detergent commercial, she suddenly slams the TV set and shouts at it (one of many violent and comic interactions between Jeanne and objects that verge on slapstick), before snuggling up with a laughing Sophie.

The film escalates the tension created by Jeanne's variations in tempo, movement and volume, performed with different interlocutors. The scene cuts to the post office where we see a customer complaining as Jeanne impassively blows her nail-polish, indifferent to the customer's complaint, another moment that might encourage a labour-oriented reading of Jeanne's humour. However, when Georges Lelièvre storms in to complain about Jeanne reading his mail, her explosive energy returns – this time verbally. She at first resists his accusation with a blasé dismissal that resembles her attitude to the previous customer; but when Georges invokes the death of her child, she confronts him with a fiery, rapid, and sexualised attack: 'Your wife was a prostitute, and your first wife wasn't much better. No wonder she killed herself!' Georges slaps Jeanne across the face then excuses himself.

Though we might be tempted to understand Georges as embodying French bourgeois patriarchal violence and misogyny and Jeanne the figure of the oppressed female worker, Huppert's comic moments as well as her placement in the film's mise-en-scène resist this reading. For one, Georges' slap recalls Jeanne's own slap of the TV in the preceding scene, just as his disdain for her is mirrored by Jeanne's sexual shaming of both Catherine and Georges' first wife. Furthermore, Jeanne is positioned against the backdrop of a poster depicting Saint-Malo's boats on the left, a map of France's north coast on the right, and a fragment of Leonetto Cappiello's 1920 poster advertising the post-war national loan programme above her head.[14] Jeanne's alignment with the geography of Saint-Malo, the French border, and a nation-building economic agenda is underscored when Sophie bursts into the post office to inform Jeanne that Georges has banned her from the house. Jeanne raises the counter to greet her friend, exposing its royal blue underside to create a 'tricolore' backdrop. But what are we to make of this association of Jeanne, whose name also recalls the Maid of Orleans, with the map, economy, and flag of France, the country's north coast, and the port of Saint-Malo? Does Sophie, who is frequently paired with Jeanne by critics, actually exist in the same relationship to geography as Jeanne, and if not, what differentiates them? Where, spatially, is the Lelièvre family in all of this? Where, and for that matter, who, are 'we'?

Numerous critics collapse Sophie and Jeanne into a single unit that emerges in opposition to the French family. Marcia Citron states that, 'the two fuse into a mindless absence and link arms in a creepy togetherness that spells trouble'.[15] For Anna Gural-Migdal, television unites 'these two delinquents' and divides them from the Lelièvre family.[16] Buss links the two in indignant subservience and is easy on their victims: 'Georges is a bit stuffy and his wife rather a snob, but their adolescent children come across as rounded personalities, with lives full of interest and promise.'[17] David Denby sees the two women as 'held together by their having gotten away ... with a serious crime', and sees the family as merely 'obsessed, like the wealthy everywhere, with food and comfort and the perfection of their personal and social arrangements'.[18]

But much of this does not seem quite right. To begin, no one recognises the profound difference between Jeanne and Sophie and the accompanying proximity between Jeanne and the bourgeois family more clearly than Huppert herself, who states, in a way that complicates Chabrol's 'last Marxist film' comment:

> Jeanne is extravagant, funny, logorrheic ... In contrast with Sophie, she is conscious of her class, of her condition, of her limitations and of the little hope that the future promises her. She is constantly aroused, she is envious, she wants everything that others have and that she doesn't. She is jealous of the bourgeois family, incarnated by Jacqueline Bisset and Jean-Pierre Cassel; conscious of the difference that there is between her and others, this has accumulated into an immense violence in her, a violence that will explode in an incredibly violent way at the end of the film.[19]

If Sophie and Jeanne are so different from each other, and if Jeanne and the Lelièvre family are so aligned in their desires, what kind of Marxist film is this? Who is supposed to be in revolt against what?

While Jeanne and Sophie do experience companionship via Sophie's television, their relationship to this medium is very different. It is Sophie alone who seems addicted to both 'télévision' (vision at a distance) and the 'télécommande' (remote control, or control at a distance), both words that naturalise the idea of remote power. If Jeanne's affect is funny, in your business, in your face, Sophie (as if the blankness Huppert exhibits in other roles has here been transferred to Bonnaire) is absent and humourless; her spatial affinities, like her télé-gaze, seem far away, elsewhere. According to the family's rather neoliberal daughter Melinda, who is keen to improve the optics of Sophie's servitude, her parents are trying to turn Sophie into 'a zombie with that television'. When Catherine responds by telling her stepdaughter how relieved she is that she doesn't have to do a thing now, not even make conversation with the maid, Melinda again invites an association of Sophie's exploited labour with slavery, and, by implication, Blackness, 'She's like a slave. She's a human being, not a robot.' There is only a single image in the film that acknowledges the presence of Black people in France, and it appears, almost subliminally, through the mise-en-scène while Sophie is watching music videos loudly on her TV up in her room to drown out the sound of the phone because she knows Georges is asking her to do a reading-based task, and puppets of Black singers appear briefly on the TV screen.

Just as puppets are objects in place of people, so Sophie, a pale zombie emissary, might be read as invoking and erasing the remote people of colour whose rebellion she seems simultaneously to mediate and make unthinkable.[20] And once we start to think about the relationship between people and words, people and objects, and people and places, this Saint-Malo home – and by extension the film – starts to seem haunted by the history and language of enslavement and littered with the material, aesthetic and intellectual afterlives of colonial and imperial geographies and histories. I regard the film object here as a complex and unwieldy articulation and management of the idea of a hermetically-sealed 'French culture'. The film contains objects, references and resonances, surely both intended and unintended by the director, that make a world beyond whiteness demonstrably present. The absence of scholarly discussion and our critical blindness to this aspect of the film tells us something about how film theory and criticism have participated in what hooks calls 'white racial domination' and invite us to develop other ways of looking and listening.

Existing readings of this film foreground Sophie's white zombie revolt, activated by Jeanne's comic catalytic energy, as the only thinkable rebellion in its all-white world. But by paying more attention to the shoreline and following the lead of King's 'geographical reading practice' that adopts 'the methodology of shoaling', other readings might come into view.[21] 'Shoaling', King insists, is 'distinct from the location of the shoal or shore on the map', surfacing 'as the disruption of the conquistador imagination and settlement, the intervening in violence and putting texts and objects together or in friction with one another'. According to King, 'shoaling' reveals, at the shoreline, 'the ways in which the attempts to secure White cartographic stability through violence and Black and Native death are tenuous and unstable practices and relations subject to intervention and revision'.[22] I am interested in bringing this method to bear on the northern shore of Chabrol's France, and to think about how Huppert's comedy, interacting with the film's mise-en-scène – its objects and its establishment of filmic space – might function as a shoal that disrupts some of the habits underlying film criticism's systems of thought.

While Sophie is a silent white zombie from elsewhere, Jeanne, by contrast, is a loquacious and playful French government employee, one repeatedly associated with France – the Tricolore – and its culture; she also happens to be played by Isabelle Huppert, who grew up in the 16th arrondissement of Paris, an area associated with wealth and prestige and who makes no effort in her performance to disguise her Parisian accent.[23] As the Lelièvres enjoy their wine (delivered by the crateful) with dinner, so Jeanne pours Sophie a glass to accompany their definitely French feast of wild mushrooms with garlic and a baguette bought fresh that day. Synching the bond between actress and role, Jeanne tells Sophie that she wants to be a film actress. Jeanne's affinity with literature distances her from the illiterate Sophie and aligns her rather with the employer's family. When Jeanne first visits the Lelièvre household, she exclaims in wonder upon entering the library, 'Look at all these books! I love reading!' Jeanne then asks if she can borrow Céline's *Journey to the End of the Night* (1932), a semi-autobiographical World War I narrative in which the protagonist wanders through colonial Africa, the United States, and Paris. This is a highly charged choice of text that associates Jeanne with an author described by Holocaust memorialist Serge Klarsfeld as both a 'great writer' and 'a despicable human being', 'the most anti-Semitic Frenchman' of his moment, adding Jewishness to the modes of otherness that the film obliquely introduces into the space of France.[24] Critics have also tended to ignore or to confuse this moment – Janet Maslin, for example, wrongly accuses Jeanne of getting Céline and Eugene O'Neill mixed up.[25] But why have reviews done so, especially as Chabrol underscores the proximity, framed as a primal relation, between Jeanne and this notoriously racist, satirical and avant-garde author by having Jeanne add (perhaps chillingly, perhaps hilariously, perhaps both), 'Céline – that's my mother's name'?

While it may be tempting to view the film within the white master-slave paradigm that Melinda invokes, moments like this, that position Jeanne as the daughter of Céline, simultaneously a symbol of European high culture and racism, invite us to look more closely at the differences between Jeanne and Sophie, and at the alignments between Jeanne, the audience and a family John Powers in *Vogue* describes as 'the charming, good-hearted Lelièvres, who are guilty of nothing worse than middle-class complacency'.[26] This critical attitude contributes, through the labour narrative, to an active process of establishing this film, and perhaps more generally, French art cinema, as a white world devoid of blackness and non-white otherness, where the conditions of enslavement and exploitation are referenced only in relation to the excessively white Sophie within the context of a geography, and by extension a history, in which the world outside of Saint-Malo and France is constantly fabricated out of the interior to create the illusion of a white nation as white world. But, inspired by Dahlia Li's recent critical project of 'finding Blackness where it seems not to exist', by David Young Kim's suggestion that our understanding of an artwork changes when we pay rigorous attention to the materials and objects in the background and by John David Rhodes's recent work on the properties of the prop, in the rest of this essay, I want to explore those aspects of the film that might illuminate the violence embedded in critical consensus and render visible the unruly geography that is unleashed on the film when we start by asserting the unthinkability not of Blackness, but of a white France.[27]

'CRITICAL HOSTILITY' AND CRITICAL BENEVOLENCE

The questions I ask about the critical reception of *La Cérémonie* are catalysed not only by King's critique of 'the violence of conquistador humanism' and the participation of academic speech in the erasure of 'gratuitous bloodletting of Black and Indigenous communities' – a critique that challenges scholars in the humanities to identify abnormal all-white-worlds when we encounter them and to pay attention to how they are maintained[28] – but also by Kristi Brown-Montesano's feminist analysis of the opera that the Lelièvres watch on television the night they are killed: Mozart's *Don Giovanni* (1787). While Chabrol seems confused about why Rendell chose this opera rather than *The Marriage of Figaro* (1786), which he thinks narratively would have worked better, Brown-Montesano, writing only about the opera and not the film, helps us see its fittingness by highlighting its uncomfortable place in the 'comic-opera category', largely because the heroine, Donna Anna, 'grips us with her seriousness' and rage, and remains throughout an unrelenting and unforgiving witness to the violence Don Giovanni has committed.[29] When considered in relation to the persistent rage that inhabits both Sophie and Jeanne, Rendell's choice of *Don Giovanni* makes total sense. But Brown-Montesano's study has also inspired my scholarly approach through her systemic tracking of how Donna Anna's relentless rage towards the opera's 'hero' has generated 'critical hostility' and 'misogynistic invention' that persists into the present (11–12), as well as her refusal of these critical habits.

Following Brown-Montesano, I want to refuse the generous critical consensus about the Lelièvre family, a generosity that enfolds the presumed 'we' invoked by reviewers. Buss finds the family 'rather attractive' and sees the Lelièvre children as 'full of interest and promise'; but promising what? The family's banter begins on the sofa as Melinda questions her parents calling Sophie 'la bonne', or 'the maid'.[30] Georges, the father, quips, 'Bonne-à-tout-faire!' ('Good-for-doing-everything'), catalysing more reflections on the new hire, such as whether she is ugly, whether Gilles wants to 'have a go at her', and whether she is 'monstrous', 'repugnant', or worse than last week's maid. (What happened to last week's maid, we may wonder.) 'That girl at the post office,' Jeanne, is treated with similar disdain. And even as Georges, a man who shares with his daughter a love of guns and hunting, is being murdered in the kitchen, his family jokes smugly about the possibility that he might be shooting 'those two loonies'. Such family chit-chat is not the exception but the rule. What exactly is there to like about this family?

Georges is obsessed with keeping Jeanne out – of his mail and his home – and bans her from the house. Yet the film's mise-en-scène pushes against Georges' effort to enforce boundaries. He announces Jeanne's exile as Sophie pours his coffee into visually striking yellow cups, cups that also play a prominent role in the murder sequence, and that establish a strong intertextual reference to Claire Denis's 1988 film *Chocolat*, in which the relationship between white French femininity and France's violent colonial legacy is also negotiated over yellow coffee cups.[31]

On hearing Georges' prohibition, Sophie drops a plate, stating, 'Look what you made me do.' This could be directed at Georges, but it could equally be a nod to Jeanne, who at various moments, operates like a mischievous poltergeist, a term that means 'noisy ghost' because of this spirit's tendency to knock and break things. In French, this ghost is an 'esprit frappeur', a knocking spirit, and Huppert's physical comedy comes into play perhaps most intensely in the wake of strange noises and breakages. Jeanne first enters the Lelièvre home after knocking at, then climbing cheekily through, the kitchen window. The script notes, 'Sophie cannot help but laugh upon witnessing Jeanne's cool but audacious manner.'[32] Her movements and humour here and throughout the film are not associated with the underdog. Rather, Jeanne's comedic energy and attitude is repeatedly associated with the power of mastery, and she often distances herself from those who rebel. For example, she comes to deliver a postcard that the family has sent to Sophie from their vacation. Jeanne reads it aloud, but when she sees they are in Corsica, she disapproves and comments that it's a dangerous place because of boat-burning pirates. The mention of Corsica invokes not only the imperial figure of Napoleon Bonaparte, who was known as 'The Corsican' and the particularly prominent role that Corsicans played in France's colonisation of both Algeria and Indochina, but also the independence struggles of the Corsican National Liberation Front, founded in 1976, which were peaking as *La Cérémonie* was made.[33] By describing these contemporary independence fighters as 'pirates', however, Jeanne not only positions herself in opposition to them, rather than in rebel alignment with them, but she also aligns Corsica, to the south of the French mainland, with the pirate, who, in the context of Saint-Malo, is associated with a threat to France's northern coast that has been commodified, rendered archaic, and turned into a tourist trinket, as we'll soon see. North and south, past and present, seem to collapse or fold in on themselves here in this increasingly claustrophobic space of the Lelièvres home.

When Jeanne and Sophie later enter the parents' bedroom during the *Don Giovanni* screening, the script describes Jeanne as 'enter[ing] the room as if it's newly conquered territory'.[34] And later, after the family has been murdered, the script says of Jeanne, 'Her movements are calm, deliberate, and almost stately.'[35] We cannot help but laugh at her behaviour as it becomes slapstick in nature – Huppert swings a shotgun around with hilarious gestures; her knees chop up and down in an exaggerated manner, her mouth scrunches, eyes pop, eyebrows arch, hips thrust back and forth, all actions fuelled by a stream of laughter and the surge of energy that comes through the yellow hot chocolate cups that punctuate the whole sequence. We laugh, but our laughter yokes us to this violence in ways that matter. As mistress of the post office, Jeanne inspects the things that come in and out of this port town. In the Lelièvre house, she talks comically to family treasures before smashing them wildly while bouncing on the bed like a child; 'urinat[es]' on the parental bed using the jug of hot chocolate as a penis, aligning herself, through mimicry, with patriarchal figures such as the pee-smelling priest and Sophie's dead father; and murders people simply because they don't want her in their home. Her actions are abominable, but they are the abominations of the coloniser, not the colonised. While she is vulnerable to the structural and physical violence of patriarchy, as we see when Georges slaps Jeanne across the face in the post office, these two are more alike than unlike and the misogyny she experiences does not cancel out her alignment with Georges and with France.

Just as Sophie both mediates and makes unthinkable Black bodies, so the discomfort of Huppert's comedy has something to do with how it reveals and conceals the relationship between European high culture, the violent occupation of space, and gratuitous murder. Until the murder, Jeanne's outrageous actions still elicit a form of laughter from the viewer, but it is not really the derisive and cathartic laughter celebrated by Virginia Woolf and playing an important continuous role in the feminist writings of scholars such as Rosalyn Deutsche, Mignon Nixon and Jacqueline Rose. Rather, the uncomfortable laughter produced by Huppert's performance makes visible the

Figure 4.2   Jeanne (Isabelle Huppert) mimicking urinating with hot chocolate, aligning herself with patriarchal violence in *La Cérémonie* (1995).

violence of the coloniser and does so in ambivalent ways. Her comedic mode lays bare the structure and horror of colonial violence, exposing it while also offering it up as a shareable pleasure for characters like Jeanne, who at other moments suffer from parallel modes of identity-based cruelty, as well as for the film viewer.

Although in cahoots with Jeanne, Sophie's relationship with space and the material world seems quite the opposite. As Jean-Claude Polack notes, 'Chabrol constantly suggests that [Sophie] sees the world differently from her masters and from the film's spectators', and he sees the Lelièvres and the film's spectators as 'isolated and rendered vulnerable by blinders' that separate them 'from any form of otherness'. In the penultimate line of the essay, Polack describes the family as 'objects of the gaze that they have now become for an aggressive third or "fourth" world,' but in Polack's essay, this 'third or "fourth"' world seems to come out of nowhere.[36] But how, and why, does this world get transferred onto the body of Sophie? In part, this happens through her interaction with the television, as suggested above; but the transfer also occurs through food. While Jeanne feasts in a stereotypically French way, Sophie repeatedly buys and eats one of the primary colonial products: chocolate. Similarly, while Jeanne avoids and fears pirates, Sophie is flanked by them when she buys sunglasses, appearing as one in a line of these internalised white outsiders that give filmic form to the sense of an imploding Empire while maintaining an entirely white world.

While Sophie eats chocolate in a manner linked with refusal and dissemblance, the Lelièvre family casually and prolifically consumes a range of colonial and imperial products, including tobacco, coffee, and (arguably) opera, and their space is cluttered by markers of Empire.[37] Although the opera they watch, *Don Giovanni*, is set in Spain, in the moments before Georges is murdered, the family sips coffee as the curtain goes up on Act II, the remote control close at hand. The scene opens onto an obelisk that suggests not only a different opera, *Aïda*, but also the way such objects visualise what Lisa Lowe describes as 'the intimacies of four continents', an understanding of which Lowe sees 'the organization of knowledge into academic disciplines' as trying to prevent.[38] Catherine personifies colonial rule as she marches around the house in her white suit that she earlier instructed Sophie to press via a written note that produced one of the early scenes of frustration, but if we adopt something like a rack focus methodology and shift our attention, as Rhodes has recently done, from the people to the rooms they inhabit, what times and spaces come into view?

In the dining room, the family's round-table revels are almost absorbed into the aristocratic round-dance scene depicted behind them on the tapestry that covers an entire wall.[39] Tristan Weddigan describes tapestry as a medium in which we find an alternative to the 'triumphal march of Renaissance

Figure 4.3   Jeanne (Isabelle Huppert) in front of a map of Saint Malo in *La Cérémonie* (1995).

Figure 4.4   The Lelièvre family in their living room featuring a tapestry covering the wall in *La Cérémonie* (1995).

central perspective from Italy throughout Europe'.[40] He highlights how this medium offered an alternative to the illusion of continuous space and allowed the coexistence of spatial and temporal 'incoherencies', including 'contradictions between fore- and backgrounds', 'spatial ambivalence', and the stacking of multiple meanings and representational modes within a single object.[41]

If we rack our critical focus, the non-unified space and logic of the tapestry works against film criticism's universalising and homogenising white world. A series of objects defining the space of this French home come into view, objects that stress the European desire to conquer, possess and fold back into itself the bodies, spaces, objects, food and drink that lie across the ocean. Framing the actors' performances, we see a map, probably 18th century, of Southeast Asia and the Indian Ocean; a slightly broken model of 3-masted bark from the late 19th century, a ship primarily used for the Australian grain trade; a Chinese or Southeast Asian liquor jar made in the classic Ming blue and white style, likely in the 19th century, for export (the angled sides denoting something made to fit into shipping crates); and finally, setting off Huppert's performance of chocolate urination, framed paintings that imitate the style of the mid-Ming Zhe painters, also most likely made in the 19th century as tourist art.[42] There is certainly something excessive in this act of over-identifying all these objects that, in their specificity, threaten to make nonsense of the film's tightly monitored story world. That is my hope.

I want here, like Jeanne-whose-thing-is-poetry, to turn towards the shores of Saint-Malo. Jacques Cartier was born in Saint-Malo in 1491 and set sail from that port in 1534 in search of a Western passage to Asia, ending up instead at the St Lawrence River. In French, the inhabitants of Saint-Malo are known as 'les malouins' and the Falkland Islands, where a territorial war was fought as recently as 1982, are known as Les Îles Malouines. Why? Because, in a 1764 act of naming-as-remote control, the French explorer Louis-Antoine de Bougainville overlaid this place that is so far from France with the name of the port from which his ships and colonists had departed: Saint-Malo.

What people, places, things and interpretations become thinkable if we watch the film with the histories of its location in mind? What discombobulated times, spaces, bodies and objects start to come into view, in part through the way Huppert's violent comedic energy indexes neither rebellion nor suppression, but rather the presence of interacting worlds? Might King's shoal methodology help to decentre the 'we' that dominates so much Anglo-European film criticism and theory in a way that could put these discourses and the complex films they engage less in the service of white supremacy and white world building? Might this turning towards the film's shoreline also help film scholarship pay more attention to the points of view of spectators outside of France, outside of cinematic hotspots, such as those spectators interviewed in Jean-Marie Teno's 2009 film *Sacred Places*, a French-Cameroonian co-production? These spectators watch 1st, 2nd and 3rd cinemas as well as soccer on a TV screen in a ciné-club that also serves as a centre for Muslim prayer in the deeply poor town of St Louis on the outskirts of Ouagadougou in Burkina Faso, a town named after the crusading King Louis IX of France (1214–1270).

Or perhaps we might imagine viewers in Louisiana, named after a different French King, Louis XIV, in 1682 (1643–1715), a state repeatedly ranked as one of the poorest regions of the United States. Although I have found no record of a public screening of La Cérémonie in New Orleans – it has never played at the French Film Festival, as part of the New Orleans Film Society's programme, or at the Shotgun Arts Cinema – I want to end by imagining a viewer of this film located in the St Bernard Parish of New Orleans, now a longstanding Filipino community.[43] This area, located in the tidal wetlands near Lake Borgne, used to be a small fishing village that was also known as Saint Malo until it was completely destroyed by a hurricane in 1915. It was named not after the French town in which Chabrol sets the film, but rather after a person for whom these wetlands provided refuge; not Jeanne, but Jean Saint Malo, an African man who escaped from and led others out of enslavement to set up a community at Bas du Fleuve, known in the 18th century as 'the Watershed'. After the American Revolution, when the slaveholding governor Esteban de Miró decided to crack down on enslaved people who had escaped, he targeted in particular the renowned and rebellious leader Jean Saint Malo, whose name, Gwendolyn Midlo Hall tells us, may be linked to the French town, the Spanish word for 'bad', or the Bambaran word for a 'charismatic leader who defies the social order'.[44] In 1784, the Spanish eventually captured and hanged him in a different *cérémonie*, along with his accomplices and female companion, in what is now known as Jackson Square. For over a century, on what we now call Juneteenth, the residents of St Bernard's parish have celebrated and remembered Jean Saint Malo, also known as Juan San Malo, as a symbol of Black freedom and resistance.[45] These real and imagined film viewers – and let's remember that the film viewers invoked in *New York Times* reviews are also imaginary – have been of little interest to mainstream film criticism and theory, and it is not clear that such viewers would have any interest in being absorbed into such texts.[46]

In this essay, the neglected comedy of Huppert's performance in *La Cérémonie* has, in ways I did not expect when I started writing, illuminated other aspects of the film that have, like her comedy, largely gone under the radar in the existing criticism, and these elements are related to each other. They include: the violence that can be embedded and occluded in critical consensus and a field's methods; the film's setting in a historically-significant French port; its preoccupation with spatial and geographic boundaries; the presence on screen of objects that simultaneously testify to, celebrate and perhaps critique – albeit softly – a long history of French colonial and imperial violence; and, perhaps most surprising of all, the film's repeated visual and narrative alignment of Huppert's character Jeanne not only with the family she kills, but with France itself.

NOTES

1. Huppert with James, 'Isabelle Huppert,' 21.
2. Ginette Vincendeau, 'Isabelle Huppert: The Big Chill,' *Sight & Sound* 16, no. 12 (2006): 38.
3. Peter Debruge, 'Femme Fatale: Isabelle Huppert,' *Variety* 334, no. 1 (November 8, 2016): 54.
4. Chabrol finds affinity with Huppert through their work modes and laughter: '[E]lle travaille exactement de la même manière que moi. On s'entend vraiment formidablement bien, on rigole beaucoup.' ([S]he works in the exact same way that I do. We understand each other extremely well, we have a lot of fun.) *La Cérémonie* Pressbook, British Film Institute Special Collections, PBS-433166. Thanks to Storm Patterson.
5. Critics have also compared the film with Jean Genet's 1947 play, *Les Bonnes* (*The Maids*), loosely based on the 1933 murders of the Papin sisters. Christopher Miles directed the 1974 film of the play starring Glenda Jackson and Susannah York. Huppert starred as Solange alongside Cate Blanchett in the Sydney Theater Company's 2014 stage version of the play. This film belongs in a transnational film history involving maids who kill, and this is the subject of my book in progress, *Murderous Maids*. In the extended version of this essay, I discuss Sophie more extensively. For a relevant essay that I regret appeared after the completion of this essay, see Salomé Aguilera Skvirsky, "Must the Subaltern Speak? On *Roma* and the Cinema of Domestic Service," *FORMA* 1, no. 2 (2020): 1-34.
6. See, for example, Robin Buss, 'La Cérémonie,' *The Times Literary Supplement*, no. 4850 (15 March 1996): 19. Royal S. Brown, 'Review: La Cérémonie,' *Cinéaste* 22.4 (1997): 51.
7. Script, BFI S 17643, 149. This comment directly echoes a line from Chabrol's earlier film with Huppert, *Violette Nozière*, the true story of a woman who kills a father who has sexually abused her. When Violette (Huppert) enters her cell and tells her cellmate what crime she has committed and why, her cell mate comments simply, 'Tu as bien fait.' The fact that this line, 'on a bien fait', is not only a citation but is also captured and replayed on the portable stereo at the end of the film underscores the idea that this narrative repeats.
8. Tiffany Lethabo King, *The Black Shoals: Offshore Formations of Black and Native Studies* (Duke: Duke UP, 2019): 20–31 and 40.
9. King, *Black Shoals*, 21.
10. Buss, 'La Cérémonie,' 19.
11. Alan Riding, 'For Chabrol, a French 'Thelma and Louise,"' *New York Times*, December 15, 1996, https://www.nytimes.com/1996/12/15/movies/from-chabrol-a-french-thelma-and-louise.html.
12. See Riding, 'For Chabrol, a French 'Thelma and Louise,"' n.p.
13. Isabelle Huppert, quoted in Suzie Mackenzie, 'I Am, Therefore I Act,' *The Guardian*, October 10, 1998: 10. Janet Maslin, 'Maid is Hired: Danger is Served,' *The New York Times*, December 20, 1996: Arts and Entertainment, Section C, p. 1. https://www.nytimes.com/1996/12/20/movies/maid-is-hired-danger-is-served.html.

14. See https://www.parismuseescollections.paris.fr/ru/node/87323#infos-princip ales. Thanks to André Dombrowski, Hassan Melehy, Nicolas Lyon-Caen, and Sam Di Lorio for helping me identify this poster.
15. Marcia J. Citron, *When Opera Meets Film* (Cambridge: Cambridge UP, 2010): 136–70; 140.
16. Anna Gural-Migdal, 'La Representation de la femme dans le cinema français des vingt dernières années: *Sans Toit Ni Loi*, *Nelly et M. Arnaud*, *La Cérémonie*,' *Women in French Studies* 9 (2001): 204.
17. Buss, 'La Cérémonie,' 19.
18. David Denby, 'Cold Maids,' *New York Magazine*, January 20, 1997, 60.
19. Isabelle Huppert in *La Cérémonie* press-book, British Film Institute Special Collections, PBS-433166, n.p. My translation. Citron also notes the difference between Jeanne and Sophie that literacy makes, 139–40. See Citron, *When Opera Meets Film*, 139–40.
20. On landscapes of 'blacklessness,' and on blackness – particularly black femininity – as unthinkable, as a haunting absence, see Katherine McKittrick, *Demonic Grounds: Black Women and the Cartographies of Struggle* (Minneapolis: University of Minnesota Press, 2006), especially 91–120. For a discussion of the zombie's transatlantic lineage, see Sarah J. Lauro, *The Transatlantic Zombie: Slavery, Rebellion, and Living Death* (New Brunswick: Rutgers University Press, 2015) and Sarah J. Lauro, *Zombie Theory: A Reader* (Minneapolis: University of Minnesota Press, 2015): ix–xi.
21. King, *Black Shoals*, 78.
22. Ibid., 78.
23. Mackenzie, 'I Am, Therefore I Act,' 10.
24. Huppert was raised Catholic, following her mother's faith, but her father was Jewish.
25. See Andrew Gallix, 'Céline: Great Author and 'Absolute Bastard,'' *The Guardian*, January 31, 2011, https://www.theguardian.com/books/booksblog/2011/jan/31/celine-great-author. See also Kim Willsher, 'Céline: French Literary Genius or Repellent Antisemite? New Film Rekindles Old Conflict,' *The Guardian*, March 12, 2016, https://www.theguardian.com/books/2016/mar/13/celine-french-literary-genius-antisemite-film.
26. John Powers, 'Bourgeoisie, Beware!' *Vogue* 186, no. 12 (December 1, 1996): 170.
27. See Dahlia Li, 'Secreting Blackness: Sweat, Dance, and the Vibrant Bodies in *A Love Supreme* (2017),' unpublished essay; David Young Kim, 'Points on a Field: Gentile da Fabriano and Gold Ground,' *Journal of Early Modern History* 23 (2019): 191–226; and John David Rhodes, 'The Prop and Its Properties,' https://www.ici-berlin.org/events/john-david-rhodes/ (lecture delivered May 20, 2019).
28. King, *Black Shoals*, 42, 44.
29. Kristi Brown-Montesano, *Understanding the Women of Mozart's Operas* (Berkeley: University of California Press, 2007), 2, 10.
30. This name also recalls Genet's *Les Bonnes* (*The Maids*).
31. In *Murderous Maids*, I will discuss further the affinities between *La Cérémonie* and *Chocolat*, as well as the film's relation to La *Noire de* … (Ousmane Sembène, 1966),

a film in which Diouana (Mbissine Thérèse Diop), a Senegalese maid in the coastal town of Antibes (so proximate to Cannes), ends up taking her own life. These affinities include Diouana's diegetic silence and what Rahul Hamid calls her 'intense, gestural performance', both of which resonate with Sophie's silent presence. In both films, the use of a preposition modifies the maid's being into either a possession or a function ('la noire *de* ...' and 'bonne-à-tout-faire'). See Rahul Hamid, 'Introduction to *Black Girl*,' *Senses of Cinema* 23, no. 78 (December 2002), sensesofcinema.com/2002/cteq/black_girl/. Thanks to Martine Tchitchihe for encouraging me to think about this parallel.
32. Script, BFI S 17643, 44.
33. Craig R. Whitney, 'France Moves to Crush Corsican Separatists,' *New York Times*, January 15, 1997, Section A, 4, https://www.nytimes.com/1997/01/15/world/france-moves-to-crush-corsican-separatists.html. Whitney notes that the Front made 8,500 attacks, resulting in 100 deaths. Corsica was granted limited autonomy in 2001.
34. Script, BFI S 17643, 48.
35. Script, BFI S 17643, 150.
36. Jean-Claude Polack, 'Chabrol and the Execution of the Deed,' transl. Annette Michelson, *October* 98 (Fall 2001): 86, 91–2.
37. For a discussion of opera and imperialism, and particularly Verdi's *Aïda*, see Edward W. Said, 'The Imperial Spectacle,' *Grand Street* 6, no. 2 (Winter 1987): 82–104.
38. Lisa Lowe, *The Intimacies of Four Continents* (Durham: Duke University Press, 2015), 1.
39. Thanks to Larry Silver and Rachel Wise.
40. Tristan Weddigen, 'Unfolding Textile Spaces: Antiquity/Modern Period,' in *Art and Textiles: Fabric as Material and Concept in Modern Art from Klimt to the Present*, ed. Markus Brüderlin (Ostfildern: Hatje Cantz, 2013): 90.
41. Tristan Weddigen, 'Unfolding Textile Spaces,' 92, 92, 95.
42. I am indebted to the expertise and generosity of Julie Nelson Davis, Stephen H. Whiteman, and David Brownlee here.
43. Thanks to Travis Bird of the Shotgun Cinema, email to author dated 26 September 2020, and to Clint Bowie, Artistic Director, New Orleans Film Society, email to author dated 1 October 2020.
44. See Gwendolyn Midlo Hall, *Afro-Creole Culture in the Eighteenth Century* (Baton Rouge: Louisiana State University Press, 1992), and Erin Elizabeth Voisin, 'Saint Malό remembered,' LSU Master's Thesis 2729 (2008): https://digitalcommons.lsu.edu/gradschool_theses/2729. See Hall, 213, quoted in Voisin 23. Voisin also points readers to the poems of Brenda Marie Osbey in *All Saints: New and Selected Poems* (Baton Rouge: LSU Press, 1997) for a different understanding of Saint Malό.
45. Lawrence N. Powell, *The Accidental City: Improvising New Orleans* (Cambridge: Harvard University Press, 2013), 237–8.
46. For a discussion of the decentring of film theory and criticism through the poetic in a different context, see Kay Dickinson, 'At What Cost 'Theory'? An Economics and Poetics of Uptake,' *Framework* 56, no. 2 (Fall 2015): 433–50.

CHAPTER 5

White Mothers on Colonised Land, or What Isabelle Huppert Makes Visible?
Erin Schlumpf

Isabelle Huppert appears in so many films that her name – perhaps only equal to that of Deneuve, Depardieu or Binoche – today has become synonymous with French stardom. Among these other internationally recognised French actors, however, Huppert stands out for a certain hardiness, a tautness, a seemingly ageless energy. In this essay, I chart how Isabelle Huppert's ability to serve as a symbol of unflagging French femininity unites two seemingly unconnected films: Rithy Panh's 2008 adaptation of Marguerite Duras's *Un barrage contre le Pacifique* (*The Sea Wall*, 1950) and Claire Denis's *White Material* (2009). I argue that Isabelle Huppert's appearance in these two films reveals the relationship between the image of French whiteness and the history of colonial Othering. Imbued with her characteristic wiry resolve – first, in the 1930s in French Indochina, and next, following the turn of the 21st century in an unnamed African country – Huppert plays a white mother on colonised or recently decolonised land. These performances reflect one another: women abandoned by the French men in their lives, left behind by the French nation, fighting for land that they will never truly own, surrounded and eventually swallowed by the fallout of imperial machinations. This uncanny doubling of Huppert at each film's centre allows Panh and Denis to pivot easily to what is truly at stake: those occupying (and relegated to) the margins. In this essay, following a line of sight starring Isabelle Huppert, I trace a particular path of destruction (and deconstruction) of what Jacques Derrida terms 'white mythology'.[1] I argue that Huppert's double billing has the surprising effect of undermining binary white/non-white (or European/non-European) imperial logic and inscribes these films with the desire to approach the Other.[2] Derrida's essay, 'White Mythology: Metaphor in the Text of Philosophy', attacks the authority grounding whiteness: western metaphysics and particularly the positivist legacy of the Enlightenment.[3] In both *Un barrage contre le Pacifique* and *White Material*, this whiteness – that which claims authority by virtue of its own logic – comes under attack. Huppert sits squarely in the centre of this attack; she is the dominant white figure in the frame, but also the victim of the white mythology which offers 'reasonable' laws constructed on the basis of theft. Both films show the basic instability in these laws as reason fails to prevail.[4] Since Huppert is both representative of white mythology and its dupe, its universal value is deconstructed from the inside, from the centre of the frame. As Huppert falters and falls, so, too, does the wisdom of white mythology.

Marguerite Duras and Claire Denis spent their childhoods in colonies. Duras was born in French Indochina in 1914 and lived in various parts of the colony with her mother and two brothers before departing at the age of 17 to attend university in Paris. Denis was born in Paris in 1946, but resided in colonial Africa (Somalia, Cameroon, Djibouti, and Burkina Faso) before returning to France for polio treatment at the age of twelve. Duras (in such works as *Un barrage contre le Pacifique* [*The Sea Wall*], *L'Amant* [*Lover*], *L'Amant de la Chine du Nord* [*The North China Lover*], among others) and Denis (most obviously in *Chocolat*, *Beau travail*, and *White Material*) are preoccupied with the spectacle (and the spectre) of French imperialism. Rithy Panh, born in Cambodia in 1964, after the departure of the French and in the midst of the Vietnam War, fled his homeland to escape the Khmer Rouge in 1979. He has since devoted his filmmaking career (in *Un barrage contre le Pacifique*, but more notably in numerous documentaries, from *Site 2* in 1989 to *Irradiated* in 2020) to revealing the impact of historical trauma – the legacy of French colonialism, the aftermath of the Cambodian genocide – on the land and people of South Asia.

Rithy Panh's adaptation of Marguerite Duras's *Un barrage contre le Pacifique* offers a portrait of childhood in a colonial present-tense in French Indochina, while Claire Denis's *White Material* (2009) discloses a postcolonial narrative in an allegorical African nation. Both narratives foreground French women – mothers – clinging to land that was never theirs. Both films cast Isabelle Huppert as these mothers. Huppert incarnates the ambivalent mother: anti-sentimental, hard, pale. We watch the translucent body of Huppert racing through the vast landscape. We witness the mother's fragility, her fierce determination, her inevitable defeat. *Un barrage contre le Pacifique* and *White Material* treat physical spaces – the foreign terrain and the body of Isabelle Huppert – in order to make visible colonialism's bad faith bargain with all of those it rendered invisible.

Un barrage contre le Pacifique and *White Material* share narrative, character and thematic arcs, but Huppert's appearance in the two films reveals a closer textual kinship between these works. On the level of narrative, both stories feature a single mother labouring to harvest a doomed crop. Her dedication to the land borders on mania; it takes priority over everything and everyone else. She confronts those who would stop her, and fights until death overtakes her. These mothers are courageous, but partly out of naivety and a sense of entitlement. They believe they have a right to the land they work, a belief containing more than one level of misconception, because the land has been doubly swindled. First, it belonged to the indigenous people. After the French claimed the land as their own, they then redistributed it to French settlers. Second, in the case of *Un barrage contre le Pacifique*, the cadastral government grants the mother a concession of land under the condition that she cultivate a crop thereon. She soon realises that her concession cannot be farmed and that she's been had; each year, the sea floods her land, ruining that year's crop of rice plants. In *White Material*, the patriarch and proprietor of the Vial Coffee Plantation, Henri Vial (Michel Subor), promises his daughter-in-law Maria (Huppert) that she will have the land after his death. This promise lacks a paper trail. Maria and André (Christopher Lambert), Henri's son, separate. André begins a relationship with another woman and sells the land to the local mayor Chérif (William Nadylam) to pay his debts and to assure his family safe passage out of the country as civil war erupts. In both texts, therefore, we have a mother struggling to hold onto something she doesn't own, betrayed by her own country, but a dubious ally of the indigenous population. She is the contaminated, diseased mother; her hapless reproduction is figured as an extension of the imperial malady.

Both films introduce Huppert as protagonist with clear visual language; it is her face in the first close-up that follows each title sequence. In *Un barrage contre le Pacifique*, we later see Huppert in profile as she regards herself

Figure 5.1   The Mother (Isabelle Huppert) regarding herself in profile in *Un barrage contre le Pacifique* (*The Sea Wall*, 2008).

in the bathroom mirror. The film pauses on this image of a woman taking stock. Huppert's expressionless, rigid, unflinching self-appraisal speaks to the mother's resolve in defiance of almost certain failure. Moving to fill the basin in front of the mirror with water, she chastises herself for falling prey to the thieving cadastral government. 'You must really be laughing now,' she says quietly, her voice bitter with irony. 'Dirty bureaucrats! I was a fool.' She splashes water on her neck; the camera pans and tracks to place the viewer behind Huppert's left shoulder, showing the delicate white bra beneath her thin white shift dress, and her hard, squinting reflection in the mirror. Her obvious physical vulnerability clashes affectingly with her blazing fury. The mother continues to wash, as if trying to cleanse herself of her bad luck, of her rotten deal with the French colonial administration. 'They're leeches,' she exclaims, wetting her cheeks and arms, her movement quickening as her indignation intensifies, until her voice breaks when she asks, 'How could they do this to me?' She dries quickly. 'It's a disaster,' she whispers. And then she repeats to herself, 'It's a disaster,' as if only by hearing her doom announced with her own voice will make the tragedy believable.

In *White Material*, we again watch Huppert and hear her voice – its slight breathiness, its subtle levels of ironic inflection – entangled in the fallout of the French imperial project. Of course, in *White Material*, the French government has cut its ties with the African nation in which the film takes place. In an early sequence, an aerial shot of a military helicopter's shadow tracks over the dirt and brush below. We hear the whirring of the helicopter's spinning blades. In the next shot, a wave of dust cascades towards the camera and black rectangular survival kits fall from the sky. The dust engulfs the camera, but over the next few shots, the helicopter's hum fades into the distance. Maria picks up a survival kit, barely inspects it, and tosses it aside scornfully. In a patterned puff sleeve blouse, silver butterfly necklace, oversized jeans, and work boots, Huppert looks like a little girl trying to pass as a seasoned labourer. Both *Un barrage contre le Pacifique* and *White Material* relish the visual tension created by this clash between Huppert's appearance and her character's ambition. Maria looks into the distance and a reverse shot captures the helicopter retreating across the sky. Walking back to the Vial compound, Maria kicks the useless survival kits that litter the ground. As she walks, Huppert's voiceover whispers, 'These whites, these dirty whites.' We follow her gaze as she glances at an African farm worker wearing a 'Café Vial' t-shirt. We wonder if she gives voice to his complaints as her commentary continues, 'They scorn us. We risk our lives for them. They're a bunch of nouveaux riches.' But the camera cuts to the inside of the departing helicopter; a young French soldier looks out the open door back at the Vial plantation. Huppert's voiceover is suddenly doubled with a man's voice: 'Pretentious, arrogant, ignorant. They don't deserve this beautiful land.'

Inside the helicopter, a new shot reveals the male speaker to be the pilot. His shared monologue with Huppert falls out of synchronization in the final sentence as her voice cracks with jagged irony and he takes off his headset in a gesture of frustration: 'They can't even appreciate it!' This sequence reveals that Maria clearly understands that the former French coloniser and the African people want her to give up and go 'home'. The voiceover suggests that she's heard these epithets ('dirty whites', 'nouveaux riches', etc.) before. Huppert speaks these lines as if in mimicry: her voice elongates certain syllables; her tone is taunting, jeering. Maria knows she's an object of contempt, and she feels equal contempt for those who would try to stop her. She can't win, but she won't concede. This is both her fatal flaw and her allure.

In these films, the depiction of the white mother as a nest of contradictions unsettles the logic of white mythology on which the empire relies. Thus, what Isabelle Huppert – in her tireless, luminous intensity – makes visible in Rithy Panh's film adaptation of *Un barrage contre le Pacifique* and Denis's *White Material* is this cycle of theft, deception and violence resulting from France's imperialist ventures. In this way, *White Material* could be called an adaptation of Duras's *The Sea Wall*, transposed to a later time and another place. Though *Un barrage contre le Pacifique* takes place in French Indochina in 1931 and *White Material* in an unnamed Francophone country in Africa sometime in the first decade of the twenty-first century, the reappearance of Huppert triggers the viewer's apprehension of the indignities of colonialism and its prolonged fallout. Placing the texts side-by-side with the common denominator of Huppert glistening, teetering in the centre, the viewer's gaze is naturally drawn first to Huppert. The work of these films, however, is to eventually erase Huppert and to draw the viewer's eye to the films' edges, to the images of the indigenous population, particularly the children who ought to inherit the land. At each film's conclusion, images of children replace those of the dying mother, leaving the future as an open question to be answered in later texts.

Before the films' conclusions, however, Huppert's image in the centre frequently recedes, allowing glimpses of the Other. In *Un barrage contre le Pacifique*, the mother and her children occasionally dress up and spend an afternoon in the company of other French colonial subjects at Chez Bart's bar and bistro. At the beginning of one such outing, the family's dilapidated car hurtles towards the camera in a mobile tracking shot. We see Huppert in the car's front passenger seat, but it's the passing landscape on the margins that catches the eye. First, the car narrowly dodges a pile of felled trees on the road. More piles of timber follow, visual reminders of the colonial plundering of natural resources in French Indochina. A reverse-shot, placing the camera in the back seat of the car, shows us what's up ahead if we look just to the side of Huppert's straw hat: thatched huts, small fires, and indigenous workers following the barked orders of uniformed men with guns. The camera now leaves Huppert behind, bringing the margins to the centre: we pass two rows of Cambodian men, their ankles chained together, marching with heads bowed.

White Material also urges the viewer to listen and look at those surrounding Huppert, the Africans who occupy the periphery of Maria Vial's story. Frustrated by the stall of the harvest, Maria stares unhappily at an idle tractor, rows of coffee beans yet to be roasted. The next shot reveals a procession of local farm workers, retreating away from the plantation on the dirt road behind her. As Huppert moves to block their passage, the workers fade and stream around her in shallow focus. 'What are you doing? Where are you going?' She implores, her hands reaching out to grab the passing bodies. Clasping hold of one man's arm, we hear him explain from the off-screen space, 'It's not good to stay. Not good at all.' Maria insists, 'But, you can't leave. We just started. Come on, let's go back.' Another worker's voice from the off-screen space explains with exasperation, 'You know it, too! You can't stay. You heard it from above.' Maria continues to argue. Tension is rising. The narrow range of focus smashes Huppert's body into the centre of the frame while the handheld cinematography intensifies her agitated pleading. Finally, a calm voice from an offscreen worker levels with Maria. 'In any case, your foremen are also leaving,' he says. The camera cuts this time to show us the speaker. Huppert, now relegated to the offscreen space, protests. The locals, some of whom likely have family who have taken up arms for one side of the civil war, take seriously the changes occurring in the country. Unlike Maria, they don't turn a blind eye to the violence. They speak reason, claim the frame, and depart before the film cuts back to Huppert.

In these sequences, Huppert – alerting us to the falseness of white mythology, decentring the image, forcing the spectator to shift their own position – materialises into a white stain. Jacques Lacan explains that the stain alerts us to the presence of the gaze, while also showing that such a gaze can be reversed. Lacan famously identifies the stain in the oblique skull at the bottom of Hans Holbein's painting 'The Ambassadors' (1533). When we tilt our heads to see the skull, we return the gaze. And, when we return the gaze, we learn something (sometimes devastating – like the reminder of death signalled by Holbein's skull), which is the impact of the real.[5] Huppert works as a stain in that she stands out against these two films' landscapes of French colonialism. The coincidence of her appearance and then reappearance causes a double take. She is in the centre of these narratives, but her uncanny recurrence removes the fiction of a singular tale. She demands that the viewer angle their view to see her 'death head' properly. We realise that she is the mark of a repetition compulsion, that of imperialism, of white mythology; not so much a singular figure, but an allegorical one. We look askance, from Huppert at the centre to the margins of the frame where we see the indigenous population. We see the disastrous consequences of French imperialism imprinted on Huppert's character once in South Asia and then again in Africa, and as she spirals out of control, our eyes leave her to see the maelstrom of devastation overtaking those who surround her.

THE DOOMED HARVEST

In Marguerite Duras's *Un barrage contre le Pacifique* and in Rithy Panh's film adaptation, we follow the mother in a desperate battle against the annual flooding of her small plantation in Indochina. The film's title sequence sets a bleak tone of impending doom: a static shot of a cloudy sky, nearly drained of colour, cracked by thunder. The next screen is black, and gives the story's setting: 'Cambodia, French Indochina. 1931, Ream Region (*Plaine de Ream*).' The extreme long shot from above reveals the tiny body of the mother (Huppert) standing in flooded fields. A local labourer employed by the family, known as The Corporal (Duong Vathon), shouts to her, 'Madame, salty water.' A close-up gives us Huppert's desolate, disgusted face. She wears a scarf and raw silk dress of deep scarlet, which emphasises the slight redness of Huppert's hair, flowing out beneath a straw hat. She examines the crumbling mud barricade which failed to keep the sea at bay. Throughout the remainder of the film, the mother will confront no end of obstacles and finally construct a stronger sea wall, which will again be bested by the ocean's waves. Panh's film emphasises the mother's relationship to the landscape and dedication to improving the farm. If she isn't in the fields inspecting the growing rice or working the garden plot next to the family's bungalow, she is inside at the table, running the numbers, drafting designs for a new sea wall. Beyond her stoicism and her increasing desperation to find a way to pay the family's debts and render the concession fruitful, the mother's interior life remains clouded. Florence Jacobowitz comments in her article on the film that the mother's lack of psychological depth

> is typical of many of the characters Huppert has played (drawing from her tendency towards a minimalist performance style and a modernist conception of characterization perfected in her great collaborations with Claude Chabrol. The effect of this is to use the individual to point to the broader social context).[6]

In the marketing of Panh's film, both the poster and DVD cover, Isabelle Huppert strides across the farm. She functions perfectly as a Trojan

Figure 5.2 A close-up gives us Huppert's desolate, disgusted face in *Un barrage contre le Pacifique* (*The Sea Wall*, 2008).

horse: drawing viewers with her international star power so that Panh may expose the indignities that French imperialism wrought upon the Cambodian population. However, the film also quickly dispels the tired trope of white mother as saviour of the indigenous population: those who rally around the mother's sea wall and her battle against the land registry officials are driven from their land and their huts are burned.

This depiction – mother as metaphor of fallible motherland – is faithful to Duras's novel, in which, typical of Duras's writing, characters' deeper motives and feelings stay largely unexplained. In the novel, the version of events aligns more closely with the point of view of the daughter Suzanne; yet, it's the mother's doomed quest that motors the narrative. With its opening description of the death of an old horse, the novel communicates a similar sense of impending doom as Panh's film. Purchased to haul goods to and from the farm, the horse lasts little more than a week: 'The horse was too old. He was much older than the mother in horse years. An old man of one hundred. He tried faithfully to do the work we asked of him and that had long been well above his strength. Then he died.'[7] As went the beast, so goes the mother: not even the most dedicated work horse will live to see the farm triumph over the laws of nature and the manoeuvres of the imperial machine.

Claire Denis's *White Material*, likewise, introduces the mother early in the film: we see Isabelle Huppert as Maria Vial against the vastness of the landscape, and (as the film flashes back to an earlier temporal point) riding a motorcycle with her hands outstretched in an expression of pure happiness and release. In James S. Williams's essay on Claire Denis's *35 Rhums* (2008), he calls attention to what he terms, with clear reference to the work of Martine Beugnet, 'Denis's cinema of the senses', which entails 'a precise choreography of movements and bodily rhythms'.[8] In *White Material*, we see this most clearly through the film's first sequences of the body of Isabelle Huppert: small in the mobile frame, running through fields in a papery, pink dress, and clenching – her bicep strained – as she holds onto the back of a moving bus. Williams, too, in a later essay, remarks on Huppert's vital central place in *White Material*. He writes, 'the sheer energy and incandescent power of its star (Huppert) propels the narrative flow'.[9] The film commands that we follow Huppert, its logic bound to her presence.

Indeed, Maria's frenetic drive to harvest the Vial coffee beans even as civil war creeps closer and finally overtakes the plantation provides the central narrative action in the film. Characteristic of Denis's work, *White Material* features the interplay of a radically mobile (frequently handheld) camera interspersed with quick static shots, and the occasional stationary or gracefully panning long take. The rhythm of this visual form – a shortness of jagged breath as the camera bumpily tracks along a dirt road, a slight slowing of inhalation and exhalation as it takes in the surroundings with a series of still images, and the momentary softening of respiration as the body returns to a place of rest and is momentarily forgotten against luxuriant vistas of sweeping landscape – physically connects the viewer to Huppert, and mimics Maria's mad devotion to the land and her escalating panic as the situation slides increasingly beyond her control.

The film's non-linear narrative, another Denisian signature, intensifies the viewer's relationship to Maria's disorientation.[10] The film's formal qualities align with what Beugnet has theorised as belonging to a subsection of French 'cinema of sensation' from the turn of the twenty-first century, which features '... cinematic corporeality – the materiality of film, bodies in film and film as embodiment', in combination with 'loose, open forms of narrations, disregard for genre boundaries, a proliferation and collage of a diversity of visual and sound material'.[11] Huppert's body leads the viewer through *White Material*'s roving narrative. Beginning at night and just before the film's brutal conclusion, the film opens like a Russian doll – flashing back to the final afternoon, then flashing back a day or two further – before essentially moving forward, nesting each piece of the past back within itself. In Denis's *White Material*, we may have a feminine cinema, in which breaks in the temporal fabric of the filmic narrative render a diegesis spun of past, present, dream and doubt, and in which the body in these determinable and indeterminable spaces is the subject.[12]

Neither of these films feature triumph over adversity; neither mother succeeds in harvesting the land's crops. These heroines fail, crumple, expire. Victims and perpetrators of a noxious system, the bad fruit of the imperial garden, they are destined to poison the land and its people, and then rot; both Duras and Denis inscribe this parable in the heart of their texts. Patricia White's essay on white womanhood and world cinema authorship argues that *White Material* and Kelly Reichardt's *Meek's Cutoff* (2011) reveal how: 'a white woman in an austere landscape triggers potent national myths of colonial entitlement. The heroines are enmeshed in history, but that history is rendered only obliquely; their partial perspectives acknowledge the costs of foreclosing on the stories that remain unnarrated.'[13] The same applies to Panh's *Un barrage contre le Pacifique*. While these films privilege the experiences of white women, corporeal 'white material', they refuse the viewer access to the motivations that would justify these women's fanatical commitment to their land. This withholding renders each woman and Isabelle Huppert, as the actor who incarnates them so fittingly and stoically, sites of spectatorial ambivalence. We are compelled to journey alongside her, but also confused and occasionally repulsed by her actions. This ambivalence mirrors the position of Denis, as a white French woman making a film 'about' Africa, and that of Rithy Panh, as a Cambodian filmmaker making a film 'about' a white woman coloniser.[14] Of course, the ambivalence in these films attacks the very concreteness of their subjects. Neither film is truly 'about' character or place; rather, each offers a glimpse of the multiple repercussions of colonial atrocity.

THE AMBIVALENT MOTHER

These multiple forms of ambivalence centre on the mother. In both *Un barrage contre le Pacifique* and *White Material*, mothers go mad. Duras's mother constructs a sea wall, which fails to keep the water out. Her crops are destroyed. Without crops, she cannot pay her taxes. But Duras is careful to leave the locus of the mother's madness an open question. She writes: 'The doctor traced her crises to the seawall's collapse. Perhaps he was wrong. Such great bitterness could only have built very slowly, year by year, day by day. There wasn't a sole cause. There were thousands, among them the seawall's collapse, the world's injustice, the sight of her children bathing in the river …'[15] The mother, a widow, refuses to accept her sorry lot. She fights the land registry officials; she writes letter upon letter pleading her case; she rebuilds the seawall; she resents her children; she attempts to reap profit by whoring out her teenage daughter Suzanne to a wealthy adult admirer; she is a bad mother. Yet, Duras's novel, which – of course – overlaps with her biography, is a love letter to this mother. The figure of the mother – blazing in passionate fury, then diminished, exhausted – is what we remember.

As Panh's film adaptation of *Un barrage contre le Pacifique* concludes, Huppert, the mother, loses everything. Her performance has chronicled the desperate concentration of her drive to keep her land, the feverous flush of her small triumphs, the ambiguous affections for her daughter and son. 'Huppert's presence sexualises the Mother', writes Jacobowitz, 'underscoring the tensions between her and her beautiful children'.[16] Her attempts to wring capital out of Suzanne's suitor result in a diamond ring, but one too flawed to garner the money necessary to save the farm. Her beloved son Joseph leaves her to live with a woman in Saigon. She pouts as he departs. The mother has failed as seductress. As she lies on her deathbed, her face sweaty, she learns that the seawall has succumbed to the waves once again. She gives Suzanne the flawed diamond ring so that she might start again elsewhere. Huppert's eyes roll back in her head. In the film's next sequence, a funeral is held at the family's bungalow. The ambivalent mother is dead.

However, as Maria Vial in *White Material*, Huppert again incarnates this bad mother. As White comments, 'Maria is a stubborn hold out who ignores everything and bullies everyone around her to bring in the year's coffee harvest as the nation implodes with ethnic violence. Her lazy, selfish son (Nicolas Duvauchelle), who is eventually driven to monstrous violence and madness, hints at her own compromised moral character.'[17] The last quarter of *White Material*, with its bloody flashes of New French Extremity that characterise many of Denis's films from the turn of the century, unfurls with a building violence as Maria's son Manuel descends into madness after his assault by rebel child soldiers.[18] This moment is coded as a rape: the castrating cutting of Manuel's blonde hair (the child soldier feels it between his fingers, and with his voice full of disgust, calls Manuel a 'yellow dog') and the suggestive image of the spear down the back of his shorts. And, in subsequent shots, we see Manuel stripped naked, reborn (or undone) by the violation. After the traumatic incident, when Maria tries to take her son back to the house on the tractor bed, we see a glimpse of a wild dog, a metaphor for her damaged, dangerous child, running between the nearby trees, and – the next time Maria turns back – Manuel is gone. As the film continues, Manuel embraces his madness, shaves his head, and attempts to 'go native'. Nonetheless, Manuel, like his mother, a product of an imperial system, must be purged.

Manuel lures the rebel child soldiers back to the plantation, saying he knows where they can find the Boxer, a hero of the rebel movement. He shares snacks with them. They eat treats and take the drugs (so many coloured candies) that they have stolen from the pharmacy. Then the children fall asleep, seeming once again like the children they are, all their violence drained from their little inert bodies. This makes their murders at the hands of the government soldiers in the next sequence even more repulsive. We see two little boys in a bathtub with the shadow of the soldiers' knife, then the bathtub filled with the boys' blood.

This violence is only equalled by the end of the film when the government soldiers push Maria into the burning remains of the family compound and she comes upon the shrivelled corpse of her son as well as her father-in-law, still alive, choking on the smoke. Her father-in-law, the dying white patriarch, the masculine coloniser, must die. Maria hacks him to death with a machete. *White Material* is about the brutal legacy of colonialism, and no one in the film is spared its viciousness: neither the rebel child soldiers, nor the masculine colonisers, nor the doubly duped Maria (who both believed she would inherit the plantation and that she belonged in Africa). As Williams explains in his essay on the film, this final sequence reveals 'a lacerating vision of a world scorched of human love and kinship, where human relations have been reduced literally to ash'.[19] Maria will perish in the burning plantation with her father-in-law's blood spattered across her face.

OTHERS MADE VISIBLE

Both *Un barrage contre le Pacifique* and *White Material* offer only bleak outcomes for white mothers on colonised land. However, as Isabelle Huppert dies a double death, the viewer can cast their eye on what's otherwise out of view, that which has been left behind and existed before: the land and its indigenous people. Both Derrida's essay on white mythology and Lacan's lecture on the gaze speak of such blind spots. Derrida suggests that western metaphysics cannot see how its proclamations of essential concepts

Figure 5.3 Maria (Isabelle Huppert) with her father-in-law's blood splattered on her face in *White Material* (2009).

rely on the very metaphors that it both created and devalues.[20] Derrida suggests that *outside* of these metaphors, before them, just out of view and earshot, there exists another history: that which has been excluded by white mythology and its 'universal' history of mankind, the story of the Other. Lacan's notion of the blind spot, too, hints at the impossibility of grasping the full story of the Other. He explains: '... *You never look at me from the place from which I see you.* Conversely, *what I look at is never what I wish to see.*'[21] But, what happens when we catch a glimpse of an object looking back? I will conclude by showing how during the final moments of *Un barrage contre le Pacifique* and *White Material*, after Huppert has occupied the light, she then transforms, metaphorises, and disappears, allowing the films to lay bare what white mythology cannot abide: that life goes on without it.

The last shots of Rithy Panh's film show Suzanne wearing her mother's straw hat. She strokes the rice stalks, just as Huppert did in the film's opening sequence. Suzanne looks into the distance, beyond the land her mother fought to keep, the land that was never hers. She smiles. A final crane shot, tilting over the fields, shows the land again, now full of Cambodian farmers. An intertitle, 'The white woman's rice fields, December 2007', ties the past to the present, the fictional to Duras's autobiography, the era of French Indochina to the Kingdom of Cambodia, and returns the stolen land.

The final shot of Denis's *White Material* also gives the land back to its own people. A mobile tracking shot shows one of the rebel child soldiers running across a grassy plain. He must have escaped the government soldiers when they invaded the Vial compound. He trips and falls. A second shot shows him crouching down. He picks up the red beret once worn by the rebel hero the Boxer. Tucking the hat into his belt, the child stands, and then, with determination, runs out of the frame. Against a black screen, Denis ends with a dedication: to the child soldiers ('aux intrépides petites marmailles') and to the film's screenwriter, the great Franco-Senegalese novelist Marie N'Diaye ('à Marie'). As Williams has written, Claire Denis is known for adapting works by male authors. Williams explains that Denis prefers the term 'grafting'. This suggests that she stitches parts of these other works into her own films: like a heart transplant into a foreign body.[22] However, *White Material* is not inspired by a male author's text, but rather by the novel *The Grass is Singing* by South African novelist Doris Lessing. And, with the film's final dedication, Denis acknowledges the influence of the woman screenwriter. The film moves from the white stain to the black screen, from the dead to the living, from the past to the future; the film's dedication makes visible the women who wrote towards this future and the children to whom this future belongs.

NOTES

1. Jacques Derrida, 'White Mythology: Metaphor in the Text of Philosophy,' trans. F. C. T. Moore, *New Literary History* 6, no. 1 (1974): 5–74.
2. Cinema privileges whiteness, equating it with the neutral or natural. As Richard Dyer has pointed out, cinema advantages whiteness both on the technical level as a 'media of light', and by following an ideological line which assumes whiteness to occupy the position of 'reality'. Thus, cinema makes whiteness the baseline, and grants white people the right to be universal subjects of its glow. As Dyer explains in the opening lines of his essays on whiteness, this 'universal' position implies other privileges in the world beyond the movie hall:

   > There is no more powerful position than that of being "just" human. The claim to power is the claim to speak for the commonality of humanity. Raced people can't do that – they can only speak for their race. But non-raced people can, for they do not represent the interests of a race.

   Dyer's project involves dismantling the false neutrality of whiteness in the cinema and rendering it strange: 'The point of seeing the racing of whites is to dislodge them/us from the position of power, with all the inequities, oppression, privileges and sufferings in its train, dislodging them/us by undercutting the authority with which they/we speak and act in and on the world.' See Richard Dyer, *White: Twentieth Anniversary Edition*, 2nd edition (New York: Routledge, 2017), 83–4, 2.
3. 'What is metaphysics?' asks Derrida. 'A white mythology which assembles and reflects Western culture: the white man takes his own mythology ... his *logos* – that is, the *mythos* of idiom, for the universal form of that which it is still his inescapable desire to call Reason.'[3] Undermining the opposition between metaphor and concept, Derrida's text challenges the hierarchy in metaphysical philosophy that renders metaphor an impoverished form of language and *mythos* subordinate to *logos*. He lambasts the assumption of stable concepts that exist outside of metaphor, suggesting that the specific details that gave birth to Western metaphysics – its *mythos* – have been erased by its *logos*: 'What is white mythology? It is metaphysics which has effaced in itself the fabulous scene which brought it into being and which yet remains, active and stirring, inscribed in white ink, an invisible drawing covered over in palimpsest.'[3] Since, as Derrida reasons, every linguistic term deploys an infinite forking branch of signifiers, cancelling out any singular meaning, even the most concrete sensory objects cannot be understood outside of allegory: be it the sun in the sky or the light of human intelligence. Derrida, 'White Mythology,' 11.
4. Following Derrida's logic, thus, 'The concept of metaphor is not a concept alien to metaphysics. It is a metaphysical concept.' See Bernard Harrison, "White Mythology' Revisited: Derrida and His Critics on Reason and Rhetoric,' *Critical Inquiry* 25, no. 3 (1999): 514.

5. Lacan writes:

   If the function of the stain is recognised in its autonomy and identified with that of the gaze, we can seek its track, its thread, its trace at every stage of the constitution of the world, in the scopic field. We will then realise that the function of the stain and the gaze is both that which governs the gaze most secretly and that which always escapes from the grasp of that form of vision that is satisfied with itself in imagining itself as consciousness. (Jacques Lacan, 'Of the Gaze as *Objet petit a*,' in *The Seminar of Jacques Lacan: The Four Fundamental Concepts of Psychoanalysis*, ed. Jacques-Alain Miller, trans. Alan Sheridan [New York; London: W. W. Norton & Company, 1981], 74.

6. Florence Jacobowitz, '*Un barrage contre le Pacifique,*' *CineAction*, no. 76 (Spring 2009): 31.
7. Marguerite Duras, *Un barrage contre le Pacifique* (Paris: Éditions Gallimard, 1950), 13. All translations from the novel are my own.
8. James S. Williams, 'Romancing the Father in Claire Denis's *35 Shots of Rum*,' *Film Quarterly* 63, no. 2 (2009): 99, https://doi.org/10.1525/fq.2009.63.2.44. Here, Williams likely refers to 'The Mise-en-scène of Desire: Towards a Cinema of Senses,' Chapter 3 in Martine Beugnet's monograph devoted to Claire Denis. See Beugnet, *Claire Denis* (Manchester; New York: Manchester University Press, 2004), 132–98.
9. James S. Williams, 'Beyond the Other: Grafting Relations in the Films of Claire Denis,' in *The Films of Claire Denis: Intimacy on the Border*, ed. Marjorie Vecchio (London: I. B. Tauris, 2014), 94.
10. Denis's non-linear narratives have been observed in the work of many scholars. Firoza Elivia, for example, employs a Deleuzian vocabulary in her analysis of Denis's 2004 *L'Intrus* (*The Intruder*), which equally illuminates the narrative strategy of *White Material*: 'In the movement-image, causes lead to actions, presenting continuity in the spatio-temporal relations between images, which fortify a knowability and understandability to the plot and narrative. In *L'Intrus*, to the contrary, there is spatio-temporal discontinuity, which flusters and dislocates the return of the same image.' Firoza Elivia, 'That Interrupting Feeling: Interstitial Disjunctions in Claire Denis's *L'Intrus*,' in *The Films of Claire Denis*, ed. Marjorie Vecchio, 189.
11. Martine Beugnet, *Cinema and Sensation: French Film and the Art of Transgression* (Carbondale: Southern Illinois University Press, 2007), 61. Although Beugnet delimits the selection of French films to those released between the years 1998 and 2006 (devoting a particularly long discussion to Claire Denis's 2001 film *Trouble Every Day*), scholars have since considered work outside of that period in concert with her theorisation of a cinema of sensation.
12. Eugenie Brinkema writes of Catherine Breillat, who like Claire Denis has been aligned with New French Extremity, 'If the phallic model of a film is cinema as monument, then cinema as rend is Breillat's counter-model.' To rend is to tear, but a rend can also be a gash, a cunt. I suggest that we might see Denis's films

as also in the model of the rend. Both Denis and Breillat make cinema that tears at its own fabric. See also Eugenie Brinkema, 'Celluloid Is Sticky: Sex, Death, Materiality, Metaphysics (in Some Films by Catherine Breillat),' *Women: A Cultural Review* 17, no. 2 (August 1, 2006).
13. Patricia White, 'Pink Material: White Womanhood and the Colonial Imaginary of World Cinema Authorship,' in *The Routledge Companion to Cinema and Gender*, eds Kristin Lene Hole et al. (Oxon: New York: Routledge, 2017), 218.
14. For a more sustained discussion of the relationship of Claire Denis to world cinema, see White, 'Pink Material.'
15. Duras, *Un barrage contre le Pacifique*, 22.
16. Jacobowitz, '*Un barrage contre le Pacifique*' 31.
17. White, 'Pink Material,' 220.
18. For the coining of this category, see James Quandt, 'Flesh & Blood: Sex and Violence in Recent French Cinema' 42 (February 1, 2004): 126–32.
19. Williams, 'Beyond the Other,' 94.
20. As Derrida notes:

> [I]t is impossible to get a grip on philosophical metaphor as such *from the outside*, since one is using a concept of metaphor which remains a product of philosophy. Only philosophy itself would seem to have any authority over its metaphorical productions. But on the other hand, and for the same reason, philosophy deprives itself of what it gives. Since its instruments belong to its field of study, it is powerless to exercise control over its general tropology and metaphorics. Indeed, they can only be perceived around a blind spot or a deaf point. (Derrida, 'White Mythology,' 28).

21. Lacan, *The Seminar of Jacques Lacan*, 102–3.
22. This, in fact, is the subject of Denis's 2004 film *L'Intrus*, adapted from a memoir of the same name by French philosopher Jean-Luc Nancy.

CHAPTER 6

Isabelle Huppert's Caring, Carefree, Careless Abortionist in Claude Chabrol's *Une affaire de femmes*
Henrietta Stanford

Set in Occupied France, Claude Chabrol's 1988 film, *Une affaire de femmes* (*Story of Women*), is based upon the story of Marie-Louise Giraud, an amateur abortionist who was tried, convicted and guillotined in 1943 for committing 'crimes against the State'. In other words, for 'depriving the country of its children',[1] thereby impeding national futures when it was women's 'vital' role under Vichy's aggressively pro-natalist and familialist social order to ensure them.[2] Incarnating the spectre of 'death in the shape of a woman, femininity as deadly',[3] to invoke Jacqueline Rose's memorable phrase, the female abortionist was in lethal contradiction not only, it seemed, to women's naturalised association with the principle of 'life', but also to the State's own sovereign authority over 'life-death' decision making. Having presided over thousands of arrests, deaths and deportations by 1943 – including, as a character in *Une affaire* will acknowledge, all 'the Jewish children sent [from France] to Germany' – the Vichy government was exercising this authority with deadly effect.

In Chabrol's film, Isabelle Huppert plays Marie Latour, a working-class mother of two small children who is struggling to survive, indeed struggling to live and thrive beyond mere survival, amidst conditions of economic precarity, material scarcity, the demands of domestic drudgery and the oppressive dictates of Vichy rule. In the film's opening sequences, Marie is weighed down, recalling, in her embodied posture, the knotted etymological roots of labour, from the Latin, *labo*, a 'burden under which one totters' and, relatedly, lassitude, *lassus*, the one 'who bends, who falls forward',[4] who posturally *inclines*. Subsumed beneath layers of tattered clothing, with stooped shoulders and a hasty, shuffling tread, Marie is introduced to us determinedly foraging for nettles on an exposed Cherbourg clifftop, impatiently berating her son, Pierrot – 'Quit whining!' – when he is stung. Soon after, we encounter her again, encumbered but staunchly, doggedly resilient, as she struggles to manoeuvre her sobbing daughter, Mouche, and a sack of potatoes, up the stairs to their tiny, sparsely furnished apartment. Surrounded by a pervasive, repressive poverty, Marie exists within a 'zone of temporality marked by ongoingness, getting by, and living on',[5] an impression reinforced by the camera's extended, unwavering focus on her repetitively effortful movements. Performing the relentlessly prosaic activities of laborious survival – the sort of care-work naturalised by the Vichy government as a gendered responsibility – Huppert's disposition and gait in these early scenes register the unabating, grinding pressures of everyday life, invoking what Jasbir Puar, parsing Lauren Berlant, has described as the chronically lived experience of debilitation.[6]

In this chapter, I repeatedly foreground *inclination*, approached as a 'bodily movement or posture' (which indexes the downward orienting force of fatigue, for example) but also as a 'posture of desire', a 'predisposition, a disposition', and, following the provocative insights of philosopher Adriana Cavarero, an 'implicit relation of care',[7] materialised in the gesture of bending over a defenceless, dependent other who demands a response. Established as a form of 'relation-to' – since the inclined body is one that either requires support and/or offers it – inclination is starkly counterposed, by Cavarero, to the presumptive verticality of masculinist individualism (or 'rectitude') and its fantasies of an impervious, rational and self-sufficient self. by focusing on Huppert's enigmatic portrayal of Marie Latour as mother, lover, friend and abortionist, this paper traces the actor's richly undecidable shifts between

Figure 6.1 Bending to pick nettles. Isabelle Huppert in *Une affaire de femmes* (*Story of Women*, 1988).

the gendered, gestural and affective registers of 'caring', 'carefree', 'careless' and 'not caring' – registers which seem to implicate, but also imbricate, different versions of inclining toward, remaining upright or leaning away from. Presenting Marie as someone who is engaged in responding to the proximate needs of others whilst searching for sustaining ways of affirming her own (the two are sometimes indistinguishable), how, I ask, does Huppert's familiarly dissonant performance in *Une affaire* expose the ties and tensions of inclined relationality – and the giving and receiving of care – amidst social and material conditions that are profoundly *un*caring? In particular, by refusing idealised framings of 'maternal' inclination and its supposedly selfless labours of care, Huppert's performance draws our attention, I will be suggesting, to those tenaciously oppressive stereotypes of self-sacrificing maternity which leave mothers unsupported (without solace or social infrastructural support) and chastised, as Marie will be, for failing to 'care' enough. Or in the wrong way. Or with too much intensity. And indeed, whilst Cavarero establishes the asymmetrical mother-child pairing as her exemplary model, and associates it with an altruistic ethic, she also remains wary of inclination's essentialising 'command and its defining grip'[8] – by which she means those devastating (hetero) patriarchal normativities which reduce care to maternal love and assign a 'burdensome self-sacrificing stereotype' to mothers, and to women more broadly.[9]

In stark contrast to the conventionalised, culturally valorised image of the mother's quietly dignified, stoic endurance and transcendence through suffering (a standard maternal imago, especially so in Vichy France), Huppert's Marie, conspicuous in her ragged, gruelling perseverance, is shown railing against the domestic servitude whose strenuous labours she deems both interminable and unscalable. 'I've been a slave since I was 14!' she protests to her unsympathetic, recently-returned POW husband, Paul, 'And I don't see how it'll change' (the focalising object of her complaint, here, is a pair of Paul's shit-stained underpants, which, bending over a bucket, she is struggling to clean). It is the oppressive weight of this daily struggle and the affective overtones it generates – exhaustion, frustration and despair – which compounds her yearning for modes and moments of embodied, relational and imaginative 'escape'. Resisting the gravitational pull of depressive withdrawal and the slumped despondency of resignation (both potential escape-routes, as the film will elsewhere attest, for those relentlessly worn down by life), Marie looks for other 'ways to exist in a world that makes it difficult to exist'.[10] In fact, 'she is always looking for an "elsewhere"'[11] suggests critic Helen Van Kruyssen of Huppert's compulsive eruptions into song, her relentless inclination for 'merrymaking', or as Marie tells the 7 year-old Pierrot as she bends to tend his nettle-stung knees: 'I need to have fun. I'm still young after all.' Immediately after this exchange and its vehemently expressed 'will to pleasure', we observe Marie inside a cramped, clandestine cafe where, shrugging off the corporeal attitude we associate with fatigue – and seemingly indifferent to judgements of maternal impropriety – she dances, tirelessly, with a friend (she leaves the children at home).

With her playfully ostentatious, almost Rabelaisian energy, Huppert's performance here reflects, in some respects, Sianne Ngai's scripting of the 'zany', an aesthetic 'highlighting the affect, libido, and physicality of an unusually beset agent' often 'in flight from precarious situations', whose 'relation to playing seems to be on a deeper level about work'.[12] But in her exuberant retreat from the depleting beat of everyday existence, Huppert also renders her character visibly, defiantly *carefree*. That is, unlike zany's undercurrent of flailing anxiety, its edge of desperation, Marie displays an irrepressible levity; she appears unburdened by the material and affective labours of care (the OED links 'care' to the Old English, *caru*, meaning 'trouble', 'concern', 'anxiety' or 'grief') and by the demands it makes on a subject's obligation to be 'responsible'.[13] She also seems indifferent to the repressive force of a radically patriarchal, pro-family ideology which, as Miranda Pollard has deftly shown, hailed the 'French Mother' as a mature, dutifully sober and uniquely responsible moral agent who renounced 'feminine frivolity' and other 'pleasures deriving from individual desires'.[14] Defying Vichy's exhortation for mothers to return to their 'authentic inclinations' inside the 'tight circle of the family',[15] Marie reaches outside its enclosures to embrace the vitalising ties of close female friendship. In fact, the lightness and ease of the women's intimacy, reinforced by the camera's lingering regard of their swooning exchange of gazes ('you got angel eyes', Marie teases), is presented as a vivifying alternative to the stultifying obligations of family life. 'One day, I'll sing on the stage,' she tells her friend, 'I can feel it.' And indeed, whilst the beleaguered Marie remains angrily, pragmatically proximate to the weight of life's pressures in these opening scenes, she is also shown evading everyday troubles, if only for a moment, by taking flight into the imagination, immersing herself in capacious, utopic daydreams about her future. Such dissociative reverie is rendered palpable by Huppert's dreamily detached facial expression, a staple of the actor's performance style which resonates, in this instance, with Marie's enduring attempts to make the unbearable liveable. Or, as Cristina Álvarez López and Adrian Martin suggest more broadly of Huppert's characters from this period, it seems she needs to 'withdraw in order to carve out … some private space for reflecting, dreaming, desiring'.[16]

When, early on in *Une affaire*, another friend requests help with 'women's business' and subsequently gifts her a gramophone, Marie assumes the role of amateur abortionist, a role that can't, she conjectures with a light shrug, be any 'harder than anything else'. Prohibited under Marshal Pétain's strident anti-abortion laws of 1942 – part of a swathe of repressive legislation subjecting women to ever-more debilitating forms of surveillance and social control – this illegality is something about which Marie, assisted by Huppert's trademark, ambiguously staged insouciance, seems not to care. In keeping with the 'inscrutability' so closely associated with Huppert's screen (and star) presence, and with Chabrol's own cultivation of an 'aesthetics of opacity',[17] her 'not caring' registers undecidably. Whether, for example, it bespeaks Marie's weary disinterest, naive ignorance or her wilful, defiant indifference – to name several interpretive possibilities – remains unclear. Either way, requests from other desperate women soon follow, and whilst Marie calmly implements what Bonnie Honig, building on Cavarero, calls an 'inclinational' model of care – she demonstrates a responsiveness to the needs of others and is simply 'helping out'[18] – her profitable sideline also resonates as a kind of bullish opportunism, which rewards the resolute Marie an escape-route out of poverty. For Honig, inclination is a postural 'geometry' specific to relationality, and mutuality, and is exemplified by the question, 'how may I be of use?'[19] And whilst the service Marie provides is consistent with this 'being useful' of care, the 'steel rod of pragmatism and bluntness that holds [her] erect'[20] and ensures she 'stop[s] at nothing'[21] – tendencies which Huppert's performance also makes visible – might appear more readily aligned with the uprightness Cavarero attributes to care's antithesis: the hegemony of ruthless individualism, masculinism and autonomous self-interest.

In these early scenes, Huppert's enigmatic Marie seems disinclined to 'give an account of herself' (an ambiguity we have come to expect and identify as a typically Huppertian trait).[22] Or, to invoke a geometrical imaginary once again, she does not appear to 'stand' for something. And without any obvious interpretive cue regarding her potential motivation or guiding purpose, we may be inclined to read her impetus to 'care' as camouflaging something more egoistic, to presume, given her evident economic acuity and attachment to profit, the urgings of a more self-serving ambition and acquisitive desire. Accentuated by Huppert's steely comportment, Marie's disciplined, entrepreneurial drive for self-enhancement is suggestive, perhaps, of the armoured self-interest that can flourish amidst uncaring conditions, when one's sense of security and comfort can feel profoundly undermined. But her determined 'resourcefulness', and the unseemliness that seems to shadow it, might also remind us of the imputations of greed so vociferously ascribed to mothers whose own devoted labours (away from the labours of parenting) are 'haunted by the specter of not good enough care for [their] child'. For the latter, writes Maggie Nelson, is expected to be 'limitless, unconditional, self-sacrificial … within systems' that, of course, render such caregiving 'difficult or impossible'.[23] Given this feminised, maternalised tethering of care to a definitionally pure and unconditional generosity, and given, as Adam Phillips and Barbara Taylor also observe, the 'widespread modern suspicion of kindness' and presumption, indeed promotion, of people as aggressively self-seeking 'by inclination' (caring, in this view, is both unrealistic and 'the saboteur of the successful life'[24]) we may be primed to view any unconventional display of care as a potential 'selfishness in disguise'.[25]

We might also note, however, the choreography of Huppert's gestures, manner and demeanour – at times, notably brusque, at others, complacent and slapdash – which are not easily assimilable to the (gendered) norms and expectations that apprehend care as a mode of feeling, arising intuitively and unbidden, an expression of sympathetic expansiveness, benevolence and compassion. For instance, in a scene whose tonalities swerve, unnervingly, between the careless and the carefree (the pieties and affective intensities often associated with care, and its performance, are missing), Marie is shown curtly instructing a woman to 'Lie down. Relax. Remove your undergarments,' before abruptly handing over to an 'assistant' and escaping to a neighbouring room. Here she jauntily sings, grins, sways goofily back and forth, and falls to the ground, in a dance of giddy jocularity performed for her German-collaborator lover, Lucien. Huppert's carefree yielding to gravity here is indicative not of weariness, with its weakly moribund posture implicitly requiring support, but might remind us, instead, of the destabilised equilibrium Cavarero associates with those 'sweeping passions' which force the 'self outside itself', irresistibly bending and dispossessing the 'I'.[26] That is, the actor's playful loss of balance provides an evocative figure for those erotic inclinations which are pleasurably felt – and sometimes feared – as undermining of the subject's 'stability'.[27] As will soon be evident, Marie's transformative move towards economic autonomy brings with it a dramatic proliferation and amplification of her passions, inclinations and desires. And these conflict with Vichy's oppressive imaginary of maternal virtue, with Huppert's character judged 'that ultimate social menace, *a bad mother*';[28] a figure who deviates – or bends – dangerously from the selfless, self-negating nature and 'authentic inclination' of maternal solicitude.

If such a figure seemed bent on prioritising her own 'self-care', as Marie's critics would surely agree, then her so-called deviance was also blamed (and explained) on her succumbing to the unruly dictates of her own drives and desires. For as Cavarero is eager to point out – and Vichy's repressive disciplinary practices attest – it is women and, indeed, anyone whose body, sexuality or appetites have traditionally faced disparagement, whose inclinations are judged irrational, insatiable and in urgent need of regulation and containment.[29] Such 'deviancy', often presented at the heart of bourgeois 'normality', is a regular stake in Huppert's roles, and here, in the eyes of her husband at least, the unfaithful Marie is unmistakably and maximally culpable for a feminine 'deviation' that involves, in Cavarero's memorable phrase, the 'scandal of maternal inclination succumbing to eros'.[30] The affair's scandalous proportions are further magnified by her brazen 'horizontal collaboration' with the charismatic Lucien, an erotic complicity Marie initiates and embraces, despite Paul's protestations and her own unbending insistence that she is 'for the Resistance!'. Refusing to care precisely when she is enjoined to, Marie flaunts her indifference – in the face of governing powers, social convention and, it would seem, her own political inclinations and desires. In fact, the breezy insouciance Huppert brings to this romantic entanglement is suggestive, perhaps, of her character's determined, fervently-sought escape from the strenuous labours of 'caring' and the charged inner states it provokes (the anxious caring, for example, about the dictates and judgements of others, a 'caring' that is often associated with, and aggressively socialised in, women).

'Who cares?' Marie declares at one point in *Une affaire*, signalling her attitudinal and affective stance towards her husband. And the simultaneously coolly noncommittal and antipathetic tenor of this phrase replays a familiar performative mode in Huppert's oeuvre. Alongside, then, the passionately zealous energy and expressivity Huppert bestows on her character, We might also consider the valences of indifference – often construed as a shortage of feeling, failure of empathy and care's opposite – which inflect Marie's actions and affect. Incorporating a nonchalant, de-dramatising disposition of 'not caring', and an unsparing determination and bravado whose imperatives and affective range might also be identified with the indifferent, Huppert's performance operates variously to render Marie ambiguously knowing and unknowing, admirable and culpable, defiant and compliant, careless and, as I also argue, *caring*. 'Who cares?'. For the women seeking abortions in *Une affaire*, the answer to that question has often appeared to be 'no one'. Facing the embodied indignities of social inequality, and without the secure infrastructures of care required to support the flourishing of life, their varied predicaments remind us that care is often entangled with the converse of care, and with failures to care, and is dependent on the 'practices and good will of others' (in effect, Marie's abortion services, despite their limited and rudimentary delivery, fill the 'caring gaps left wide open by an uncaring state').[31] Ultimately, I wish to argue, by drawing attention to Marie's expanding relationality, that is, her leaning out towards others, seeking and offering support (and sometimes failing to provide it), Chabrol's film elaborates a version of coalitional, cooperative survival and, to use Honig's phrase, 'inclinational care'.[32] And this incorporates both unwieldy, unconventional care practices *and* the negative affect of 'not caring' – a crucial, carefully orchestrated component of Huppert's performance here – as part of a broader effort to refuse, and defuse, the violent imperatives of a cruelly patriarchal world. That effort, for Marie, will prove costly.

Up until her arrest, however, and following the material success of her abortionist enterprise and growing number of clients, Marie is presented as blithely indifferent to the risks. Ostensibly without caution or concern, and heedless of consequence, she doesn't, we might say, 'take care'. Increasingly resplendent in bright floral dresses, curled hair and red lipstick – accoutrements of femininity whose clichéd, spectacularised cadences register as 'excessive' – she luxuriates in the carefree leisure and pleasure of daytime idleness, the sensuous charms of material plenitude and the heady rush of an illicit extramarital affair. She revels, publicly and unabashedly, in the comforts and convivial pleasures of consumption. For example, in one singularly evocative scene, Marie and her children are shown devouring spoonfuls of jam (then a luxury) smothered abundantly on cake and licked gleefully off fingers. Elsewhere, she abandons herself to the soaring rhythms and thrills of a garishly painted carousel. In fact, the film's increasingly luminous colour palette – in marked contrast to the muted tones that dominate earlier scenes – provides an aesthetic and expressive analogue to the pleasurable intensity of Marie's burgeoning desire. No longer tethered to the burdens of domestic labour (she has employed a housekeeper, outsourcing these labours of care to someone else) she spends time playing, boisterously, with her daughter. With the enlivening rhythms of non-productive – and non-reproductive – time now supplanting the grim labours of routinised endurance, Marie appears ebullient, and galvanised, too, by the communal delights of newly forged, non-familial intimacies. 'Got to make time for pleasure!' remarks local prostitute Lulu, a resonant presence within the film, and one of the many women now in Marie's life. Women who, like Marie, are exposed to the cascading psychic and material impacts of insecurity, poverty, marginalisation and the unrelenting burdens of reproductive and other forms of labour delegated as a woman's purview. Portrayed as a pragmatic source of acceptance, wry humour and cooperative support, it is the sex-worker Lulu with whom Marie establishes a particularly close, sustaining bond and mutually rewarding (and illegal) commercial arrangement.

In fact, Marie soon invites her into the family apartment by renting her a room, a gesture which jubilantly bends the conventions of normative domesticity and opens up 'the family' to alternative modes of intimate alliance and support (the women's solidarity also hints at the expansion and redistribution of care away from the maternal subject and from sanctioned marital-reproductive models of kinship). In one languidly carefree encounter, Marie and Lulu lean in to chat irreverently together in the kitchen, a domestic enclosure now transformed, albeit temporarily, from a locus of oppressive constraint into one of intimate, reciprocating solidarity. Newly released from the enervating pressures of precarity and material

Figure 6.2 Enjoying jam and biscuits. Isabelle Huppert in *Une affaire de femmes* (*Story of Women*, 1988).

privation, Huppert's 'carefree' countenance is accompanied, we might say, by her character's greater 'freedom to care, to respond to the world'.[33] For the kitchen is also where Marie practices her abortions, conducts the 'business' of the film's title, and, as I wager here, where she cultivates the supportive ties of inclined relationality – however fragile, temporary and situationally specific these may be. When Marie embarks upon her flagrant relationship with Lucien, however, this triggers an enraged reprisal from the ailing, ineffectual and pyjama-clad Paul (radiating dejection and defeat, he is the affective antipode of Huppert's audacious, pleasure-seeking Marie). 'Being with whores has made you a whore' he hollers, a description not altogether inaccurate given her now striking resemblance to Lulu.[34] Soon after this, Paul returns home to find a disorderly scene of apparently careless excess and over-indulgence, with the lovers asleep, languorously entwined, on the marital bed, and Lulu napping contentedly on a couch. The next day, as Huppert walks purposively, and with a quiet exultance, to her character's first singing lesson and we anticipate Marie's creative ambitions reaching some kind of fulfilment, we hear Paul reciting, in a flat, disembodied voiceover, a letter denouncing his wife's activities. The consequences of this betrayal will prove fatal, as Marie is swiftly arrested and, in subsequent scenes, imprisoned, transferred to State court in Paris and, in *Une affaire*'s final dramatic moments, executed for treason (her anticipated last gesture – of lowering her head into the guillotine – is precluded from view).

As Noah McLaughlin has argued in his commentary on the film, the resentful Paul – whose forceful entreaties for intimacy Marie has repeatedly spurned – elects to use 'the tools of the state in a cowardly fashion to exact revenge'.[35] And by calibrating our attention to a maternal subject who is audaciously desiring and agentive, whose behavioural and affective attributes openly flout Vichy's repressive conventions of marital propriety, femininity and family, Huppert's performance invites us to view Marie's desperate fate as punishment, too, for these 'transgressions'. Performed by Huppert with an irrepressible energy and sometimes jarring intensity, the film's iterative emphasis on Marie's corporeal, sensorial enjoyment, her carefree 'over-investment' in the pleasures of consumption, for example, or 'illicit' carnal experiences, frames this behaviour as a scandal of (feminine) appetite, as something that, given Vichy's disavowal of 'feminine decadence',[36] would be deemed extravagant, unbridled and incompatible with the gendered norms and decorum of responsible conduct. This is rendered powerfully legible when the staunchly Catholic sister-in-law of a client who previously died (following an abortion performed by Marie) visits the apartment, accompanied by two of the woman's orphaned children. A forceful emblem of Vichy's pro-natalist, familialist vision, her overt disapproval, modest clothing and self-sacrificing pledge to raise the six children herself, is presented in stark contrast to Huppert's determinedly flamboyant Marie, who is seen leaving her children as she rushes to meet Lucien, her extravagant trappings of sensuality 'unabashedly displayed'.[37] As such, and at a moment when, as Leah D. Hewitt points out, 'Vichy propaganda [was] condemning individualism, materialism, and immorality, especially in women',[38] Marie's 'wayward' pleasures are shown becoming the target of moral disapprobation in much the same way, then, as her abortionist activities do. 'When the world turns ugly, when it cannot bear to confront its own cruelty, the punishing of mothers darkens and intensifies',[39] Jacqueline Rose has observed, and Marie's unpardonable 'crimes' would provide a ready scapegoat for a government eager, as her ineffectual lawyers later remark, to take 'revenge ... on their own cowardice. On theirs, on mine, on yours', a government whose corruption and duplicity had given it a 'pressing need for moral restoration'.

According to Colo Tavernier O'Hagan, the film's screenwriter, Huppert's character is 'playful and childish ... a flighty creature. She earned money rapidly and spent it quickly.'[40] And indeed, Huppert's expressions of lively enjoyment often project the semblance of an exorbitant, self-indulgent or 'childish' elation which appears, at times, unweighed by anxiety and real-world consequences ('carefree'), and, at others, in thrall to bourgeois idealities and their commercial, individuating inducements to pleasure (crucially, this does not mean Marie invests in the norms of bourgeois propriety). In other words, we detect the standard, denigrated figures of a resoundingly feminine 'excess' transmuting themselves across her person. Through a certain interpretive lens, we might connect Huppert's febrile, joyfully inflated performance here to the demystifying imperatives of parody, with its exaggerated proportions bespeaking an inclination towards denaturalising and dislodging stereotypically gendered images and assumptions (the all to familiar stereotype aligning femininity with consumption, fantasy and the surrender to pleasure, for instance). Catherine Dousteyssier-Khoze suggests something similar when she alludes to the 'touch of falseness, incongruity ... that seems to emanate from [Huppert's] characters ... which introduce cracks in the diegetic world'.[41] As Eve Kosofsky Sedgwick would prominently point out, the distinctly 'paranoid' logics of parody are habitually linked with 'camp', whose subversive protocols and pastimes coincide with a desire to mockingly expose, and depose, the workings of an oppressive status quo. But with her striking evocation of 'surplus beauty, surplus stylistic investment', Huppert's appearance and conduct may appear equally apposite alongside Sedgwick's own alternative, reparative reading of camp, as a practice whose decorative accretions, 'over'-attachments and exaggerated flourishes follow the contours of a different desire, that is, to 'confer plenitude' on a worldly reality 'inadequate or inimical to [one's] nurture'.[42]

Perhaps, then, a generative way to approach Huppert's rendition of her character's audacious inclinations, which she performs deliberately, defiantly and with considerable delight, might be as a dramatisation of Marie's refusal, or *dis*inclination, to accommodate herself to a callous reality – its gendered exploitations and compounded precarities – by deviating and striving to conjure one less punitive. Accordingly, the refusal inscribed in Marie's violation of Vichy's anti-abortion edicts – via her acts of inclinational care, her support of women's reproductive rights – might be construed as a continuation and intensification of the refusals she practices elsewhere in the film. Whether eluding and refusing expectations of marital and maternal virtue, immersing herself in the dissident pleasures of daytime indolence, or initiating unconventionally caring, non-familial affinities, these together reflect, we might suggest, a determinedly resistive mode of being and living. In other words, and in keeping with the joyous noncompliance associated with some of Huppert's most memorable roles, her performance conveys both the weight of Marie's discontent, and her refusal to bend – or acquiesce – to the rhythms and roles imposed by a patriarchal society. Pointedly, much of this refusal is staged 'inclinationally' – rather than vertically, if we adopt Cavarero's schema – in the sense that it engages relationality, interdependency and the giving (and receiving) of care. And indeed, at salient moments in the film, Marie is shown, quite literally, 'on the incline'[43]: whether bending low over a client, straining forward to speak conspiratorially with Lulu, playing rambunctiously with Mouche on a newly purchased mattress or lying supine in bed after sex (incidentally, Cavarero will inform us that inclination is etymologically related to the Greek, *kline*, for 'bed' or 'couch'). In effect, then, and in contrast to those dominant, verticalised understandings of 'refusal' that associate it with the austerely stative condition of remaining upright, immobile and firm, or with the dynamic action of 'standing up for yourself', Huppert's performance foregrounds physical and affective modes of 'leaning' as part of her character's expansive expressions of care and/as dissent.

Alongside this, however, and hard to ignore, is the actor's intimation of a certain ruthless self-reliance, fervent self-gratification and ostensibly 'uncaring' disregard of others (a leaning away from) suggested, for example, by Marie's showy indifference towards her husband's own suffering – as he struggles with PTSD and loses his job – and by the carelessness which distinguishes some of her exchanges with Pierrot, on which more later. In other words, pressed up against scenes which broadcast care's relational arrangements and solidarities, are instances when Huppert's performance invokes the insistent, self-enclosed verticality of masculinist individualism and its consummate lack of care. If this hints at the potentially ambiguous tensions and intersections of 'rectitude' and 'inclination' – contra Cavarero, who sets them 'completely apart'[44] – then it surely also gestures towards the vertiginous intimacy of compliant and resistant (female) subjectivities amidst conditions of precarity and patriarchal constraint, when concrete, material survival might be at stake. Summoning unsettling questions about women's own role as supporters and accomplices of patriarchal power, Marie's ethically inflammatory relationship with Lucien – who performs 'favours for Nazis' – also captures the potential asymmetry between a subject's desiring inclinations and her (professed) political allegiances. Savouring her erotic investment in the tyrannical Lucien whilst explicitly renouncing him politically ('I'm for the Resistance!'), Marie acts upon libidinal impulses which seem to run counter to the forms of oppositionality she enacts elsewhere. Testifying, then, to the complex realities of our lives and minds, and the pull of contradictory impulses, Marie is shown flouting Vichy's patriarchal norms and laws, whilst signalling her apparently blithe unconcern at forming a passionate attachment with Lucien – a brash representative of that same system of oppression.

Of course, as Judith Butler deftly points out, there is no guaranteed causality between the urgencies of one's instinctual life, or drives, and the literal, bodily actions we go on to perform. Our aggressive impulses need not, as she elaborates in her writings on 'aggressive nonviolence', manifest in embodied acts of violence on the wider social stage. In fact, finding ways of acknowledging and 'working through' those destructive inclinations which emerge in one's relation with oneself, and with others, and in response to the 'recognition of our interdependency',[45] is a fundamental part of the struggle that animates, and potentially imperils, any caring relationship – especially those we cherish most. Huppert's performance in *Une affaire* is particularly striking, we might suggest, for its rendering of this ambivalent mutuality, that is, the twinned destructive and loving inclinations which mark our affective ties, including the maternal ties that Cavarero so strategically valorises. Performed by Huppert to connote ambiguous shifts between the gestures of protecting and resenting, abandoning and impinging, supporting and obstructing, Marie's interactions with her children might remind us that although, for Cavarero, the mother's responsiveness is tied firmly to pacifism, and to altruism, she also leaves open the possibility that no response, or a potentially harmful one, might be forthcoming. As she puts it: 'the alternative between care and wound, as well as that between love and violence, is ... entirely inscribed in inclination as a predisposition to respond.'[46] The challenging ambiguities that characterise Huppert's depiction of maternal care might also remind us, however, that in Donald Winnicott's favoured developmental story 'caring' and 'wounding' are not, as Cavarero implies, entirely distinct or oppositional, and care emerges in psychic life as a result of managing, and destructive, states of mind. In his famous narration of 'good-enough' mothering, the caregiver's onerous everyday challenge is to recognise and accommodate her child's incessant demands, hostility and aggression (which might entail hating the child in return) without acting upon the inclination to abandon or retaliate; without, that is, severing the relationship.[47]

Equally important, in Winnicott's account, is the mother's responsiveness in recognising and mirroring the child, and his feelings, 'giving back to the baby the baby's own self'[48] – although there may be various factors that impede her capacity to do so. These include, for example, the mother's depression (Winnicott cites the unresponsive maternal visage 'fixed' by a depressed mood[49]), her frustration connected to unfulfilled needs and desires, or, we might add, the impact and unrelenting pressures of precarity and poverty. Notably absent in Marie's relationship with Pierrot, it would seem, is Winnicott's maternal gaze of reflective recognition – a consistently open, patient and confirming gaze that holds the child fully in its grasp and allows him to 'feel real'[50] – since Pierrot undoubtedly feels 'unseen' by his mother. In fact, throughout *Une affaire* we are made palpably aware of the boy's wounded sense of exclusion, frustration and yearning for maternal affection, and often encounter him searching for Marie's elusive affirmation (he is therefore closely identified with Paul, whose feelings of loss, jealousy and displacement are equally evident). In the film's opening sequence, for example, as Marie tenderly props up her daughter whilst avowing, to a friend, that Mouche is her 'one success', the next shot, framed statically and in sudden close-up, reveals Pierrot, wide-eyed and perplexed as he silently apprehends this conversation (shortly after this, Huppert shows Marie recognising his distress and offering gentle reassurance).[51] But whilst the relation of attentive care inscribed in Winnicott's scripting of maternal 'mirroring' may appear unevenly evidenced in Marie's care for her son, it often seems more overtly present with her clients, whose speech and self-narratives – as they recount their reasons for requesting an abortion – are sustained and contained by the silent, deeply listening Marie.

That said, although Huppert demonstrates a semblance of firm responsiveness during these interactions, there remain moments when her impassive, steady gaze and countenance of self-enclosed blankness threaten to transition into an idiom of response more reminiscent of the rigid indifference of 'not caring' than of Winnicott's reliably attentive, mirroring gaze of recognition. As we've seen, elsewhere in *Une affaire* Marie's affective neutrality becomes an attitude she wields and inflicts upon others, deployed to broadcast, for instance, her pronounced lack of sympathy in the face of Paul's own suffering. And her indifference also resonates as a determined form of refusal: the defiantly staged rebellion of refusing to care precisely when one is obliged to. An altogether different iteration of Huppert's oft-cited 'blankness', however, is established in one of the film's most memorable and quietly devastating scenes; in those brief, desperate moments prior to her execution when a stunned, ashen-faced Marie, weighed down by shackles, waits alone in an empty prison cell. 'Hail Mary, full of shit,' she intones with a concentrated resolve, 'rotten is the fruit of your womb,' before forcefully ripping off a Catholic communion medal presented to her by a fellow inmate. Whilst this curtly-delivered statement wavers tremulously under the weight of an apparently barely restrained defiance and disgust – at the Church, the punitive control it exercises over women's bodies and lives, and its own complicity in condemning her – Huppert's features remain tautly impassive, her wide, tear-filled eyes fixed somewhere off camera. Accompanying the strained indifference of her facial expression, however, are the actor's shuffling tread, jerkily-uncoordinated movements, and sudden, incongruous action of leaning up against the wall – a propulsive forward motion with arms outstretched which, in this particular variation of 'inclination', invokes Marie's acute physical and psychic distress. Or rather, the agitation and unpredictability of Huppert's gestural repertoire and her expression of tensed neutrality together register Marie's precarity as she struggles to both 'stand' and defensively withstand the insupportable pressures of an unbearable, and soon-to-be deadly, reality.

Returning, in my closing remarks, to the film's earlier kitchen abortion scenes, we might note that Huppert's tensely diffident facial expression

Figure 6.3 Listening to her neighbour as she recounts her reasons for wanting an abortion. Isabelle Huppert in *Une Affaire de femmes* (*Story of Women*, 1988).

here does not appear redolent of profound anguish, nor does it signal her character's failed compassion, noncompliance or an oppressive non-rapport (although we might glimpse elements of these in the subtle modulations of her performance). Instead, appearing to lodge no demonstrable complaint, preference or inclination, her restrained bearing during these encounters evinces an impression of impartial neutrality, another version, then, of 'Who cares?'. Conferred without justification or differentiation, Huppert's gaze is apparently disregarding of difference; it is, in this particular sense, 'indifferent'. At a time when women, and especially marginalised women, were denied access to reproductive healthcare services and the support of caring infrastructures and economies (a situation of systemic carelessness increasingly and harrowingly familiar to us today), Marie's levelling 'indifference' represents a counter, in a sense, to the prevailing ways in which care, as a socially organised capacity and practice, is differentially imagined and allocated. Attesting to her character's seemingly non-judgemental attitude – her 'not caring' about these women's varied circumstances or motivations for ending their pregnancies – Huppert's nuanced evocation of 'indifference' is suggestive not, as we might expect, of a deplorable lack of feeling, intervention, or failure to respond to suffering. Instead, it invokes an inclinational care that 'seek[s] to make ourselves useful to others'[52] – whilst challenging the assumption that care must be practised or performed in empathy's terms. As Marie bluntly, and supportively, tells Lulu: 'If you're ever in trouble, I could help.'

NOTES

1. Leah D. Hewitt, *Remembering the Occupation in French Film: National Identity in Postwar Europe* (New York: Palgrave Macmillan, 2008), 134.
2. She was an impediment, in other words, to the reprofuturity which conflates the future with imperatives of procreation and parental care. See Lee Edelman, *No Future: Queer Theory and the Death Drive* (Durham and London: Duke University Press, 2004).
3. Jacqueline Rose, *The Haunting of Sylvia Plath* (London: Virago, 1991), 3.
4. See Roland Barthes's discussion of 'weariness' in *The Neutral: Lecture Course at the Collège de France (1977–1978)*, eds Thomas Clerc and Éric Marty, trans Rosalind E. Krauss and Dennis Hollier (New York: Columbia University Press, 2005), 16.
5. Lauren Berlant, *Cruel Optimism* (Durham and London: Duke University Press, 2011), 99.
6. Jasbir Puar, *The Right to Maim* (Durham and London: Duke University Press, 2017).
7. This is Judith Butler's summation of inclination within Cavarero's postural ethics of nonviolence. Judith Butler, 'Leaning Out, Caught in the Fall: Interdependency and Ethics in Cavarero,' in *Toward a Feminist Ethics of Nonviolence: Adriana Cavarero, Judith Butler and Bonnie Honig, with Other Voices*, eds Timothy J. Huzar and Clare Woodford (New York: Fordham University Press, 2021), 46–62.
8. Adriana Cavarero, *Inclinations: A Critique of Rectitude* (Stanford: Stanford University Press, 2016), 10.
9. Ibid., 13. The 'mother' here represents the person (of any gender) who is called upon to respond to the ethical choice of either care or abandonment, but is acknowledged by Cavarero as a role traditionally occupied by women.
10. Sara Ahmed, *Living a Feminist Life* (Durham and London: Duke University Press, 2017), 239.
11. Helen Van Kruyssen, 'Review of *Une affaire de femmes*,' *52 French Films*, February, 5, 2015, https://52frenchfilms.org/2015/02/05/une-affaires-de-femmes-a-story-of-women/.
12. Sianne Ngai, *Our Aesthetic Categories: Zany, Cute, Interesting* (Cambridge: Harvard University Press, 2012), 7, 182. As others have noted, a 'volcanic, hysterical energy' is a habitual feature of Huppert's performances, even 'her most glacial'. Cristina Álvarez López and Adrian Martin, 'Isabelle Huppert: The Absent One,' *The Third Rail* 10 http://thirdrailquarterly.org/isabelle-huppert-the-absent-one/.
13. As Catherine Audard points out, the word 'care' also designates 'the effort to anticipate a danger ... by acting responsibly.' Catherine Audard, *Dictionary of Untranslatables: A Philosophical Lexicon*, eds Barbara Cassin, Emily Apter, Jacques Lezra and Michael Wood (Princeton: Princeton University Press 2014), 125.

14. Miranda Pollard, *Reign of Virtue: Mobilizing Gender in Vichy France* (Chicago: University of Chicago Press, 1998), 42.
15. Ibid., 13.
16. Álvarez López and Martin, 'The Absent One.'
17. Catherine Dousteyssier-Khoze, *Claude Chabrol's Aesthetics of Opacity* (Edinburgh: Edinburgh University Press, 2017).
18. Bonnie Honig, *A Feminist Theory of Refusal – Mary Flexner Lectures of Bryn Mawr College* (Cambridge: Harvard University Press, 2021), 102.
19. Ibid., 46. Honig notably diverges from Cavarero's text in her attempt to shift inclination from a maternal gesture of pacifist care towards a 'sororal agonism'.
20. Van Kruyssen, 'Review of *Une affaire*.'
21. Janet Maslin, 'Huppert as an Abortionist, in Chabrol's *Story of Women*,' *The New York Times*, October 13, 1989, Arts and Entertainment, Section C, 17, https://www.nytimes.com/1989/10/13/movies/review-film-huppert-as-an-abortionist-in-chabrol-s-story-of-women.html.
22. Judith Butler, Giving an Account of Oneself (New York: Fordham University Press, 2005).
23. Maggie Nelson, *On Freedom: Four Songs of Care and Constraint* (London: Jonathan Cape, 2021), 69.
24. Adam Phillips and Barbara Taylor, *On Kindness* (London: Penguin, 2010), 2.
25. Phillips and Taylor, *On Kindness*, 6–7.
26. Cavarero, *Inclinations*, 7.
27. Ibid., 6.
28. Devorah Baum, *Feeling Jewish: (A Book for Just About Anyone)* (New Haven and London: Yale University Press, 2017), 193.
29. Cavarero, *Inclinations*, 3–7.
30. Ibid., 9.
31. Lisa Baraitser, *Enduring Time* (London: Bloomsbury, 2017), 15; The Care Collective, *The Care Manifesto: The Politics of Interdependence* (London: Verso, 2020), 57.
32. Honig, *A Feminist Theory*, 71.
33. Sara Ahmed, *The Promise of Happiness* (Durham and London: Duke University Press, 2010), 222.
34. This serves to visually reinforce the women's reciprocal attachment.
35. Noah McLaughlin, *French War Films and National Identity* (Amherst: Cambria Press, 2010), 45.
36. Pollard, *Reign of Virtue*, 73.
37. Leah D. Hewitt, 'Vichy's Female Icons: Chabrol's *Story of Women*,' in *Gender and Fascism in Modern France* (Hanover: University Press of New England, 1997), 161.
38. Hewitt, *Remembering the Occupation*, 131.
39. Jacqueline Rose, *Mothers: An Essay on Love and Cruelty* (London: Faber and Faber, 2018), 188.
40. Colo Tavernier O'Hagan, cited in Mary E. McCullough, '*Une affaire de femmes* (*A Story of Women*, 1988): Profile of an Abortionist Executed Under the Vichy

Regime,' in *War, Revolution and Remembrance in World Cinema: Critical Essays*, ed. Nancy J. Membrez (Jefferson: McFarland and Company, 2021), 41.
41. Catherine Dousteyssier-Khoze, 'Huppert and Chabrol: Opacity, Dissonance, and the Crystal-Character,' in *Isabelle Huppert: Stardom, Performance, Authorship*, eds Darren Waldron and Nick Rees-Roberts (New York: Bloomsbury, 2021), 143–4.
42. Eve Kosofsky Sedgwick, in *Novel Gazing: Queer Readings in Fiction*, ed. Eve Kosofsky Sedgwick (Durham: Duke University Press, 1997), 28.
43. Honig also elaborates a specifically feminist version of 'inclinational refusal' in her reading of Euripides' *Bacchae*. See *A Feminist Theory*, 45–71.
44. Cavarero, *Inclinations*, 173.
45. Butler, 'Leaning Out,' 61.
46. Cavarero, *Inclinations*, 105.
47. For 'only then can the subject, the baby, conceive of her, the object, as beyond its power and therefore fully real', Katherine Angel explains. Katherine Angel, *Daddy Issues* (London: Peninsula Press, 2019), 100.
48. D. W. Winnicott, *Playing and Reality* (London and New York: Routledge, 2005), 158.
49. Ibid., 152.
50. Ibid., 158.
51. By repeatedly foregrounding the perspective of Pierrot (through conspicuous point-of-view shots), the film also permits us to reframe Marie's (lack of) care as evidence of the son's own weighted or constructed vision.
52. Honig, *A Feminist Theory*, 102.

CHAPTER 7

Horn | Huppert | Horn
Lutz Koepnick

After watching a series of films with Isabelle Huppert in 2004, American artist Roni Horn wrote to the French actor: '[W]atching you is like looking out a window – but a window that opens onto a different view each time one looks. The window itself – constant, but what's beyond – changing. Perhaps you are a medium.'[1] Though Horn goes on to applaud Huppert's radiant transparency, her present-ness in front of the camera, she also understands the actor's intensity as a form of camouflage. Huppert appears to be herself whenever she exists on screen as someone other; she assumes the role of others in the very appearance of herself. Such camouflage could not be more different from what we know about the iconicity of other famous actors. It categorically challenges what theorists of acting since Greek antiquity have come to think about the relation of face and mask, subjectivity and role, identity and personhood. Marilyn Monroe remained Marilyn Monroe in each of her films and was revered by her audiences as such. Not so Isabelle Huppert. To present herself as other, for her, is to become herself. The frenetic pace of her performances, of taking on different roles, is the work of an exceptional con artist, however fragile her persona on screen may appear, however nuanced the voices may sound that resonate through her image. Huppert is an anti-icon. Rather than embodying an object of speechless devotion, of presenting the divine and transcendental in visual form, Huppert defies any effort to get a hold of her identity at close range. To arrest her image. To attach her to our expectations or attach us to her projected life. Window and medium alike, what defines Huppert as Huppert is her provocative ability to escape the audience's grasp in plain sight. She 'uses the visible as the place to hide'.[2]

Some of the central questions of Horn's remarkable work as a photographer, writer, sculptor, and book and installation artist since the 1980s have been: Can we sustain identity over time, and if so, how? How much change can something – the face of a teenager, the surface of a passing river, a landscape amid changing weather conditions – afford before we begin to perceive it as other? And conversely and perhaps more importantly: to what extent do we require marks of difference to experience the identity of a particular object, its semblance of sameness, in the first place?

A 'woman of many faces',[3] Isabelle Huppert's career since the 1970s has been hailed as bold, daring and experimental; as zealous to meet the camera and return its gaze, yet also as impermeable and riddled by secrets; as at once uniquely skilful and intuitive, controlled and impulsive, intensively present and strangely withdrawn, transparent and enigmatic. The central questions that haunt Huppert's work as an actor for the past decades have thus been: what holds the many images together we know of Huppert? If she exists only in her roles, as different characters she embodies across a wide range of generic registers, as difference incarnated, does it make sense to speak of 'Isabelle Huppert' at all? Adamantly present and absent alike, is the identity of Huppert a mere figment of her viewers' imagination? A mere mirror telling us more about our expectations and denials as spectators than about the object of our gaze?

Though dedicated to different mediums and audiences, Horn's work and Huppert's performances over the last four decades have raised questions that resonate with each other. At heart, both ask their viewers to mistrust any concept of identity coupled to conventional ideas of temporal stability, intentional self-expression and essential sameness. In the work of both, still and moving images figure as much more than mere representations or signs of the real. They instead animate and diffract passing realities and shape the place of human and nonhuman objects within larger ecologies of perception. Both entertain certain affinities to the legacy of minimalism, but in the work of both deliberate strategies of reduction, of apparent blankness, blandness and repetitiveness, of refusing the overly dramatic and subjective, all clearly serve maximalist goals. They investigate nothing less than the question of what it means to register and exist amid the vagaries of time, and they do so by directing our attention to the extent to which different environments and atmospheres – what Horn, as we will see, calls 'weather' in the broadest possible sense – shape and inflect our understanding of the human.

It therefore comes as no real surprise that artist and actor collaborated for a project in 2005, entitled *Portrait of an Image*, later exhibited in Frankfurt am Main in 2013 as an exhibition of photographs shown in the rotunda of the Schirn Kunsthalle and, without caption and context, at local bus stations, inside subway cars, and on billboards across the entire cityscape of Frankfurt. *Portrait of an Image*, as exhibited at the Schirn, gathered one hundred photographs of Huppert, organised into twenty series of five sequential portraits. For each of these series, Huppert replayed for the camera from memory an expression, a feeling, or an attitude associated with one of her former roles and characters: the figures of Erika in *La Pianiste* (*The Piano Teacher*, 2001), Claire in *La Vie moderne* (*Modern Life*, 2000), Mika in *Merci pour le chocolat* (*Nightcap*, 2000), Emma in *Madame Bovary* (1991), Charlotte in *Signé Charlotte* (*Sincerely Charlotte*, 1984), Lena in *Entre nous* (*Coup de foudre*, 1983), Isabelle in *Sauve qui peut (la vie)* (*Every Man for Himself*, 1980), and Pomme in *La Dentellière* (*The Lacemaker*, 1977). Often captured only split seconds apart, the shots of each series typically capture minute, albeit nuanced, differences. Each image offers a different take that appeals to the viewer's curiosity, urges us to read individual portraits against each other, and leaves little doubt about the fact that neither acts of recollection nor of becoming other can produce singular and immutable truths. In contrast to the contemplative setting at the Schirn, the display of select images from these series across the city of Frankfurt employed ordinary advertising spaces to provoke unexpected encounters and cause citizens mid-stride to wonder about what they were seeing and be startled by the sight of a somewhat familiar face turning its gaze on their everyday movements.

Portrait of an Image is neither a work about Huppert's roles nor about the actor Huppert. It instead taps into the rich history of portrait painting and photography in the West since the Renaissance in order to probe what

Figure 7.1   Figure 7.1 *Roni Horn*, Portrait of an Image (*Frankfurt*), 2013(detail). 16 images from *Portrait of an Image (with Isabelle Huppert)*, 2005. Commissioned by Schirn Kunsthalle, Frankfurt. December 12, 2013 – January 26, 2014. Photo: Norbert Migueletz. © Roni Horn. Courtesy the artist and Hauser & Wirth.

media-saturated cultures of the twenty-first century consider as image, and it deploys the unique temporality of photographic images in order to unsettle representational expectations we might have about the logic of a portrait. Huppert serves Horn as window and medium to explore these issues, yet in approaching Huppert not as star image or icon but as a mere window and medium Horn ironically stays true to what, in her eyes, Huppert is all about after all. Inspired by this curious dialectic, the following pages explore this productive meeting of artist and actor, portrait and image, in greater detail in order to better understand what it may mean to be a medium and thereby hide in plain sight. This essay is neither about Horn nor about Huppert. It is about the space in between them, the windows they open onto each other, the interfaces that simultaneously connect and separate their work as image-makers.

MEDIUM | MEDIA

Roni Horn's artistic practice since the 1980s has been irreverently agnostic about the issue of media specificity, the mantra of modernist art of the twentieth century. In pursuing the mutability of subjectivity across time and what Horn herself with some Borgesian irony calls 'the idea of an encyclopedia of identity',[4] Horn has approached media such as photography, sculpture, the book or drawing simply as different environments to stage transformations of sensory experience, not as mediums that may claim self-reflexive gestures of attention to guard art against the world's interference. Mediums no doubt matter for Horn, but they do not matter on their own terms. Their task instead is to provide means to mediate different catalogues of experience and draw our attention to the manifold ways in which inanimate objects interact with their surrounding spaces, human faces echo atmospheric conditions and natural landscapes fold subjects into unsteady ecologies of perception we cannot fail but to control.

Consider *Doubt Block*, a solid, rectangular glass sculpture from 2005 with matte sides, a deep amber interior and a clear surface on the top. Meant to sit directly on the floor of a given exhibition space, *Doubt Block* at once deflects, refracts and inflects the viewer's gaze, lures and repels our curiosity about what may reside inside. While its top mirrors the sculpture's exhibition environment and thereby invites the viewer, by taking up shifting positions, to frame and reframe possible reflections, the block's textured sides – seemingly illuminated from the inside, yet nevertheless obstructing any sense of transparency – emphasise a greater sense of stasis, of groundedness, the extremely slow process by which geological time makes and marks the non-human time of the elements. *Doubt Block* thus results in a dual splitting of time and space. Its luminous and enigmatic materiality appeals to viewers at once eager to explore the relation of memory and perception ('Is this the same block when I view it from a different angle and as its surface reflects a different view?') and to engage with the question of what it means to centre oneself in one's place without insisting to attain one timeless truth ('How much sameness and stability is necessary to recognise the vagaries of time and place?').

Horn has investigated similar concerns and questions in other media as well. Yet to say that *Doubt Block*'s medium of glass – a material made from sand that due to Horn's long-standing work in and about Iceland alludes to the island's foundational presence of volcanic lava – is secondary to the work's phenomenological aspirations misses the point. Instead, *Doubt Block* draws acute attention to what Craig Dworkin discusses as the dual paradox of what twentieth-century art has come to consider as artistic medium.[5] First, we cannot think of or ever locate a specific medium in isolation. Mediums become recognisable as mediums through various acts of inscription and contextualisation: *Doubt Block* requires the viewers' movements and the gallery's architectural structures – the work of other mediums – to become what it aspires to be in the first place. Second, though we consider mediums as the material substrate of certain artistic practices, we are misled to think of them as mere objects. 'Indeed, the closer one looks at the materiality of a work – at the brute fact of its physical composition – the more sharply a social context is brought into focus.'[6] Certain materials become legible as mediums only under certain conditions, in contexts that allow us to approach them as such. *Doubt Block*'s glass sheds light on the fact that mediums in art are both nature and culture, matter and discourse.[7] They provide the condition – the quasi-natural base – for the possibility of aesthetic expression or perception, but they at the same time present and frame their nature as a product of historically situated acts of human meaning-making and experience.

Portrait of an Image follows the paradoxes Horn's work with and about different mediums has addressed over time and thereby allows us to understand Horn's designation of Huppert as a medium and window in greater detail. Similar to *Doubt Block*, Horn's images of Huppert involve viewers in complex processes in which a certain splitting of temporal and spatial registers create curiosity and unease at once. Whether placed in an interior gallery setting or across public spaces, the portraits of Huppert – most of them tightly cropped below the actor's chin and below the top of her forehead – stage puzzling acts of memory and recollection. They show an actor trying to recall former acts, perform a previous performance, without indicating what these roles may have been, nor what precise moment of a certain film Huppert reenacts for the camera. Photography here remediates the operations of moving images, as much as memory recontextualises the past within a multiply mediated present. Minute differences between images and across different series in the gallery setting cause viewers to want to read one image against another, even if they will often be unable to see more than a few images within their field of vision. To remember what you saw before thus deeply affects what you see now; what you see now may transform what you have seen before. Not one view will ever be the same because time interferes at all times, similarly to how a different position will cause us to see and see something in *Doubt Block* very differently.

But there is more. Analogous to *Doubt Block*'s tension between transparency and obscurity, reflectiveness and deflection, Huppert's images specifically in buses, subways and on advertising billboards present much more than mere visual surfaces meant to mesmerise the gaze of unsuspecting onlookers. Because Huppert during the shooting directly reciprocated the gaze of the camera, Horn's images are in fact experienced as entities that look at and look back at their viewer and thus structure our sense of place within the urban fabric. They reflect the city as much as they reflect on our own act of viewing. Whether displayed much larger than life or roughly at human scale, they all place claims on their viewers to negotiate some sense of mutuality, of co-existence, with them. What may strike some viewers as unwelcome events of recognition and surveillance, may leave others with a surprising sense of attachment and entanglement. Or both at once. In this, what these portraits accomplish is not simply to provide objects of to-be-looked-at-ness and consumption, but to inflect the city's very ecology of seeing, the way in which viewers and viewed co-constitute each other. Huppert's images, in other words, aren't just representations, or even representations of representations. Horn instead positions them as agents and actants within the expanded field – the environment – of still and moving images we have come to call modern media culture. They comment on how cinema in the twenty-first century, as a medium of artistic expression and as a media of mass communication, has come to permeate each and every space of our social, economic, and political lives. And they reflect on the extent to which in our contemporary world we need to think of both mass media and artistic mediums, not as mere objects, but as elemental forces, as curious hybrids of the natural and the cultural that shape the very way in which we perceive the world in the first place. Medium and media alike, Horn's Huppert recognises images as – in the words of John Durham Peters's philosophy of elemental media – 'vessels and environments, containers of possibility that anchor our existence and make what we are doing possible'.[8]

For Horn to speak of Huppert as a medium, then, implies much more than to describe Huppert's unique ability to be and become other while staying the same. Or to secure some sense of sameness, of identity, by embodying the ever different. It instead sheds light on how Huppert joins what is natural and cultural about her body to explore the contours of subjectivity today, and how this deployment reflects and refracts the ubiquity of moving images in our contemporary moment. Reminiscent of *Doubt Block*, Horn's Huppert is a medium because she invites us to view and re-view our present in ever-changing ways and thereby probe what it means to place oneself in one's times. To act, for her, is to absorb, mirror and modulate different environments of being rather than to assume postures of calculated self-expression. It is to ask questions, to trade in doubt, rather than to deliver lasting impressions. It is to unsettle any desire to be seen and approached as an object of the viewer's gaze. Similar to Horn's glass sculpture of 2005, Horn's Huppert is at once luminous and tangible, transparent and impermeable. We can never own her image because whatever we call image today resides in multiple temporal and spatial realms at once and remains continually suspended between what we see and what we remember or anticipate, between the appearance of compelling presence and a profound sense of absence, of vacantness.

In the work of aesthetic modernists mediums aspired to 'rescue from cognitive and rational oblivion our embodied experience and the standing of unique, particular things as the proper objects of such experience, albeit only in the form of a reminder or promise'.[9] Horn may no longer situate herself in this tradition, and yet, precisely in shunning modernism's self-reflexive obsession with issues of medium-specificity, her work with Huppert offers potent insights about the place of subjectivity amid our post-media condition.[10] Horn's Huppert is a medium because she enables her viewers to bring into focus, not simply what surrounds her (and them), but what it means to become and be ecological in a contemporary world in which media and technologies of communication equally belong to the worlds of culture and of nature. Rather than to bathe her viewers in the presumed comforts of the past, Horn's Huppert encourages audiences to experience the expanded landscape of cinema today as a unique container of possibility: as a vessel and environment that, in the form of a reminder or promise, can deliver subjectivity from the many burdens the drive of human self-assertion and exceptionalism has historically placed on the subject.

WEATHER | SUBJECTIVITY

When discussing acting, character and role play in cinema, film scholarship has long struggled to develop a vocabulary as theoretically rich and demanding as the one used, for instance, to address editing, cinematography or plot construction. Haunted by one-dimensional understandings of identification, critical writing on film has often shunned serious examinations of the relation between actors and their cinematic characters, not least of all because such examinations may have aligned scholarly work all too closely with the affects of general audiences – their presumed desire for identifying with particular actors and their roles – and thereby betrayed what defined scholars as scholars. To discuss character seemed to privilege content over form, emotional absorption over criticality, and hence to deflate film studies' formative indebtedness to the legacy of modernism and its ethos of formal experimentation, self-reflexivity, estrangement and distantiation. At best, film scholarship mobilised complex repertoires of psychoanalytic concepts from Freud, Lacan or Mulvey to show that identification with individual characters and/or their actors seduced viewers into twisted, albeit culturally symptomatic forms of complicity. At worst, it simply declared any focus on character and the dynamics of identification as politically regressive and abstained from any detailed discussions of how specific actors and stars use their bodies as masks to present – to 'sound through' (lat. *per-sonare*) – their roles and characters.

The discussion of character in cinema begs the question of identification, yet as a form and structure of attachment, the concept of identification begs for serious reconsideration itself. It is much messier than often assumed. And the attachments between viewers, characters and actors it is meant to describe can be many things and many things at once: ironic and sentimental, moral and political, driven by or disregarding the drive of a particular narrative. As Rita Felski has recently argued with regard to acts of reading, identification describes an affinity based on some sense of similarity.[11] But in the context of cinema it is difficult to sort out whether that sameness is about a character's psychological or physical traits, about actor or role, about a character's function within a particular narrative or a much larger dynamic in whose context certain characters or actors have become part of our everyday lives beyond the limits of an individual text. 'Characters', Felski argues,

> are movable, teleporting into new media and milieus, times and places. They swarm among us, populating the world with their idiosyncrasies, accessories, trademarks, sidekicks, and sayings. They are not just inside books, awaiting our attention to spring to life, but also outside books, beings we may bump into without expecting it. They differ from persons yet are easily recognizable as akin to persons, objects of widespread devotion (or dislike). In short, they form part of an Umwelt.[12]

What holds for literary characters and our identification with them as readers, certainly applies for the image of the actor on screen as well. To think of cinematic characters as an *Umwelt* not only means to conceive of them as part of a dynamic and open-ended process, but to rethink identification as a reciprocal, often highly contingent, situated and unpredictable process. As Felski concludes:

We act on this Umwelt – that is, surrounding world – in interacting with it; the environment as it concerns us is a networked array of phenomena. Characters matter to us and yet are not simply 'in our minds'; they come to us as if from elsewhere; they possess a degree of solidity, permanence, and force.[13]

Never hesitant to add yet another role and register to her repertoire, Isabelle Huppert's perhaps most consistent trademark is to create different characters in front of the camera as laboratories – as environments – to investigate the nature of identification in cinema. '[W]hen I act', Huppert noted in an interview in 2016, 'I don't think about anything. My acting depends on the staging: you know, you put the camera in front of me, and I do it.'[14] Though often drawn to work with filmmakers who remain faithful to the rhetoric of auteurism, Huppert tends to approach her own acting neither in terms of Stanislavski's or Strasberg's methodological exploration of specific feelings and shared experiences, nor according to Brechtian or Benjaminian concepts of reflective detachment and deliberate testing. For her, to act, to assume a role and character, is to attune body and voice to a setting, a larger choreography, an environment as much defined by the presence of other actors, spatial locations and atmospheric milieus as the observing gaze of the recording apparatus. It is to let go of the protocols of control, criticality and self-determination shared by dominant visions of acting and art filmmaking, and instead take on characters as figures that gain solidity and force precisely because they absorb and are being absorbed by what exceeds the contours of subjectivity.

It would seem reasonable to locate Huppert's art in her unique ability to activate spontaneity and intuition if such concepts didn't detract from what I, with Felski, would like to understand as Huppert's ecology of character and identification, her profound ontological blurring between actor and role, interiority and exteriority. Huppert's characters matter to us even beyond their presence in individual films, they gain permanence and provide sites of identification, because they defy any reliable stability and invite their audiences to act on them, to live with them and in living with them to change them. We attach to Huppert's characters, not because we know or grasp them (we don't, ever!), but because they provide worlds in which the familiar and the strange, the obvious and the obscure co-exist in variable constellations. Greta Garbo's face at once embodied and transcended classical ideas of beauty. The drama of her countenance, according to Roland Barthes, resulted from the interplay of what was mask – defined as a sum of lines – and what was face – understood as the thematic harmony of the mask's graphic lines.[15] Marlene Dietrich's face, due to its mimetic assimilation to the cinematic apparatus, displayed a sense of effortlessness and malleability that anticipated the role of the morph, the cyborg. Mimesis of body and machine, her face was essentially protean.[16] Huppert's face is of a very different order. It is neither classical nor posthuman. In each of its different appearances, it provides her audiences with a sun-dial of the worlds and environments that surround her. Viewers attach to and identify with this face because it registers what exceeds the frames of the visible and thereby, in the midst of what we want to identify as 'Huppert', connects us to what is neither her nor her roles. 'Every performance', writes Kristin Schrader, 'exists only as something that is relational, only as something that occurs through the presence of the recipient. It needs others as an audience.'[17] Huppert's face takes on different characters only to reveal the extent to which no character and no act of identification ever exists independent of its environment. To identify with her and her characters – the landscapes of her face – is to recognise subjectivity as an ecology of dispersed and open-ended interactions in which all kinds of agents, be they human or nonhuman, constantly and unpredictably act on each other.

Which returns us to the work of Roni Horn, her work with Huppert in *Portrait of an Image*, but also how this work picks up what has driven Horn's photographic practice since the 1990s. The hundred images of *Portrait of an Image* are all tightly cropped around Huppert's face, so closely that in some we don't even see the white background in front of which Huppert posed. The lighting is even and diffuse, no visible make up softens or dramatises Huppert's facial features. Some of the more generously framed images reveal Huppert's neck, collar bones, and shoulders, her skin in full view and not obscured by clothes or jewellery. Though in each of the images Huppert gazes right into and is visibly aware of the presence of the camera, and even though not one photo masks the reflection of artificial light in her eyes, Huppert in all of Horn's hundred images radiates 'naturalness': a face not made up for the camera, an appearance that has nothing to hide precisely because it does not encounter the camera – and by extension, the viewer – as a source of antagonistic interference.

Pushing against photography's illustrious chase after decisive moments, the seriality and grouping of *Portrait of an Image* have reminded many reviewers of Horn's *This is Me, This is You* (1999–2000), a series of ninety-six

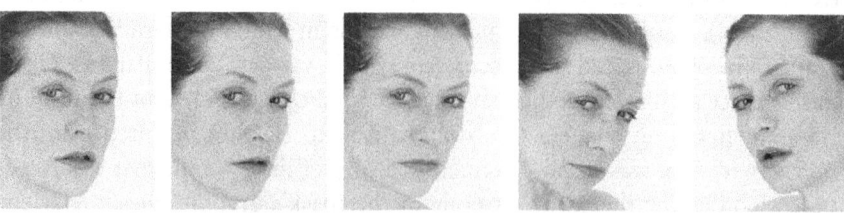

Figure 7.2   *Roni Horn, Portrait of an Image (with Isabelle Huppert)*, 2005–6 (detail). Courtesy the artist and Hauser & Wirth. © Roni Horn.

images Horn took of her niece Georgia over a period of two years. Each image is paired with another taken a few seconds later. In all images we see Georgia trying out different personalities for the camera – some quiet, pensive and brooding, others loud, provocative and teasing – as if to probe various portals into adulthood and thereby reveal the multiplicity that lies dormant in all of us.[18] An even more pertinent and illuminating analogue in Horn's work, however, can be found in *You Are the Weather* (1994–95): one hundred photographic images of a young woman – Margrét Haraldsdóttir Blöndal – who holds the camera's gaze as we see her immersed in various natural pools in Iceland amid challenging weather conditions. The framing of Margrét is as tight as that of Huppert. Though the lighting conditions vary somewhat across the earlier series due to different outdoor settings, Horn prioritised the impression of diffuse over direct light sources, an even softness of the visible over any dramatizing or expressive use of shadows. Unlike Georgia or Huppert, Margrét was not asked to assume different roles and perform memories of other performances for the viewer, whether such impersonation was achieved through utter absorption into a character or through distant and detached re-presentation, through empathetic dissolution or utterly controlled self-management. Yet similar to the Huppert series, *You Are the Weather* presents its principal subject's face as a space seemingly void of civilizational markers. In most images, we see water either in parts of the background or reaching up Margrét's neck. Yet in all images the focus is entirely on its subject's unembellished and unmarked presence, communicating a form of intimacy and austerity that, even more strongly than the Huppert series, evokes some sense of 'naturalness'.

Similar to *Portrait of an Image*, the focus of *You Are the Weather* is quite obsessively on one face only, however different it may appear over time. Deliberately captured amid the rough environmental conditions around 66° North – fog and rain, snow and ice, steam and massive skies – Margrét's face in the earlier project emerges as no more and no less than an interface to what surrounds and structures her subjectivity yet cannot but remain invisible, as a landscape that echoes, extends and recasts the landscape and its atmospheric fickleness beyond the frame. The geographic and climatic conditions of Iceland have been central concerns in Horn's work since the 1980s.[19] Iceland and its weather, for Horn, have the status of a verb, of actions; they raise open-ended questions about what it takes to centre oneself. As importantly, in their unpredictability and harshness, they often take on the quality of a labyrinth. As Horn wrote in a short text from 1991:

> The weather or even the roads here, which are more like paths, are labyrinths. Things that lead away, forcing you out into the world and more in upon yourself. What this island is defines you.

> As long as you don't stop – there's no getting lost in a labyrinth, through there is the illusion. The labyrinth razes all distinctions. Disorientation comes quickly. Your sense of place breaks down. Your relation to the world becomes tenuous. Go on long enough and doubt may isolate you. Go on long enough and clarity will become you.[20]

Horn's photographs of Margrét Haraldsdóttir Blöndal study a labyrinthian maze whose complexity we tend to obscure when using words such as subjectivity or identity. Margrét may be lost in isolation and disorientation, but her tenuous relation to the world outside the frame offers a powerful promise of clarity. We may want to read her face as closely as we can to detect some stable sign of selfhood, yet in the end it's the island and its weather that critically define who she is. Distinctions might break down, place seems to become elusive, but truly lost are only those who think they can own space and place, self and identity like immutable objects. To be someone, here, is to take on the maze of one's location however intractable and capricious it may be. It is to face, with some sense of tenacity, what exceeds the domain of individual control and prediction, rather than to display your face as a container, a billboard, of unquestionable distinctions and individual property rights. We have come to think of the Minotaur, the labyrinth's mythological occupant, as a monster. In Horn's version that monster is us, the other that is in and beyond us and that we demonise in order to hold on to illusions of permanence.

Monsters remind, warn, instruct or foretell us of things we seek to forget or repress. It is tempting to think of Horn's Huppert in such terms as well. Horn's images of Huppert remind us of the fact that identity becomes monstrous if severed as a fixed image from its environments, its relationality. Horn's Huppert warns us not to think of repetition in radical opposition to difference and of identity as the opposite of flux. She asks us instead to explore the generative power of repeating differences and to remain steady in our eagerness to attune to varying conditions of being. She instructs her viewers to abandon the modern history of the portrait – its rhetoric of orchestrated self-performance – unless they want to uphold notions of human agency that have caused lasting havoc to our planet and social fabrics. And she foretells in form of a promise a future in which we can relax the screens of subjectivity and fearlessly assimilate to and co-exist with what is not us. Huppert's image does not instil terror. It isn't scary. But – like a monster – it deeply unsettles what we typically take for granted and mediates truths we are eager to keep at bay. As seen by Horn, Huppert at heart opens a window onto a world that no longer essentially pivots around the figure of the human. Huppert, in this view, is medium and mediated at once. She registers the weather as much as she is this weather.

Horn's 2007 *Vatnasafn/Library of Water* in Stykkishólmur uses a converted old library to exhibit twenty-four columns of water gathered from different glaciers in Iceland, all threatened by the impact of climate change. The building's rubber floors display a multitude of words in English and Icelandic describing the weather – atmospheric conditions that may as well apply to human moods and temperaments as well. 'Horn has likened the work', writes Briony Fer, 'to a lighthouse in which the viewer is the light. But it also acts as a kind of gigantic optical instrument, the distorting lenses of the columns picking up, like so much residue or sediment, the fractured view that looks both inward, inside ourselves, and outward, to water.'[21] Horn's Huppert is such a lighthouse as well. She makes us look inward and outward. And as she reflects the visible and refracts what exceeds its frames, she makes us realise that nothing might produce more monstrous returns of the repressed than our impulse to keep the inward and the outward, subject and environment, viewer and viewed, the visible and the invisible tidily apart.

AFTER-IMAGE

At least two films of her sprawling career show Isabelle Huppert behind as much as in front of a photographic camera. In Hong Sangsoo's *La Caméra de Claire* (*Claire's Camera*, 2017), Huppert plays the film's eponymous Claire, a Parisian high school teacher who visits Cannes during the film festival and upon arrival befriends Manhee, a young Korean woman just fired from her position as a film sales assistant. A slow-paced ensemble piece centred around prolonged dialogues between Claire, Manhee, film director So Wansoo, and Kim's boss Yanghye, *Claire's Camera* offers at once comedic and contemplative views on the power of image-making. Claire's polaroid camera is its central agent. It harbours magic qualities that not only disturb the chronological telling of the film's story, but in the end manage to reverse the firing of Manhee in the film's opening. When Manhee asks amateur photographer Claire why she takes pictures, Claire answers philosophically: 'Because the only way to change things is to look at everything again very slowly.' Photographs do not merely capture the real. They re-train how we look at and engage with the world. They suspend the normal course of things, yet in doing so they open up alternate ways of telling the past and shaping the present. To borrow Benjamin's famous metaphors: photographers are simultaneously magicians and surgeons. Their images elicit awe and incite contemplative acts of looking as much as they have the power to restitch the social fabric and reengineer the world.

In Joachim Trier's *Louder than Bombs* (2015), Huppert is Isabelle Reed, a famous and restless war photographer whose suicide drives her family to the brink of disintegration. Her images are replete with scenes of violence, suffering, and trauma, but she is remembered by her husband Gene (Gabriel Byrne) and her sons Jonah (Jesse Eisenberg) and Conrad (Devin Druid) mostly through her absence, her emotional distance, her gestures of affective departure rather than arrival. Isabelle's images are dramatic, highly stylised documents of human agony. They show families in Middle Eastern war zones mourning the dead; domestic spaces invaded by armed military; and most iconic (and printed in black and white): a mother grieving her deceased child, captured from a stark overhead angle with the mother's face cut out of the frame. Huppert is not the film's central figure, and yet her images and her own family's memories are what hold *Louder than Bombs* uneasily together. Conrad's somewhat surreal visions and recollections stand out. Once he sees her floating amid ruins after she was injured during a shoot. Once he recollects her car crash in utter slow motion from multiple angles, as if secretly knowing, yet also deliberately repressing its suicidal intent. We see the photographer's head violently thrown backward and forward, from the rear and from the side, while the windshield's glass bursts into a thousand pieces that drift towards and around her head and face. Though restaging her death as a destruction of screen and frame, the utter slo-mo of Conrad's memorialisation starkly indicates the highly mediated nature even of Isabelle's final image. What Conrad envisions is not a moment of immediacy and intimacy, but an image of a portrait. His mother is in full sight, and yet recedes from the picture. The car's window might break, but the photographer's face and body – for Conrad, as much as for the viewer – continue to offer a window onto the demolition that prevails around and finally catches up with her.

'What is striking is your transparency', Roni Horn wrote in her 2004 letter to Isabelle Huppert, 'a simple almost fragile quality and your always-clear and transparent presence that carries with it the paradox of something both specific and unknown'.[22] Horn's insight seems to hold even when we approach the world through the eyes of Huppert's cameras, when Huppert herself is shown as an image-maker. Huppert's cameras don't just picture but make worlds. They slice into the fabric of space and time, not to arrest images viewers can simply and safely hold onto, but to rearticulate the ecologies of their lives and attachments. These images don't hide anything, and yet in their praise of unmitigated presence, they always remain enigmatic, puzzling, ungraspable. Images of and by Huppert bring to light that even at our most intimate we never escape the logic of mediation, of open-ended entanglement.

What we, with Huppert, call image today is no different than what we say about the weather in the age of the Anthropocene. Neither images nor the weather are external to us, a mere tool or object we can use to achieve certain goals. They have become what we are, they are us. They reflect on us as much as we reflect on them.

> Some say talking about the weather is talking about oneself. This seems to hold true in a general sense on an individual level. But for entire populations as well the weather is reflection and measure. In this century, as young as it is, we have merged into a single, global us; with each passing day we can watch as the weather actually becomes us.[23]

The image of Huppert is the weather that is us. It is the reflection of a world whose inhospitality reveals the limits of human wilfulness and agency. And it provides measures for alternate lives in which we can centre ourselves amid the unknown without dominating or devastating what is not us.

NOTES

1. Kristin Schrader and Max Hollein, eds, *Roni Horn: Portrait of an Image* (Frankfurt/M.: Schirn Kunsthalle, 2014), 52.
2. Schrader and Hollein, *Roni Horn*, 52.
3. Ronald Chammah and Serge Toubiana, eds, *Isabelle Huppert: Woman of Many Faces* (New York: Harry N. Abrams, 2005).
4. Roni Horn, 'Roni Horn: You Are the Weather,' interview by Claudia Spinelli, Kunstforum International (June-August 1997): 156–9.
5. Craig Dworkin, *No Medium* (Cambridge, MA: MIT Press, 2013).
6. Dworkin, *No Medium*, 30.
7. For more on the artistic mediums as interfaces between nature and culture, materiality and consciousness, see also J. M. Bernstein, *Against Voluptuous Bodies: Late Modernism and the Meaning of Painting* (Stanford: Stanford University Press, 2006).
8. John Durham Peters, *The Marvelous Clouds: Toward a Philosophy of Elemental Media* (Chicago: University of Chicago Press, 2015), 2.
9. Bernstein, *Against Voluptuous Bodies*, 7.
10. Rosalind Krauss, *A Voyage on the North Sea: Art in the Age of the Post-Medium Condition* (London: Thames & Hudson, 1999).
11. Rita Felski, 'Identifying with Characters,' In Amanda Anderson, Rita Felski and Toril Moi, *Character: Three Inquiries in Literary Studies* (Chicago: University of Chicago Press, 2019). Kindle file.
12. Felski, 'Identifying with Characters,' n.p.
13. Felski, 'Identifying with Characters,' n.p.
14. Andrew Pulver, 'Isabelle Huppert: 'When I act, I don't think about anything,'' *The Guardian* April 21, 2016, https://www.theguardian.com/film/2016/apr/21/isabelle-huppert-when-i-act-i-dont-think-about-anything.

15. Roland Barthes, 'The Face of Garbo,' in *Film Theory and Criticism*, eds Gerald Mast, Marshall Cohen, and Leo Braudy (New York: Oxford University Press, 1992), 628–31.
16. Lutz Koepnick, 'Dietrich's Face,' in *Dietrich Icon*, eds Gerd Gemünden and Mary R. Desjardins (Durham: Duke University Press, 2007), 43–59.
17. Kristin Schrader, 'Portrait of an Image – On Finding the Other,' in Schrader and Hollein, *Roni Horn*, 61.
18. Elisabeth Lebovici, 'Faces that Speak Volumes: Roni Horn,' *Tate Etc.* 15 (Spring 2009), https://www.tate.org.uk/tate-etc/issue-15-spring-2009/faces-speak-volumes.
19. Mark Godfrey, 'Roni Horn's Icelandic Encyclopedia,' *Art History* 32, no. 5 (2009): 932–53.
20. Roni Horn, 'Island and Labyrinth,' in *Vatnasafn / Library of Water*, eds James Lingwood and Gerrie van Noord (London and Göttingen: Artangel / Steidl Verlag, 2009), 136.
21. Briony Fer, 'Complete with Missing Parts,' in *Roni Horn aka Roni Horn: Catalogue*, ed. Beth Huseman (New York and Göttingen: Whitney Museum of Art / Steidl Verlag, 2009), 37.
22. Schrader and Hollein, *Roni Horn*, 52.
23. Horn, 'An Introduction,' in *Vatnasafn / Library of Water*, 107.

Bibliography

Ahmed, Sara. *The Promise of Happiness*. Durham: Duke University Press, 2010.
Ahmed, Sara. *Living a Feminist Life*. Durham and London: Duke University Press, 2017.
Álvarez López, Cristina and Adrian Martin. 'Isabelle Huppert: The Absent One.' *The Third Rail* 10 http://thirdrailquarterly.org/isabelle-huppert-the-absent-one/.
Angel, Katherine. *Daddy Issues*. London: Peninsula Press, 2019.
Asibong, Andrew. *François Ozon*. Manchester: Manchester University Press, 2008.
Audard, Catherine. *Dictionary of Untranslatables: A Philosophical Lexicon*, edited by Barbara Cassin, Emily Apter, Jacques Lezra and Michael Wood. Princeton: Princeton University Press 2014.
Aumont, Jacques. *Du visage au cinéma*. Paris: Éditions de l'étoile, 1992.
Bachmann, Ingeborg. *'Todesarten' – Projekt*, edited by Robert Pichl, Monika Albrecht and Dirk Göttsche. Munich: Piper, 1995.
Baraitser, Lisa. *Enduring Time*. London: Bloomsbury, 2017.
Barthes, Roland. 'The Face of Garbo.' In *Film Theory and Criticism*, edited by Gerald Mast, Marshall Cohen, and Leo Braudy, 628–31. New York: Oxford University Press, 1992.
Barthes, Roland. *The Neutral: Lecture Course at the Collège de France (1977–1978)*, edited by Thomas Clerc and Éric Marty. Translated by Rosalind E. Krauss and Dennis Hollier. New York: Columbia University Press, 2005.
Barthes, Roland. *Mythologies*. Translated by Annette Laver. London: Vintage, 2009.
Balázs, Béla. *Theory of Film: Character and Growth of a New Art*. Translated by Edith Boone. New York: Dover Books, 1970.
Baum, Devorah. *Feeling Jewish: (A Book for Just About Anyone)*. New Haven and London: Yale University Press, 2017.
Berlant, Lauren. *Cruel Optimism*. Durham: Duke University Press, 2011.
Berlant, Lauren. 'Structures of Unfeeling: Mysterious Skin.' *International Journal of Politics, Culture, and Society* 28, no. 3 (September 2015): 191–213.

Bernstein, J. M. *Against Voluptuous Bodies: Late Modernism and the Meaning of Painting*. Stanford: Stanford University Press, 2006.

Beugnet, Martine. *Claire Denis*. Manchester: Manchester University Press, 2004.

Beugnet, Martine. *Cinema and Sensation: French Film and the Art of Transgression*. Carbondale: Southern Illinois University Press, 2007.

Birchall, Bridget. 'From Nude to Metteuse-en-scène: Isabelle Huppert, Image and Desire in *La Dentellière* (Goretta, 1977) and *La Pianiste* (Haneke, 2001).' *Studies in French Cinema* 5, no. 1 (2005): 5–15.

Bonnaud, Frédéric. 'French Filmmaker François Ozon Directs an All-Femme All-Star Cast.' *Film Comment* 38.2 (March 1, 2002): 23.

Brinkema, Eugenie. 'Celluloid Is Sticky: Sex, Death, Materiality, Metaphysics (in Some Films by Catherine Breillat).' *Women: A Cultural Review* 17, no. 2 (August 1, 2006): 147–70.

Brinkema, Eugenie. *The Forms of the Affects*. Durham, NC: Duke University Press, 2014.

Brinkema, Eugenie. 'A Mother Is a Form of Time: Gilmore Girls and the Elasticity of In-Finitude.' *Discourse* 34, no. 1 (Winter 2012): 3–31.

Brooks, Peter. *The Melodramatic Imagination*. New Haven and London: Yale University Press, 1976.

Brody, Richard. 'The Literary Frenzy of Werner Schroeter's *Malina*.' *The Front Row* (Blog). *The New Yorker*, November 15, 2020. https://www.newyorker.com/culture/the-front-row/the-literary-frenzy-of-werner-schroeters-malina.

Brown-Montesano, Kristi. *Understanding the Women of Mozart's Operas*. Berkeley: University of California Press, 2007.

Brown, Royal S. 'Review: *La Cérémonie*.' *Cinéaste* 22.4 (1997): 50–51.

Buss, Robin. 'La Cérémonie.' *The Times Literary Supplement*, no. 4850 (15 March 1996): 19.

Butler, Judith. *Giving an Account of Oneself*. New York: Fordham University Press, 2005.

Butler, Judith. 'Leaning Out, Caught in the Fall: Interdependency and Ethics in Cavarero.' In *Toward a Feminist Ethics of Nonviolence: Adriana Cavarero, Judith Butler and Bonnie Honig, with Other Voices*, edited by Timothy J. Huzar and Clare Woodford, 46–62. New York: Fordham University Press, 2021.

Cardullo, Bert, Jonathan Rosenbaud, and Michael Stern. '"An Unhappy Happy End": Douglas Sirk,' in *Action!: Interviews with Directors from Classical Hollywood to Contemporary Iran*, edited by Gary Morris. London: Anthem Press, 2009.

Care Collective, The. *The Care Manifesto: The Politics of Interdependence*. London: Verso, 2020.

Cavarero, Adriana. *Inclinations: A Critique of Rectitude*. Stanford: Stanford University Press, 2016.

Cavell, Stanley. *The World Viewed: Reflections on the Ontology of Film*. Cambridge: Harvard University Press, 1979.

Cavell, Stanley. *Pursuits of Happiness: The Hollywood Comedy of Remarriage*. Cambridge: Harvard University Press, 1981.

Cavell, Stanley. 'Psychoanalysis and Cinema: The Melodrama of the Unknown Woman.' In *Images in Our Souls: Cavell, Psychoanalysis, Cinema*, edited by Joseph Smith and William Kerrigan, 11–43. Baltimore: Johns Hopkins University Press, 1987.

Cavell, Stanley. *In Quest of the Ordinary: Lines of Skepticism and Romanticism*. Chicago: University of Chicago Press, 1988.

Cavell, Stanley. *Contesting Tears. The Hollywood Melodrama of the Unknown Woman*. Chicago: University of Chicago Press, 1996.

Chammah, Ronald and Serge Toubiana, eds, *Isabelle Huppert: Woman of Many Faces*. New York: Harry N. Abrams, 2005.

Cho, Michelle. 'Face Value: The Star as Genre in Bong Joon-Ho's *Mother*.' In *The Korean Popular Culture Reader*, edited by Kyung Hyun Kim and Youngmin Choe, 168–94. Durham, NC: Duke University Press, 2020, 172.

Citron, Marcia J. *When Opera Meets Film*. Cambridge: Cambridge University Press, 2010.

Corrigan, Timothy. 'Werner Schroeter's Operatic Cinema.' *Discourse* 3 (Spring 1981): 46–59.

Corrigan, Timothy. 'On the Edge of History: The Radiant Spectacle of Werner Schroeter.' *Film Quarterly* 37, no. 4 (Summer 1984): 6–18.

Dargis, Manohla and A. O. Scott, 'The 25 Greatest Actors of the 21st Century (Thus Far).' *New York Times*, November 25, 2020. https://www.nytimes.com/interactive/2020/movies/greatest-actors-actresses.html.

Debruge, Peter. 'Femme Fatale: Isabelle Huppert.' *Variety* 334, no. 1 (November 8, 2016): 53–4.

Deleuze, Gilles and Félix Guattari. *Mille plateaux*. Paris: Les Éditions de Minuit.

Denby, David. 'Cold Maids.' *New York Magazine*, January 20, 1997, 60–61.

Deneuve, Catherine. '"8 femmes": "L'arbre de Noël d'Ozon."' Interview by Gérard Lefort. *Libération*, August 12, 2020. https://www.liberation.fr/cinema/2002/02/06/catherine-deneuve-8-femmes-l-arbre-de-noel-d-ozon_392926/.

Derrida, Jacques. 'White Mythology: Metaphor in the Text of Philosophy.' Transated by F. C. T. Moore. *New Literary History* 6, no. 1 (1974): 5–74.

Dewey, John. *The Public and Its Problems: An Essay in Political Inquiry*, edited by Melvin L. Rogers. University Park, PA: Pennsylvania State University Press, 2012.

Devor, Aaron. *Gender Blending: Confronting the Limits of Duality*. Bloomington: Indiana University Press, 1989.

Dickinson, Kay. 'At What Cost "Theory"? An Economics and Poetics of Uptake.' *Framework* 56, no. 2 (Fall 2015): 433–50.

Diderot, Denis. *The Paradox of Acting*. Translated by Walter Herries Pollock. London: Chatto & Windus, 1883.

Diderot, Denis. 'Observations sur une brochure intitulée Garrick ou Les Acteurs anglais (1770).' In *Paradoxe sur le comédien*. Cork: Éditions Ligaran, 2018. ProQuest Ebook Central.

Donadio, Rachel. 'The Enduring Allure of Isabelle Huppert.' *New York Times Style Magazine*. November 30, 2016. https://www.nytimes.com/2016/11/30/t-magazine/isabelle-huppert-elle-movie-interview.html.

Dousteyssier-Khoze, Catherine. *Claude Chabrol's Aesthetics of Opacity*. Edinburgh: Edinburgh University Press, 2017.
Dworkin, Craig. *No Medium*. Cambridge: MIT Press, 2013.
Duras, Marguerite. *Un barrage contre le Pacifique*. Paris: Éditions Gallimard, 1950.
Dyer, Richard. *Stars*. London: British Film Institute, 1979.
Dyer, Richard. *Heavenly Bodies: Film Stars and Society*. New York: Macmillan, 1986.
Dyer, Richard. *White: Twentieth Anniversary Edition*. New York: Routledge, 2017.
Edelman, Lee. *No Future: Queer Theory and the Death Drive*. Durham and London: Duke University Press, 2004.
Ehrlich, David. 'Who Is the Greatest Actress in the World? – IndieWire Critics Survey.' *Indiewire*. December 5, 2016. https://www.indiewire.com/2016/12/best-actress-in-the-world-isabelle-huppert-tilda-swinton-greta-gerwig-1201752582/.
Ehrlich, David. 'Killer Instinct: Why Isabelle Huppert Is Still the Most Dangerous Actress in the World.' *IndieWire*. February 28, 2019. https://www.indiewire.com/2019/02/isabelle-huppert-interview-greta-1202047935/.
Enelow, Shonni. 'The Great Recession.' *Film Comment* 52, no. 5 (2016): 56–61.
Felski, Rita. 'Identifying with Characters.' In Amanda Anderson, Rita Felski and Toril Moi, *Character: Three Inquiries in Literary Studies*. Chicago: University of Chicago Press, 2019.
Fleishman, Ian. *An Aesthetics of Injury: The Narrative Wound from Baudelaire to Tarantino*. Evanston: Northwestern University Press, 2018.
Gallix, Andrew. 'Céline: Great Author and "Absolute Bastard."' *The Guardian*, January 31, 2011. https://www.theguardian.com/books/booksblog/2011/jan/31/celine-great-author.
Godfrey, Mark. 'Roni Horn's Icelandic Encyclopedia.' *Art History* 32, no. 5 (2009): 932–53.
Gorelik, Mordecai. 'Bertolt Brecht's "Prospectus of the Diderot Society."' *Quarterly Journal of Speech* 47.2 (April 1961): 113–17.
Gorfinkel, Elena. 'The Body's Failed Labor: Performance Work in Sexploitation Cinema.' *Framework* 53, no. 1 (2012): 79–98.
Grundmann, Roy, ed. *Werner Schroeter*. Vienna: Österreichisches Filmmuseum, 2018.
Grusin, Richard A., ed. *The Nonhuman Turn*. Minneapolis: University of Minnesota Press, 2015.
Gural-Migdal, Anna. 'La Representation de la femme dans le cinema français des vingt dernières années: *Sans Toit Ni Loi, Nelly et M. Arnaud, La Cérémonie*.' *Women in French Studies* 9 (2001): 193–206.
Hall, Gwendolyn Midlo. *Afro-Creole Culture in the Eighteenth century*. Baton Rouge: Louisiana State University Press, 1992.
Hamacher, 'Afformative, Strike: Benjamin's "Critique of Violence."' Translated by Dana Hollander. In *Walter Benjamin's Philosophy: Destruction and Experience*, edited by Andrew Benjamin and Peter Osborne, 110–38. Manchester: Clinamen Press, 2000.

Hamid, Rahul. 'Introduction to *Black Girl*.' *Senses of Cinema* 23, no. 78 (December 2002). sensesofcinema.com/2002/cteq/black_girl/.
Handyside, Fiona. 'Melodrama and Ethics in François Ozon's *Gouttes d'eau sur pierres brûlantes/Water Drops on Burning Rocks* (2000).' *Studies in French Cinema* 7. 3 (2007): 207–18.
Haneke, Michael. 'Michael Haneke Talks About *The Piano Teacher*.' Interview by Karin Schiefer. https://www.austrianfilms.com/news/en/bodymichael_haneke_talks_about_the_piano_teacher_body.
Heidegger, Martin. *Unterwegs zur Sprache*. Pfullingen: Verlag Günther Neske, 1959.
Hewitt, Leah D. 'Vichy's Female Icons: Chabrol's *Story of Women*.' In *Gender and Fascism in Modern France*. Hanover: University Press of New England, 1997.
Hewitt, Leah D. *Remembering the Occupation in French Film: National Identity in Postwar Europe*. New York: Palgrave Macmillan, 2008.
Harrison, Bernard. '"White Mythology" Revisited: Derrida and His Critics on Reason and Rhetoric.' *Critical Inquiry* 25, no. 3 (1999): 505–34.
Hoberman, J. 'Pill-Popping Prostitute Driven Mad by Crashing Piano Chords.' *Village Voice*. February 24, 2004. https://www.villagevoice.com/2004/02/24/pill-popping-prostitute-driven-mad-by-crashing-piano-chords.
Honig, Bonnie. *A Feminist Theory of Refusal – Mary Flexner Lectures of Bryn Mawr College*. Cambridge: Harvard University Press, 2021.
hooks, bell. *Black Looks: Race and Representation*. Boston: South End Press, 1992.
Horn, Roni. 'Roni Horn: You are the Weather.' Interview by Claudia Spinelli. Kunstforum International (June-August 1997): 156–59.
Horn, Roni. 'Island and Labyrinth.' In *Vatnasafn / Library of Water*, edited by James Lingwood and Gerrie van Noord. London and Göttingen: Artangel / Steidl Verlag, 2009.
Hornby, Louise. *Still Modernism: Photography, Literature, Film*. Oxford: Oxford University Press, 2017.
Huppert, Isabelle. '"Ich treibe die Teufel aus": André Müller spricht mit der Schauspielerin Isabelle Huppert.' Interview by André Müller. *DIE ZEIT*, July 4, 1991. https://www.zeit.de/1991/02/ich-treibe-die-teufel-aus.
Huppert, Isabelle. 'I am, therefore I act.' Interview by Suzie Mackenzie. *The Guardian*, October 10, 1998.
Huppert, Isabelle. "La pianiste est une mutante." Interview in *l'Humanité*, September 5, 2001. https://www.humanite.fr/isabelle-huppert-la-pianiste-est-une-mutante-251729.
Huppert, Isabelle. 'Isabelle Huppert (I).' Interview with Christopher Cook. *The Guardian*, November 11, 2001. https://www.theguardian.com/film/2001/nov/11/londonfilmfestival2001.londonfilmfestival1.
Huppert, Isabelle. '"Ich nenne das eine Art von Unschuld": Isabelle Huppert im Interview.' Interview by Daniel Kothenschulte. *Frankfurter Rundschau*, July 26, 2009. https://www.fr.de/panorama/ich-nenne-eine-unschuld-11485025.
Huppert, Isabelle. 'I don't have a reputation for being difficult. Because I've been shrewd enough not to let it show.' Interview by Robert Chalmers. *Independent on Sunday* (July 4, 2010): 10–12, 14.

Huppert, Isabelle. 'Isabelle Huppert.' Interview by Nick James. *Sight & Sound* 26, no. (September 2016): 18–23.
Huseman, Beth, ed. *Roni Horn aka Roni Horn: Catalogue*. New York and Göttingen: Whitney Museum of Art / Steidl Verlag, 2009.
Ince, Kate, ed. *Five Directors: Auteurism from Assayas to Ozon*. Manchester: Manchester University Press, 2008.
Jacobowitz, Florence. '*Un barrage contre le Pacifique/The Sea Wall*.' *CineAction*, no. 76 (Spring 2009): 31.
Jelinek, Elfriede. *Isabelle Huppert in Malina: Ein Filmbuch. Nach dem Roman von Ingeborg Bachmann*. Frankfurt am Main: Suhrkamp, 1991.
Jelinek, Elfriede. *Die Klavierspielerin*. Reinbek bei Hamburg: Rowohlt Taschenbuch Verlag, 1998.
Joudet, Murielle. *Isabelle Huppert: Vivre ne nous regarde pas*. Paris: Capricci, 2018.
Kim, David Young. 'Points on a Field: Gentile da Fabriano and Gold Ground.' *Journal of Early Modern History* 23 (2019): 191–226.
King, Tiffany Lethabo. *The Black Shoals: Offshore Formations of Black and Native Studies*. Duke: Duke University Press, 2019.
Kleist, Heinrich von. 'Puppet Theatre (1810).' *Salmagundi*, no. 33/34 (1976): 83–8.
Kleist, Heinrich von. 'On the Gradual Productions of Thoughts Whilst Speaking.' In *Selected Writings: Heinrich von Kleist*, edited by David Constantine (London: J. M. Dent, 1997), 405–9.
Kohut, Heinz. 'Thoughts on Narcissism and Narcissistic Rage.' In *The Search for the Self. Selected Writings of Heinz Kohut: 1950–1978*, edited by Paul H. Ornstein, vol. 2, 615–58. Madison, Connecticut: International Universities Press, Inc., 1978.
Koepnick, Lutz. 'Dietrich's Face.' In *Dietrich Icon*, eds Gerd Gemünden and Mary R. Desjardins, 43–59. Durham: Duke University Press, 2007.
Krauss, Rosalind. *A Voyage on the North Sea: Art in the Age of the Post-Medium Condition*. London: Thames & Hudson, 1999.
Krauss, Werner. 'Über den Zustand unserer Sprache.' In *Die Innenseite der Weltgeschichte: Ausgewählte Essays über Sprache und Literatur*, ed. Helga Bergmann. Leipzig: Reclam, 1983.
Kristeva, Julia. *Le Plaisir des formes*. Paris: Seuil, 2003.
La Feria, Ruth. 'Isabelle Huppert: The Best Way to Please Is Not to Please.' *The New York Times*. February 23, 2017. https://www.nytimes.com/2017/02/23/fashion/isabelle-huppert-oscar-nominee-elle.html.
Lacan, Jacques. 'Of the Gaze as *Objet petit a*.' In *The Seminar of Jacques Lacan: The Four Fundamental Concepts of Psychoanalysis*, edited by Jacques-Alain Miller. Translated by Alan Sheridan. New York: W. W. Norton & Company, 1981.
Langford, Michelle. *Allegorical Images: Tableau, Time and Gesture in the Cinema of Werner Schroeter*. Bristol, United Kingdom: Intellect Books, 2006.
Lauro, Sarah J. *The Transatlantic Zombie: Slavery, Rebellion, and Living Death*. New Brunswick: Rutgers University Press, 2015.
Lauro, Sarah J, ed. *Zombie Theory: A Reader*. Minneapolis: University of Minnesota Press, 2015.

Lebovici, Elisabeth. 'Faces that Speak Volumes: Roni Horn.' *Tate Etc.* 15 (Spring 2009). https://www.tate.org.uk/tate-etc/issue-15-spring-2009/faces-speak-volumes.

Li, Dahlia. 'Secreting Blackness: Sweat, Dance, and the Vibrant Bodies in *A Love Supreme* (2017).' Unpublished essay.

Lowe, Lisa. *The Intimacies of Four Continents*. Durham: Duke University Press, 2015.

Lübecker, Nikolaj. *The Feel-Bad Film*. Edinburgh: Edinburgh University Press, 2015.

Maslin, 'Huppert as an Abortionist, in Chabrol's *Story of Women*,' *The New York Times*, October 13, 1989, Arts and Entertainment, Section C, 17. https://www.nytimes.com/1989/10/13/movies/review-film-huppert-as-an-abortionist-in-chabrol-s-story-of-women.html.

Maslin, Janet. 'Maid is Hired: Danger is Served.' *The New York Times*, December 20, 1996. Arts and Entertainment, Section C, p. 1. https://www.nytimes.com/1996/12/20/movies/maid-is-hired-danger-is-served.html.

McCullough, Mary E. '*Une affaire de femmes* (*Story of Women*, Chabrol 1988): Profile of an Abortionist Executed Under the Vichy Regime.' In *War, Revolution and Remembrance in World Cinema: Critical Essays*, edited by Nancy J. Membrez, 37–49. Jefferson: McFarland and Company, 2021.

McKittrick, Katherine. *Demonic Grounds: Black Women and the Cartographies of Struggle*. Minneapolis: University of Minnesota Press, 2006.

McLaughlin, Noah. *French War Films and National Identity*. Amherst: Cambria Press, 2010.

Mulhall, Stephen. *Stanley Cavell: Philosophy's Recounting of the Ordinary*. Oxford: Oxford University Press, 1998.

Nelson, Maggie. *On Freedom: Four Songs of Care and Constraint*. London: Jonathan Cape, 2021.

Ngai, Sianne. *Our Aesthetic Categories: Zany, Cute, Interesting*. Cambridge: Harvard University Press, 2012.

Noveck, Jocelyn. 'Isabelle Huppert: I'm Not an Artist, I'm the Canvas.' *AP News*, February 15, 2017. https://apnews.com/article/971f97e64e8a44988ef17dd93dca3122.

Parker, G. 'The Lacemaker.' *Film Quarterly* 32, no. 1 (Fall 1978): 51–5.

Perloff, Marjorie. *Wittgenstein's Ladder: Poetic Language and the Strangeness of the Ordinary*. Chicago: University of Chicago Press, 1996.

Peters, John Durham. *The Marvelous Clouds: Toward a Philosophy of Elemental Media*. Chicago: University of Chicago Press, 2015.

Phillips, Adam and Barbara Taylor, *On Kindness*. London: Penguin, 2010.

Polack, Jean-Claude. 'Chabrol and the Execution of the Deed.' Translated by Annette Michelson *October* 98 (Fall 2001): 77–92.

Pollard, Miranda. *Reign of Virtue: Mobilizing Gender in Vichy France*. Chicago: University of Chicago Press, 1998.

Pomerance, Murray and Kyle Stevens, eds. *Close-Up: Great Cinematic Performances Volume 1: America*. Edinburgh: Edinburgh University Press, 2018.

Poppelreuter, Walther. *Psychokritische Pädagogik. Zur Überwindung von Scheinwissen, Scheinkönnen, Scheindenken usw.* Munich: C.H. Beck'sche Verlagsbuchhandlung, 1933.

Poppelreuter, Walther. *Hitler der politische Psychologe.* Langensalza: Herman Beyer & Söhne, 1934.

Powell, Lawrence N. *The Accidental City: Improvising New Orleans.* Cambridge: Harvard University Press, 2013.

Powers, John. 'Bourgeoisie, Beware!' *Vogue* 186, no. 12 (December 1, 1996): 170.

Puar, Jasbir. *The Right to Maim.* Durham and London: Duke University Press, 2017.

Pulver, Andrew. 'Isabelle Huppert: "When I act, I don't think about anything."' *The Guardian* April 21, 2016. https://www.theguardian.com/film/2016/apr/21/isabelle-huppert-when-i-act-i-dont-think-about-anything.

Quandt, James. 'Flesh & Blood: Sex and Violence in Recent French Cinema.' 42 (February 1, 2004): 126–32.

Quandt, James. 'Magnificent Obsession: The Films of Werner Schroeter.' *Artforum* 50, no. 9 (May 2012): 253–61.

Rees-Roberts and Darren Waldron, eds. *Isabelle Huppert: Stardom, Performance, Authorship.* London: Bloomsbury, 2021.

Rhodes, John David. 'The Prop and Its Properties.' https://www.ici-berlin.org/events/john-david-rhodes/. Lecture delivered May 20, 2019.

Rickels, Laurence A. *Aberrations of Mourning: Writing on German Crypts.* Detroit: Wayne State University Press, 1988.

Rickels, Laurence A. *Nazi Psychoanalysis: Only Psychoanalysis Won the War.* Minneapolis: University of Minnesota Press, 2002.

Rickels, Laurence A. *The Psycho Records.* New York: Wallflower Press, 2016.

Rickels, Laurence A. *Critique of Fantasy, Volume 1: Between a Crypt and a Datemark,* Santa Barbara: Punctum Books, 2020.

Rickels, Laurence A. *Critique of Fantasy, Volume 3: The Block of Fame.* Santa Barbara: Punctum Books, 2020.

Riding, Alan. 'For Chabrol, a French "Thelma and Louise".' *New York Times,* December 15, 1996. https://www.nytimes.com/1996/12/15/movies/from-chabrol-a-french-thelma-and-louise.html.

Rose, Jacqueline. *The Haunting of Sylvia Plath.* London: Virago, 1991.

Rose, Jacqueline. *Mothers: An Essay on Love and Cruelty.* London: Faber and Faber, 2018.

Said, Edward W. 'The Imperial Spectacle.' *Grand Street* 6, no. 2 (Winter 1987): 82–104.

Schilt, Thibaut. *François Ozon.* Urbana, IL: University of Illinois Press, 2011.

Schoonover, Karl. 'Histrionic Gestures and Historical Representation: Masina's Cabiria, Bazin's Chaplin, and Fellini's Neorealism.' *JCMS: Journal of Cinema and Media Studies* 53, no. 2 (2014): 93–116.

Scott, A. O. 'Review: Isabelle Huppert Is Great in "Things to Come." Discuss.' *New York Times,* December 1, 2016. https://www.nytimes.com/2016/12/01/movies/things-to-come-review-isabelle-huppert.html.

Schrader Kristin and Max Hollein, eds, *Roni Horn: Portrait of an Image*. Frankfurt/M.: Schirn Kunsthalle, 2014.
Schroeter, Werner. '"Gegen das Rohe und Brutale steht die Verfeinerung": Werner Schroeter auf der Viennale 2008.' Interview by *artechock* Filmmagazin. https://www.artechock.de/film/text/interview/s/schroeter_2010.
Schroeter, Werner with Claudia Lenssen, *Days of Twilight, Nights of Frenzy: A Memoir*. Translated by Anthea Bell. Chicago: University of Chicago Press, 2017.
Sedgwick, Eve Kosofsky, ed. *Novel Gazing: Queer Readings in Fiction*. Durham: Duke University Press, 1997.
Sedgwick, Eve Kosofsky. *Touching Feeling: Affect, Pedagogy, Performativity*. Durham: Duke University Press, 2002.
Sieglohr, Ulrike. 'Why Drag the Diva into It? Werner Schroeter's Gay Representation of Femininity.' In *Triangulated Visions: Women in Recent German Cinema*, edited by Ingeborg Majer O'Sickey and Ingeborg von Zadow, 163–72. Albany: State University of New York Press, 1998.
Sieglohr, Ulrike. 'Divine Rapture.' *Film Comment* 48, no. 3 (May/June 2012): 50–5.
Solomon, Alisa. 'It's Never Too Late to Switch.' In *Crossing the Stage: Controversies on Cross-Dressing*, edited by Leslie Ferris, 144–54. London: Routledge, 1993.
Stacey, Jackie. 'Crossing Over with Tilda Swinton – the Mistress of "Flat Affect".' *International Journal of Politics, Culture, and Society* 28, no. 3 (September 2015): 243–71.
Stern, Lesley and George Kouvaros, eds, 'Introduction: Descriptive Acts.' In *Falling for You: Essays on Cinema and Performance*. Sydney: Power Publications, 1999.
Stewart, Kathleen. 'Atmospheric Attunements.' *Environment and Planning D: Society and Space* 29, no. 3 (2011): 444–54.
Taylor, Alison. 'Isabelle Huppert in *The Piano Teacher*,' in *Close-Up: Great Cinematic Performances*, edited by Murray Pomerance and Kyle Stevens, 217–227. Edinburgh: Edinburgh University Press, 2018.
Terada, Rei. *Feeling in Theory: Emotion After the Death of the Subject*. Cambridge: Harvard University Press, 2003.
Marjorie Vecchio, ed. *The Films of Claire Denis: Intimacy on the Border*. London: I. B. Tauris, 2014.
Van Kruyssen, Helen. 'Review of *Une affaire de femmes*.' *52 French Films*, February, 5, 2015. https://52frenchfilms.org/2015/02/05/une-affaires-de-femmes-a-story-of-women/.
Vincendeau, Ginette. 'Isabelle Huppert: The Big Chill.' *Sight & Sound* 16, no. 12 (2006): 36–9.
Viviani, Christian. 'Permanence Du Mélo: Variations Folles et Élaborées.' *Positif: Revue Mensuelle de Cinéma* 507 (May 2003): 70–4.
Waldron, Darren. '"Une Mine d'or Inépuisable": The Queer Pleasures of François Ozon's 8 Femmes/8 Women (2002).' *Studies in French Cinema* 10, no. 1 (2010): 69–82.
Weddigen, Tristan. 'Unfolding Textile Spaces: Antiquity/Modern Period.' In *Art and Textiles: Fabric as Material and Concept in Modern Art from Klimt to the Present*, edited by Markus Brüderlin, 88–95. Ostfildern: Hatje Cantz, 2013.

Weyergans, François. 'Isabelle Huppert: Drapée dans son mystère.' *Paris-Match* 2885 (September 2, 2004): 50–59.

Wheatley, Catherine. 'Isabelle's Espadrilles. Or, *les chaussures d'Huppert.*' In *Shoe Reels: Footwear on Film*, edited by Elizabeth Ezra and Catherine Wheatley. Edinburgh: Edinburgh University Press, 2020.

White, Patricia. 'Pink Material: White Womanhood and the Colonial Imaginary of World Cinema Authorship.' In *The Routledge Companion to Cinema and Gender*, edited by Kristin Lené Hole, Dijana Jelača, E. Ann Kaplan, and Patrice Petro (London: Routledge, 2016), 215–26.

Whitney, Craig R. 'France Moves to Crush Corsican Separatists.' *New York Times*, January 15, 1997, Section A, 4. https://www.nytimes.com/1997/01/15/world/france-moves-to-crush-corsican-separatists.html.

Winnicott, D. W. *Playing and Reality*. London and New York: Routledge, 2005.

Winnicott, D. W. *Deprivation and Delinquency*, eds Claire Winnicott et al. London and New York: Routledge, 2000.

Willsher, Kim. 'Céline: French Literary Genius or Repellent Antisemite? New Film Rekindles Old Conflict,' *The Guardian*, March 12, 2016, https://www.theguardian.com/books/2016/mar/13/celine-french-literary-genius-antisemite-film.

Wojcik, Pamela Robertson, ed. *Movie Acting: The Film Reader*. New York: Routledge, 2004.

Yuan, Jada. 'Isabelle Huppert is Having a Great Fall,' *Vulture*, December 1, 2016. https://www.vulture.com/2016/12/isabelle-huppert-is-already-having-a-great-fall.html.

Index

Adler, Laure, 2
affect
    affect/emotion distinction, 36–7, 38, 54
    affective excess, 53–4
    affective labour of care, 106–7, 108
    affectivity of Huppert-puppet, 37–8
    flat affect, 49–50, 51–2, 53–4, 57, 61
    flat affect's disruption of gender, 61–3
    melodrama as an affective genre, 32–3
Ahmed, Sara, 62
Almodóvar, Pedro, 32
Álvarez López, Cristina, 2, 5, 10, 23, 24, 25, 51, 52, 57, 108
Asibong, Andrew, 31–2
Aumont, Jacques, 24

Barthes, Roland, 17, 24, 26, 131
Bellaïche, Carole, 16
Berlant, Lauren, 9, 51–2, 53–4, 57, 62, 63–4, 106
Beugnet, Martine, 97
Black feminism, 71
blankness
    flat affect, 49–50, 51–2, 53–4, 57, 61
    Huppert's blank expression, 5, 49, 50–2, 62–3, 64
    Huppert's self-description as a blank canvas, 48, 50, 63
    not-caring in *Une affaire de femmes*, 117, 118–19
    performative blankness in *La Pianiste*, 28, 50–1
    Pomme's muteness and withdrawal in *La Dentellière*, 20–3
    symptomaticity and, 63–4
Brinkema, Eugenie, 38
Brody, Richard, 2, 56
Brown-Montesano, Kristi, 79
Butler, Judith, 116

Caméra de Claire, La, 135
Cannes Film Festival, 1
Captive (Mendoza), 9
Catherine Deneuve, 30
Cavarero, Adriana, 106, 109, 110–11, 115, 116, 117
Cavell, Stanley, 15, 17, 18, 22, 24, 25
Cérémonie, La (Chabrol), 4, 23, 24, 70–88
    French colonial violence, 77–8, 79, 80, 81–5
    physical and verbal comedy, 24, 71, 72–3, 74, 80–2, 85
    whiteness of, 71–2, 76–8, 79
Chabrol, Claude, 70
    La Cérémonie, 4, 23, 24, 70–88

Chabrol, Claude (*cont.*)
  Une affaire de femmes (*Story of Women*), 105–22
Chalmers, Robert, 50
Chéreau, Patrice, 17
Cho, Michelle, 4
Citron, Marcia, 75
Claire's Camera, 9
class politics, 72, 73, 76, 78, 79
colonialism
  colonial consumer products, 80, 82
  colonial Othering in *Un barrage contre le Pacifique*, 89, 93–4
  colonial Othering in *White Material*, 89, 93, 94
  Derrida's white mythology, 89, 100–1
  French colonial violence in *La Cérémonie*, 77–8, 79, 80, 81–5
  Lacan's white stain, 94, 100, 101
  post-colonial narrative of *White Material*, 90–1, 92
  power and privilege of white femininity, 9, 98
  violence of white mythology, 89–90, 93, 94–5, 99–100
  see also White Material
Copacabana, 4
corporeal performativity
  diminutive gestures and expressions, 5–6, 23, 25, 95
  Huppert's physicality in *White Material*, 92, 96–7
  inclination (bodily), 106–7, 110, 115–16
  inclination (care), 106–7
  physical and verbal comedy in *La Cérémonie*, 24, 71, 72–3, 74, 80–2, 85
  physical mobility, 24–5, 33, 59
  in *Une affaire de femmes* (*Story of Women*), 105–6, 109, 110
  zany, 108

Dargis, Manohla, 7
Davis, Bette, 15, 16–17
Deleuze, Gilles, 38, 40–1, 43
Denby, David, 75
Denis, Claire
  adaptations, 101
  Chocolat, 80, 90
  non-linear narratives, 97
  35 Rhums, 96–7
  time in colonial Africa, 90
  see also White Material
Dentellière, La (*The Lacemaker*), 19–20, 22, 23–4, 26–7, 28, 125
  facial close-ups in, 22, 23, 24, 26–7, 28
  gaze to the camera, 22, 23, 24, 26–7, 28
  Huppert's performative style, 28
Derrida, Jacques, 89, 100–1
Deux, 48–9, 57–60, 62
Diderot, Denis, 36, 44
Dietrich, Marlene, 131–2
Dix pour cent (*Call My Agent!*), 1–3
Don Giovanni (Mozart), 79
doubles
  in *Deux*, 48–9, 57–60
  in *Malina*, 48–9, 53, 55
Dousteyssier-Khoze, Catherine, 115
Duras, Marguerite, 89, 90, 98
Dworkin, Craig, 127
Dyer, Richard, 4

Edelman, Lee, 9
8 Femmes, 24, 30–44
  facial close-ups in, 33–4
  as melodrama, 31, 32, 40
  melodramatic/mechanic relationship, 30, 40, 43–4
  psychological readings of, 35–6, 40
Elle, 4, 6, 19, 28, 50
emotional performativity
  affect/emotion distinction, 36–7, 54
  Huppert's film choices, 4
  Huppert's range, 2–3
  non-identification/acting as a process, 49, 53, 131
  techniques of good acting, 36–7
Enelow, Shonni, 8

facial close-ups
  distinctiveness of the actor's face, 24–5
  in *8 Femmes*, 33–4
  Garbo's face, 17, 24, 25, 26, 131
  in *La Dentellière*, 22, 23, 24, 26–7, 28
  in *Portrait of an Image*, 127, 132
  screen/spectator relationship, 25
  in *Un barrage contre le Pacifique* (*The Sea Wall*), 91–2
  viewer identification with Huppert, 132
Fassbinder, Rainer Werner, 31, 43
Felski, Rita, 130–1
Fer, Briony, 135
Foucault, Michel, 54–5
French cinema, 9

Garbo, Greta
  Barthes's essay on her face, 17, 24, 26, 131
  Grand Hotel, 17
  Huppert's portraits as, 15–17, 26, 28
  unknowability of, 26
gender
  of care work, 106
  depictions of femininity in Schroeter's works, 61–2
  female inclination/masculine verticality, 106–7, 109, 116
  flat affect's disruption of, 61–3
  see also motherhood; women
Giraud, Marie-Louise, 105
Greta, 23, 24, 28, 50
Guattari, Félix, 40–1, 43
Gural-Migdal, Anna, 75

Hewitt, Leah D., 114
Hoberman, J., 5, 50
Honig, Bonnie, 109, 111
hooks, bell, 72, 77
Horn, Roni, 123–38
  Doubt Block, 126–7, 128, 129
  Portrait of an Image, 123, 124–9, 132, 134

This is Me, This is You, 132–3
Vatnasafn/Library of Water, 135
You Are the Weather, 133–4
Hornby, Louise, 26
humour
  comedies of remarriage, 18, 20, 22
  in Huppert's work, 70
  physical and verbal comedy in *La Cérémonie*, 24, 71, 72–3, 74, 80–2, 85
Huppert, Isabelle
  acting as therapy, 52–3
  as auteur, 10, 48, 70, 131
  career and public persona, 1–2, 4, 27–8, 123–4
  as herself in *Dix pour cent*, 1–3
  international standing, 1, 6–7, 9
  off-screen privacy, 3, 4, 52
  portraits as Greta Garbo, 15–17, 26, 28
  star image, 3–4, 9, 22, 23, 25, 89
  see also performative style (of Huppert)

Ibsen, Henrik, 18
images
  image-making in *La Caméra de Claire*, 135
  Portrait of an Image (Horn), 123, 124–9, 132, 134
  of violence in *Louder Than Bombs*, 135–6
  see also Horn, Roni
In Another Country, 9
Ince, Kate, 32
international art cinema, 3, 7

Jacobowitz, Florence, 95
James, Nick, 70
Joudet, Murielle, 20–1, 22

Kael, Paul, 50
Kahn, Cédric, 1
Kim, David Young, 78

King, Tiffany Lethabo, 71, 72, 77, 79, 84
Kleist, Heinrich von, 37, 40–1, 44
Kouvaros, George, 6
Kristeva, Julia, 7
Kruyssen, Helen Van, 107

Lacan, Jacques, 94, 100, 101, 130
Langford, Michelle, 58
Larsson, Andreas, 16
L'Avenir (*Things to Come*), 6, 19
Les soeurs fâchées (*Me and My Sister*), 4
Lessing, Doris, 101
Li, Dahlia, 78
Louder Than Bombs, 9, 135–6
Lowe, Lisa, 82

Ma Mère, 4
Madame Bovary, 35, 125
Malina (Schroeter), 19, 28, 48–9, 53, 54–7, 59, 62
Malo, Jean Saint, 85
Martin, Adrian, 2, 5, 10, 23, 24, 25, 51, 52, 57, 108
Maslin, Janet, 73
McLaughlin, Noah, 114
melodramas
   as an affective genre, 32–3
   8 Femmes as, 30, 31
   genre, 31, 32–3
   melodramatic/mechanic relationship in *8 Femmes*, 30, 40, 43–4
   unknown woman, 17–18, 20, 22
Mendoza, Brillante, 9
Merci pour le chocolat, 4, 125
meta-acting, 35–6, 37–8, 44
motherhood
   care/wound dialectic, 116–17
   doomed mother figures, 90–1, 95–9, 100
   feminine deviancy in *Une affaire de femmes*, 110–15
   'good-enough' mothering, 117
   reconceptualisations of care in *Une affaire de femmes*, 107, 109–11
   stereotypes of self-sacrificing maternity, 107
   in Vichy France, 105, 107, 108, 110, 114
Mulhall, Stephen, 18

Naqvi, Fatima, 54–5
Nelson, Maggie, 109
Ngai, Sianne, 108

O'Hagan, Colo Tavernier, 114
Ozon, François, 30, 31
   8 Femmes, 24, 30–44

Panh, Rithy, 90
   Un barrage contre le Pacifique (*The Sea Wall*), 9, 89–98, 100, 101
performance
   acting as therapy, 52–3
   actor/character relationship, 129–31
   characters and viewer identification, 130–2
   cultural contexts, 8
   emotional inaccessibility, 8–9
   the presentation of self, 123
   techniques of good acting, 36–7, 44
   see also puppets
performative style (of Huppert)
   acting as moulding a performance, 37–8
   affective intensity, 5–6, 9
   diminutive gestures and expressions, 5–6, 23, 25, 95
   dissociation, 49, 53, 64
   emotional discontinuity in, 2–3, 49
   extreme/deviant roles, 4–5
   gaze to the camera, 22, 23, 24, 25, 26–7, 28
   Huppert as auteur, 10, 48, 70, 131
   Huppert's onscreen opacity, 4, 7–8, 9
   interiority, 51
   negative aesthetic, 9–10
Phillips, Adam, 109–10
Pianiste, La (*The Piano Teacher*), 4, 19, 23, 28, 35, 50–1, 70, 125

Polack, Jean-Claude, 82
Pomerance, Murray, 3
Portrait of an Image (Horn), 123, 124–9, 132, 134
Powers, John, 78
Puar, Jasbir, 106
puppets
    the actress as puppet in *Deux*, 60
    the actress as puppet-doll in *8 Femmes*, 42–4
    affectivity of Huppert-puppet, 37–8
    the great actor as puppet, 36–7, 44
    in *La Cérémonie*, 76–7
    puppet-machinery aesthetic in *8 Femmes*, 30, 40, 41–3

Quandt, James, 48
queerness
    figure of the unhappy queer, 62
    parody's link with camp, 115
    Swinton's androgyny, 61, 64

race
    deconstructions of whiteness, 9, 89–90
    power and privilege of white femininity, 98
    violence of white mythology, 89–90, 93, 94–5
    whiteness in *La Cérémonie*, 71–2, 76–8, 79
Rees-Roberts, Nick, 3
Rhodes, John David, 78, 82
Rose, Jacqueline, 105, 114

Sangsoo, Hong, 135
Schrader, Kristin, 132
Schroeter, Werner
    control/chaos balance, 55–7
    depictions of femininity, 61–2
    Deux, 48–9, 57–60, 62
    dislike of psychology, 54–5
    relationship with Huppert, 48, 49
    stylistic excess, 49, 53
Scott, A. O., 7, 10

Sedgwick, Eve Kosofsky, 51, 64, 115
ShinRedDear, 16
Sieglohr, Ulrike, 61
Sirk, Douglas, 22, 32, 42, 43
Solomon, Alisa, 62
Sontag, Susan, 7
Stacey, Jackie, 49–50, 61, 62–3, 64
Stanwyck, Barbara, 18, 23
stardom
    the actor's face, 24
    distinctness of great film stars, 17, 26
    Huppert's star image, 3–4, 9, 22, 23, 25, 89
Stern, Lesley, 6
Stevens, Kyle, 3
Stewart, Kathleen, 6
Swinton, Tilda, 61, 62–3

Taylor, Alison, 36, 50–1
Taylor, Barbara, 109–10
Trier, Joachim, 9, 135

Un barrage contre le Pacifique (*The Sea Wall*) (Panh), 9, 89–98, 100, 101
    facial close-ups in, 91–2
    Huppert's doomed mother figure, 90–1, 95–6, 97–9, 100
    violence of white mythology, 89–90, 93, 94–5
Une affaire de femmes (*Story of Women*) (Chabrol), 105–22
    corporeal performativity, 105–6, 109, 110
    feminine deviancy and appetite, 110–15
    inclination (bodily), 106–7, 110, 115–16
    motherhood in Vichy France, 105, 107, 108, 110, 114
unknowability
    gaze to the camera, 26–8
    of Isabelle Huppert, 15
    melodramas of the unknown woman, 17–18
    theatricalisation of the self, 18, 24

Valley of Love, 23
Vie promise, La (*The Promised Life*), 5
Vincendeau, Ginette, 4, 9, 50
Violette Nozière, 23
Viviani, Christian, 32, 34, 44

Waldron, Darren, 3
war machines, 40–1
Weddigan, Tristan, 82–3
White, Patricia, 9, 98
White Material, 9, 89–101
White Material (Denis)
   colonial Othering, 89, 93, 94
   Huppert's doomed mother figure, 90–1, 96–8, 99, 100
   violence of white mythology, 89–90, 93, 94–5, 99–100
'White Mythology: Metaphor in the Text of Philosophy' (Derrida), 89–90

Williams, James S., 96–7, 100, 101
Wilson, Robert, 15–16, 26, 28
Winnicott, Donald, 117, 119
Wojcik, Pamela, 3
women
   abortion and deadly femininity, 105
   anti-abortion laws, 108–9
   comedies of remarriage, 18, 20, 22
   doomed mother figures, 90–1, 95–9, 100
   feminine deviancy and appetite in *Une affaire de femmes*, 110–15
   gendered care work, 106
   marriage, 18, 19
   melodramas of the unknown woman, 18, 20, 22
   power and privilege of white femininity, 9, 98
   see also motherhood

EU representative:
Easy Access System Europe
Mustamäe tee 50, 10621 Tallinn, Estonia
Gpsr.requests@easproject.com

www.ingramcontent.com/pod-product-compliance
Lightning Source LLC
Chambersburg PA
CBHW071433160426
43195CB00013B/1884